Nation-Building Unraveled?

Nation-Building Unraveled?

Aid, Peace and Justice
in Afghanistan

Edited by
**Antonio Donini, Norah Niland,
and Karin Wermester**

A PROJECT SUPPORTED BY THE INTERNATIONAL PEACE ACADEMY

Kumarian
Press, Inc.

Nation-Building Unraveled? Aid, Peace and Justice in Afghanistan

Published 2004 in the United States of America by Kumarian Press, Inc., 1294 Blue Hills Avenue, Bloomfield, CT 06002 USA

Copy editing, design, and production by Joan Weber Laflamme, jml ediset, Vienna, Va.
Index by Barbara J. DeGennaro.
Proofread by Phil Trahan, The Sarov Press.
The text of this book is set in 10/12 Sabon.

Printed in the United States of Amerca by Thomson-Shore, Inc.
Text printed with vegetable oil-based ink.

∞The paper used in this publication meets the minimum requirements of the American National Standard for Information Sciences—Permanence of Paper for Printed Library Materials, ANSI Z39.48-1984.

Library of Congress Cataloging-in-Publication Data

Nation-building unraveled? : aid, peace and justice in Afghanistan / edited by Antonio Donini, Norah Niland and Karin Wermester.
      p. cm.
Includes bibliographical references and index.
   ISBN 1–56549–180–7 (pbk. : alk. paper) — ISBN 1–56549–181–5 (cloth : alk. paper)
   1. Afghanistan—Politics and government—2001– 2. Humanitarian assistance—Afghanistan. 3. International relief—Afghanistan. 4. Human rights—Afghanistan. I. Donini, Antonio. II. Wermester, Karin. III. Niland, Norah. [date]
   DS371.4.N37 2003
   958.104'6—dc22

                                        2003016534

---

13 12 11 10 09 08 07 06 05 04   10 9 8 7 6 5 4 3 2 1   First Printing 2004

*To the memory
of the Afghan and non-Afghan aid workers
who paid the ultimate price for their commitment
to humanitarianism since the beginning of the war.
A special tribute is due to the ten Afghan colleagues
who, among scores of innocent civilians,
were brutally killed in Yakawlang in January 2001.*

Contents

PART TWO
POLITICS AND HUMANITARIANISM
AFTER SEPTEMBER 11

CONCLUSION

Foreword

It is difficult to imagine a time in which there could have been a greater gap between the norms that, formally at least, govern the conduct of international relations and the realities of the world. Read the Universal Declaration of Human Rights, the United Nations Convention on the Rights of the Child, or the Geneva Conventions, and realize that most nations in the world have agreed to be bound by them, and you might be forgiven for imagining that the world was already a comparatively decent place and was likely to become still better. But look at the facts of the world, at least the vast majority of it outside a few relatively privileged corners of East Asia, Europe, and North America, and it is hard to believe in the promise of progress, let alone in its reality. Misery is a constant, and in many places it is growing worse, whether because of the rigged game favoring the global North that is the essence of the international trading system, of AIDS, or the debt overhang. And from the Democratic Republic of Congo, to Aceh, to Afghanistan, the crises that seem to dwarf even the "everyday" horrors of the poor world appear to be increasing almost exponentially.

Whether this is an accurate perception or not is of course doubtful. Anyone with enough historical memory and imagination to understand what really occurred during the Middle Passage, the colonization of Africa, or, for that matter, the Wars of Religion in Europe in the seventeenth century, rightly will be unpersuaded by the claim. But equally, there can be no question that a growing consensus has arisen both within the rich countries of the West and the United Nations system which, window-dressing aside, does their bidding, that these crises cannot be ignored, as, arguably, they might once have been. To this extent at least, the new normative universe of individual rights, and the conviction that nations do not have the right to treat their subjects in any way they see fit as long as they do not menace their neighbors (the old "Westphalian" consensus), has prevailed.

But to what end? Before decolonization, management of crises on the periphery was viewed by imperial powers as their mandated responsibility. In the immediate aftermath of decolonization, the hope burned brightly that colonial domination would be replaced by a just world of effective, law-abiding nation-states. In some places, that has happened. But in many others neocolonialism replaced colonialism, as morose discontent replaced revolutionary unrest, while in still others the horror of colonialism was replaced by a horror without even some of the material benefits of imperial rule. Until the end of the Cold War, this was of scant concern to the great powers in whose hands the fate of the world rests. But after the demise of the Communist empire, this disorder came to seem somehow morally and politically intolerable.

The "whys" of this are complicated. The existence of a United Nations ideal, if by no means of that entirely fictitious entity called the international community, doubtless played a role. So did economic globalization with its concurrent weakening of the nation-state system on which the Westphalian order had been based. And surely, the role of human rights in the moral imaginations of "enlightened" Western people is another key element to the story. After all, human rights became far more central as Communism was discredited and Christianity continued to wane as a living moral force. It might have been a poor light, as Locke said of reason, but it often seemed as if, morally speaking, it was all there was.

And it was enough to motivate many decent people, both within the United Nations system and the seemingly ever expanding world of nongovernmental organizations (NGOs), both those committed to human rights and those committed to development and/or emergency relief, to insist that a Somali famine, a Rwandan genocide, or the vast humanitarian needs of war-torn Afghanistan are to be dealt with, not ignored. As a result, in the 1990s the United Nations, an abysmal failure as a peace and security institution, but a tremendous success at being what the late Sir Anthony Parsons once called "a vast decolonization machine," became, for all intents and purposes, a vast alleviation machine—albeit one at least formally committed to the furtherance of human rights and sustainable development rather than exclusively to emergency humanitarian relief.

From Bosnia to East Timor, Kosovo to the Democratic Republic of the Congo (and, in all likelihood, to Iraq as well before the story ends), not to mention dozens of other venues in which the United Nations operates to the general indifference of powerful states, versions of this new dispensation in crisis management can be observed and anatomized. Each has its own peculiarities, not to mention widely varying abilities to garner economic resources, political attention, and media focus. Nonetheless, a broad outline of the new system is emerging. Its ostensible commitments are to those authentic and sincere notions of good—largely human rights based—that dominate the enlightened imaginations of Western people these days. Of course, it is unfortunate that they are conventionally described in a social scientist "newspeak" that is every bit as offensive as the euphemistic language of the modern military. There may once have been, and doubtless still is, both some thought and some heart behind such phrases as *conflict prevention, rule of law, conflict resolution,* and their ilk, but to use them is to do more than enter a terminological wasteland; it is to enter a cognitive one as well, for these phrases almost invariably mask more than they explicate. But the main point is elsewhere.

As is so often the case, the ostensible and the real are not the same. For the real logic of all these pious sentiments and good intentions, the endless think-tank evaluations, academic study groups, and university specializations, has been one of recolonization. Usually, the great powers—first and foremost the United States—grant the United Nations what in another era was the purview of some great colonizing nation's colonial office (the fact that this is not the way UN officials want to see their role and, indeed, is one that makes the best of them profoundly uncomfortable and often furious, is irrelevant). Sometimes, as in Afghanistan or Iraq, they turn over that power after a war. But either way, the deep reality of the new system remains largely unalterable. If anything, the increasing vocation of the United States for intervention in the "humanitarian" crisis zones, at least if it continues to enjoy support domestically and success in its expeditionary endeavor, is likely only further to transform the United Nations into the colonial office of the twenty-first century American empire, and the NGOs into its subcontractors.

Such a development may well be inevitable. The United Nations is a subaltern organization; some have argued it is powerless by design. It is certainly powerless to resist the United States. As for the European Union, at least at present it is unwilling to constitute itself as a counterweight to American military power (as it has already and effectively constituted itself a counterweight to US economic power). As for the NGOs, they are dependent on the great powers for funding, whether directly or through the UN system, and on an increasingly monopolistic and commercialized media for the coverage needed to mobilize popular opinion in the West. Is there an alternative to the current system of institutionalized and bureaucratized aid often delivered courtesy of national militaries with little or no understanding of, or commitment to, even the most basic of humanitarian principles, legal or customary? Can something be done about dubious development practices and insincere commitments to local democracy that, in any case, are incompatible with the proconsular realities of places like Afghanistan, or Kosovo, let alone Iraq, and that further the hidden agenda of governments delivered under the flag of convenience of human rights? Perhaps it is not too optimistic to insist that it is too soon to tell. And whatever the future holds, what is occurring should not be allowed to go unchallenged. The best, or at least the first way, to challenge the emerging recolonizing consensus effectively is to dissect it through concrete analysis of how it works. And yet, surprisingly, such efforts have been few and far between, which alone should testify to the extent of the consensus.

Perhaps the most important of the many merits of *Nation-Building Unraveled? Aid, Peace and Justice in Afghanistan* is that it does just that, and with the authority of contributors who were among the principal decision-makers on humanitarian and human rights issues in Afghanistan, both during the Taliban regime and in the aftermath of the American war. Written with passion, with intellectual verve, and with stunning moral seriousness, the book is not only immensely important for its discussion of what actually happened in Afghanistan and for its teasing out of the political and institutional implications of the Afghan experience for other humanitarian interventions in the crisis zones, it is also a profound work about power in the twenty-first century.

DAVID RIEFF

Acknowledgments

It is customary for editors to thank an army of friends, intellectual sparring partners, and colleagues who contributed, in one way or another, to the initiation and production of a book that is finally ready to go to press. We will not attempt to do so here. The energy that propelled this book into being is due in no small part to the divergent views, tendencies, and perspectives that dominated discourse on the future of Afghanistan in the early months of 2002. The editors and all but one of the contributors to this book were fortunate to have had front-row seats in the unfolding drama of the tentative rebirth of Afghanistan. Many of the ideas and insights discussed in the following pages were born in face-to-face verbal combat with protagonists in the fledgling government, UN agencies, NGOs, and the donor community. Discussions were heated on occasion and often continued well beyond curfew in the sheltered gardens of UN and NGO staff houses in Kabul, Herat, Kandahar, Jalalabad, Bamyan, and Mazar. Thus any listing of individuals who have wittingly or unwittingly contributed to this book runs the risk of embarrassing some or regenerating hard-won debates!

Nevertheless, special thanks are due to the International Peace Academy for providing moral and financial support at an early point in this book's genesis and for organizing a workshop for the editors, some of the authors, and a select group of UN and international NGO experts in New York in February 2003. The workshop greatly facilitated reflection on and clarification of contending views and theories. Particular thanks are due to the president and vice-president, David Malone and Necla Tschirgi respectively, in addition to Karen Ballentine, who provided valuable comments on material related to this volume. Those funders who provided generous support for this project as part of the Economic Agendas in Civil Wars Programme are due warm thanks, including: the Canadian Department of Foreign Affairs and International Trade (DFAIT), the Canadian International Development Agency (CIDA), the Department for International Development (DFID) of the United Kingdom, the International Development Research Centre (IDRC) of Canada, the Government of Norway, the Government of Switzerland, the Government of Sweden, the Rockefeller Foundation, and the United Nations Foundation.

The Watson Institute for International Studies at Brown University and the Institute for Human Security at the Fletcher School of Law and Diplomacy, Tufts University, also proved congenial and intellectual homes for two of the editors, who also benefited from the kind and stimulating support provided by their respective directors, Tom Biersteker and Peter Uvin. In addition, Karin Wermester was able to conduct research in Afghanistan from May through September 2002 thanks to the support of the Centre for Humanitarian Dialogue. David Bryer in particular deserves warm thanks for his kind and unerring support.

The authors and editors are also indebted to Guy Bentham and Krishna Sondhi as well as Joan Laflamme and Erin Brown at Kumarian for their tenacity in believing in a project with many moving parts.

Finally, special thanks are due to Alexander Costy, whose early editorial contributions were invaluable.

Acronyms

AACA	Afghan Assistance Coordination Authority
AHRC	Afghanistan Human Rights Commission
AIA	Afghanistan Interim Authority
AREU	Afghanistan Research and Evaluation Unit
ATA	Afghanistan Transitional Authority
CG	Consultative Group
CJCMOTF	Coalition Joint Civil-Military Operations Task Force
DDR	Disarmament, Demobilization, and Reintegration
DHA	(UN) Department of Humanitarian Affairs (now OCHA)
DRC	Democratic Republic of the Congo
ECHO	European Commission Humanitarian Office
HPG	Humanitarian Policy Group (at ODI)
HPN	Humanitarian Practice Network
HRW	Human Rights Watch
ICG	International Crisis Group
ICRC	International Committee of the Red Cross
IDP	Internally Displaced Person
IMF	International Monetary Fund
IRC	International Rescue Committee
ISAF	International Security Assistance Force
ISI	Inter-Services Intelligence (Pakistan's military intelligence wing)
ITAP	Immediate and Transitional Assistance Programme for Afghanistan
MOU	Memorandum of Understanding (between the UN and the Taliban, May 1998)
MoWA	Ministry of Women's Affairs

MSF	Médecins sans Frontières
NDF	National Development Framework
NGO	Nongovernmental Organization
OCHA	(UN) Office for the Coordination of Humanitarian Affairs (formerly DHA)
ODI	Overseas Development Institute
OECD	Organisation for Economic Cooperation and Development
OHCHR	(UN) Office of the High Commissioner for Human Rights
PCP	Principled Common Programming
PDPA	People's Democratic Party of Afghanistan
POW	Prisoner of War
PRT	Provincial Reconstruction Team
PSYOPs	Psychological Operations
RAWA	Revolutionary Association of the Women of Afghanistan
SF	Strategic Framework
SRSG	Special Representative of the Secretary-General (UN)
UNAMA	UN Assistance Mission in Afghanistan
UNCO	UN Coordinator's Office
UNDP	UN Development Programme
UNHCR	UN High Commissioner for Refugees
UNICEF	United Nations Children's Fund
UNOCHA	United Nations Office for the Coordination of Humanitarian Assistance to Afghanistan
UNSMA	UN Special Mission in Afghanistan
USG	Under-Secretary-General
WHO	(UN) World Health Organization
WFP	(UN) World Food Programme

AFGHANISTAN

CHINA

TAJIKISTAN

UZBEKISTAN

TURKMENISTAN

ISLAMIC REPUBLIC OF IRAN

PAKISTAN

INDIA

Jammu and Kashmir

Islāmābād

AFGHANISTAN

Dushanbe

Feyẕābād
BADAKHSHĀN

Tāloqān
KONDŌZ TAKHĀR
Kondōz
Baghlān
BAGHLĀN

SAMANGĀN
Samangān

Mazār-e Sharīf
BALKH

JOWZJĀN
Sheberghān

Sar-e Pol

SAR-E POL

Meymaneh
FĀRYĀB

Qaleh-ye Now
BĀDGHĪS

Chaghcharān
GHOWR

Herāt
HERĀT

Farāh
FARĀH

Zaranj
NĪMRŪZ

Lashkar Gāh
HELMAND

Tarīn Kowt
ORUZGĀN

Qalāt
ZĀBOL

Kandahār
KANDAHĀR

BĀMIĀN
Bāmiān

Mahmūd-e Rāqī
Chārīkār
PARVĀN
KĀPĪSĀ
Meydān Shahr
VARDAK

Ghaznī
GHAZNĪ

Sharan
PAKTĪKĀ

Gardīz
PAKTĪĀ
Pol-e 'Alam
LOWGAR

KHOWST
Khowst

KĀBUL
Kābul

NŪRESTĀN
Mehtarlām
LAGHMĀN
Asadābād
KONAR
Jalālābād
NANGARHĀR

National capital
Provincial capital
National boundary
Provincial boundary

0   50   100   150   200   250 km
0   50   100   150 mi

Map No. 3958.1 UNITED NATIONS
November 2002

Department of Public Information
Cartographic Section

1

Introduction

ANTONIO DONINI, NORAH NILAND,
AND KARIN WERMESTER

Prior to the events of September 11, 2001, visitors arriving in Kabul were greeted with the following words of welcome: "Put your watch back half an hour . . . and go back in time a thousand years." Since the collapse of the twin towers in New York, and the momentous changes that followed, it is the French dictum—somewhat ironically—that has acquired new resonance upon arrival in Afghanistan: "Plus ça change, plus c'est la même chose" (The more things change, the more they stay the same). Time present and time past, in Afghanistan as elsewhere, are key determinants of time future. While there has been rapid and dramatic change on several fronts, many of the factors that shape Afghan society have shown remarkable resilience over the arc of a twenty-five-year crisis.

This volume deals with the challenges of aid, peace, and justice in Afghanistan and with the perils and opportunities of the international response to the Afghan crisis. It is intended to contribute to critical debate on the direction and effectiveness of international approaches to the management of crises. The volume focuses on Afghanistan's experience as an illustration of the way in which emerging international "ordering" practices are affecting the role and policy of international organizations, their interaction with national authorities and local communities, and their ability to generate just and sustainable social outcomes.

Drawing primarily on the experiences of key international and Afghan practitioners and analysts who have been directly involved in the political, assistance, and human rights aspects of post–September 11 (and in some instances pre–September 11) Afghanistan, this volume offers a series of disparate views from the field on the costs and benefits, challenges and opportunities, tradeoffs and compromises, involved in responses to conflict, injustice, and chronic insecurity. Situating the discussion within broader scholarly and practitioner debates on peace-building, transitional justice, and humanitarian action, the contributors bring a unique perspective on themes of global relevance by telling the inside story of the Afghan crisis.

While the story deserves to be told in its own right, Afghanistan's quarter century of crisis and responses to it also has wider resonance. Afghanistan stands out as a defining moment (post-Kosovo—pre-Iraq) in the evolution of the theory and practice of global ordering. Here, regime change, nation-building, the quest for justice, humanitarian and development assistance, and support for a fragile peace overlap and interact with domestic and international agendas in ways that are certain to influence future thinking about the role of external actors in conflict and transition settings. Only time will tell how deeply, for example, the practice of humanitarian action will be altered by precedents set in post–September 11 Afghanistan, but there can be no doubt that the history of external interventions in complex crises will be divided into pre–September 11 and post–September 11 periods.

GLOBAL ORDERING
AND THE QUEST FOR COHERENCE

International responses to complex crises have evolved significantly in the post–Cold War period. Since the early 1990s, many have charted the evolution of more robust and comprehensive external interventions, often led by UN peace operations, in complex crises.[1] Such changes have been accompanied by more profound shifts in international response that have seen the United Nations, in association with other "benign" international actors, take on quasi-state functions in places such as Kosovo and East Timor as "transitional authorities" and, more recently and in a qualitative leap from the past, in Afghanistan and Iraq under the banner of "regime change." Together, such trends have widened and deepened the nature of the international community's response in the global periphery. The underlying objectives of such interventions—peace, stability, development, accountable governance—have become steadily more ambitious, wide ranging, and trusteeship-like than in the past. Partly as a result, Western decision-makers who fund and essentially call the shots in such operations have pressed international economic, political, and military instruments to work more closely together in what are described as "coherent" and "comprehensive" strategies and mechanisms geared to mending failed or dysfunctional states.

The trend toward coherence has sparked considerable debate across the international assistance, conflict resolution, and human rights communities.[2] However, what coherence means, its underlying assumptions, its attempted operationalization, and whether it is effective at delivering desired outcomes, is still subject to ambiguity, debate, and dissension. At stake are fundamental issues concerning the rationale of peace-making and peace-building efforts as well as the purposes, principles, and functions of assistance in post-ceasefire or post-regime-change situations.

At its most basic, coherence refers to the attempt to coordinate, bring together, or join political intervention with other relevant types of action, including humanitarian and human rights actions.[3] At its most developed, coherence suggests the harmonization or merging of objectives, strategies, and programming tools within and across relevant actors so that they are all geared toward the pursuit of a common end goal or are in line with an articulated vision. From this perspective, as Nicholas Stockton says, integration is understood as the organizational attempt to enact coherence through managerial methods and/or institutional or structural reform.

There is both a normative and an organizational dimension to the search for coherence. On the one hand, coherence is employed as a global public good that is value neutral. Synonymous with the pursuit of greater efficiency and effectiveness, it is touted as desirable both as a process and an outcome. Such normative considerations have contributed to, and been a result of the merging of development and security responses as a means of governing "the periphery"—namely, those states of little geostrategic relevance to major powers.[4] On the other hand, though often relatedly, coherence has become an ordering concept for organizations, both internally and among themselves. In this sense its operationalization lies at the intersection of common understandings of *coordination* and *strategy;* it is deemed necessary to "work together" because the absence of coordination creates opportunities for opposing agents to exploit gaps and thereby to obstruct, or upset, commonly agreed strategies.[5]

Afghanistan in the late 1990s represented a high point in the quest for coherence and integration of the various "regimes" of international action in response to a complex crisis. The Strategic Framework (SF) experiment, tailored to the very specific situation of Taliban-ruled Afghanistan, was a deliberate attempt to reduce the disconnects between the peace-making, humanitarian, and human rights functions of the United Nations. Its underlying assumption was that better synergies based on agreed-upon objectives and principled interventions would make for better peace prospects. Similarly, the UN Assistance Mission in Afghanistan (UNAMA), which replaced the SF and became operational in

Afghanistan in early 2002 with the broad objective of supporting the implementation of what has become known as the Bonn Agreement of December 2001, is arguably the most institutionally and normatively advanced integrated mission fielded by the United Nations in one of its most high-profile interventions. Its success, perceived or actual, as well as the effectiveness of the broader regime consolidation effort, will likely have major implications on the evolution of global ordering practices well beyond the UN system.

As the chapters that follow suggest, one of the lessons of Afghanistan is that while coherence is a laudable objective in and of itself—who could object to better coordination and synergies among external actors in crisis countries?—it does not necessarily lead to effective, principled, and predictable responses or to just and durable outcomes. One of the more unfortunate findings in this volume is that when the crunch comes, expedient politics nearly always trumps universal principles. It is unlikely that the tensions among the international actors that derive their legitimacy from time-bound Security Council resolutions and those who claim their legitimacy from international treaties and international humanitarian law will evaporate like morning mist anytime soon. However, it is the hope of the editors that the exploration of these and other tensions and tradeoffs in the Afghan context will serve to provide a better understanding of the issues at stake—many of which are relevant also in other crisis situations—and how they can be addressed to the best advantage of the victims of crisis and conflict.

BRIEF OVERVIEW: THEMES AND CHAPTERS

In the opening chapter Nicholas Stockton offers a provocative interpretation of the Afghan crisis in the context of changes in the international security environment—from the Cold War to the "war on terrorism"—that have influenced assistance objectives, and defined humanitarian interaction with the political realm over the past decade and more. Stockton offers a critical analysis of the evolving role of aid as a tool in peace-consolidation efforts and of the institutional and policy adjustments that this has triggered among leading international organizations. He points to the limited capacity of the aid arena to measure its impact in terms of lives lost or saved and the huge gap that often exists between actual requirements and response; in so doing he questions the conventional wisdom that greater coherence among political, humanitarian, and human rights action necessarily leads to more effective peace-building strategies and outcomes.

Part One is clustered around the theme of prioritization of imperatives in the context of the post–September 11 response in Afghanistan. While there are various ways in which aid, peace, and justice interventions can complement one another, there are also instances in which imperatives informing the responses of each can differ depending on how priorities are defined, ordered, and sequenced, and by whom. In Afghanistan, if pragmatism and the pursuit of stability have been the guiding tenets of the peace-implementation process since the signing of the Bonn Agreement, the implications of this have not been limited to the political or security sphere. The decision-making that determines political strategies informs, defines, or has implications for assistance and justice interventions that are equally important in terms of securing a just and sustainable peace. In effect, the strategies and relationships among aid, peace, and justice in Afghanistan have in many ways been structured by political choices, resulting in an implicit hierarchy in the relationship between, and decisions made regarding, aid and justice interventions.

In Chapter 3 J. Alexander Thier, who conducted research for the International Crisis Group on post-Bonn political processes in Afghanistan, sets the political stage that has defined the parameters of the international community's response in Afghanistan since the signing of the Agreement on Provisional Arrangements in Afghanistan Pending the Re-establishment of Permanent Institutions—the Bonn Agreement—in December 2001. The chapter examines the vision of the Bonn process for the transition from war to peace and assesses the intertwined strands of intervention and entropy—the (re)creation of a central state, the continuing war on terrorism, and a relapse into division and conflict in the countryside—as the story of Afghanistan's first year of post-Taliban political transformation.

Chapter 4 examines Afghanistan's human rights experience and its relevance to the broader quest for justice. As a former United Nations human rights adviser in Afghanistan, Norah Niland looks at the trajectory of human rights issues and responses in Afghanistan from an insider's perspective. Focusing primarily on the urgency of addressing the justice vacuum that was institutionalized under the Taliban, Niland argues that decision-making on human rights in Afghanistan has changed very little despite the unique opportunity that emerged in the wake of the Taliban's fall. Just as before, human rights have been relegated to back-burner status despite the desire for change among citizens. Recognizing the challenges of managing the delicate and often perilous transition to peace with justice, she advocates the need for a clear and conspicuous commitment to tackling the twin problems of impunity and ongoing human rights violations as part of a larger justice package that addresses structural inequalities and the need for judicial reform.

In Chapter 5 Kate Clark, who was the BBC correspondent in Afghanistan prior to and during the fall of the Taliban, presents a unique view of intervention in Afghanistan from the media's perspective. Clark examines the instrumentalization, by design and by default, of the media and provides a fascinating account of how the media contributes and responds to the shaping of political imperatives.

In the final chapter of Part One, Sippi Azarbaijani-Moghaddam examines the oft-discussed but, it seems, little understood role of women in the perpetuation and transformation of violent conflict. Delving beyond the "burqa issue," she presents a critical historical analysis of the situation of women in Afghanistan. She argues that the historical evolution of the changes in their situation suggests that the trends are linked to state actors' efforts at exercising centralized control. This chapter, based on a series of interviews with Nancy Hatch Dupree, who has lived and worked in and around Afghanistan since the 1950s, traces some of the patterns and intersections of social change and political dynamics with external interventions over the past hundred years, focusing specifically on the opportunities and challenges of the post-Taliban era.

Together, the chapters in Part One are suggestive of the underlying challenges—and various points of contention that arise at normative, policy, and operational levels—of attempts to lend coherence to aid, peace, and justice interventions in a given context.

From the humanitarian perspective, keeping an informed but practical distance from partisan political activity is perceived as necessary to ensure that relief is provided to those in most need and that lives and livelihoods are protected. At the same time, political actors (both at home and in the area of intervention) have often found it useful to coopt humanitarian actors in the pursuit of political objectives or simply to marginalize them altogether. The cultural and institutional differences that characterize their respective agendas only compound the more fundamental distinction between pragmatism and principle that has traditionally defined the respective work of political and humanitarian actors.

Part Two of the volume addresses different facets of the political and humanitarian action problématique in the Afghan context. Since the end of the Cold War the issue of instrumentalization or politicization of the humanitarian enterprise that can result from too great proximity to political activity—whether among local power holders, donors, and the diplomatic community, or the United Nations—is fiercely debated and often contested, though often on the margins of major debates on peacebuilding and transition.[6] The trend toward coherence as a major global ordering practice has, however, generated a critical mass of voices and views on the extent and nature of the interaction and proximity, perceived or actual, of the two traditionally distinct forms of intervention.

In Chapter 7 Antonio Donini, who worked as a senior UN official in Afghanistan in the 1990s and early 2000s, provides a historical overview of the politicization of humanitarian action throughout the different phases of conflict there. He argues that the manner in which the international community responded to humanitarian need and to the human rights dimension of the crisis, and the fluctuations of the response over time, were heavily influenced by political agendas that were often at odds with humanitarian objectives. This has ranged from relatively benign conditionality from governments to the overt manipulation of humanitarian action for partisan purposes. In the late 1980s, cross-border "humanitarian" activities were part of Cold War efforts to weaken the Soviet Union; under the Taliban, principles were hostage to the fortunes of a reviled regime and to its demonization by various interest groups abroad; post–September 11, the anti-terrorism agenda and realpolitik have coalesced to put pragmatism before principle, with possible long-term consequences for the stability of Afghanistan (and the future of humanitarianism).

Picking up on many of the points raised by Donini, Alexander Costy in Chapter 8 analyzes the contemporary—post–September 11—dimensions of the interaction between political and humanitarian action as they have played out in the Afghan context. As a UNAMA official during its nascent stages, Costy provides an inside but balanced perspective. Placing the role, actual or desirable, of the state at the center of the debate, his chapter outlines the main patterns of "integration" between external political and assistance initiatives concerned with peace-building in Afghanistan in 2002 and highlights two issues that have caused significant debate over "humanitarian space" in the post-Taliban transition. The first is the leadership role claimed by the Afghan Interim and Transitional Administrations in managing international assistance in Afghanistan. The second is the heatedly contested direct involvement of external military combat forces in the delivery of relief and recovery activities.

The following two chapters offer opposing perspectives on many of the issues raised in Costy's chapter. Nicholas Leader, seconded from UNAMA as an adviser to the Afghan interim and transitional administrations, and Haneef Atmar, a former NGO worker who was appointed Minister for Rural Reconstruction and Development in mid 2002, analyze the humanitarian and development enterprise from the Afghan government's perspective. Paul O'Brien of CARE-USA, on the other hand, offers a view from an international NGO perspective. Together, these two chapters are suggestive of the range of issues that are brought up in relation to the management of humanitarian crises in countries in which there is a disconnect between the roles, responsibilities, and capacities of humanitarian actors—mainly the United Nations and international NGOs—and those government ministries responsible for the provision of basic services to citizens.

In the concluding chapter Bruce D. Jones teases out and analyzes many of the key themes highlighted in the volume from a broader institutional—primarily United Nations—peace-building perspective. He examines the nature of decision-making and the tradeoffs that accompany UN interventions in crisis and post-crisis situations and also the organizational imperatives and cultures that condition and set the parameters of response. In particular, he offers perspectives on the relationship between the United States and the United Nations—a crosscutting theme that is in many ways the canvas on which the chapters of this book are drafted.

NOTES

[1] See Stephen John Stedman, Donald Rothchild, and Elizabeth Cousens, eds., *Ending Civil Wars: The Implementation of Peace Agreements* (Boulder, Colo.: Lynne Rienner Publishers, 2002).

[2] Joanna Macrae and Nicholas Leader's seminal work *Shifting Sands: The Search for "Coherence" Between Political and Humanitarian Responses to Complex Emergencies* has been important by lending coherence, as it were, to disparate but related strands of thought on this topic (HPG Report 8 [London: ODI, August 2000]). For a discussion of various perspectives on coherence, see also *Disasters: The Journal of Disaster Studies, Policy and Management* 25/4 (2001); and Devon Curtis, *Politics and Humanitarian Aid: Debates, Dilemmas, and Dissension*, HPG Report 10 (London: ODI, April 2001).

[3] Centre for Humanitarian Dialogue, *HD Report: Politics and Humanitarianism: Coherence in Crisis?"* (February 2003). These definitions were informed by lengthy discussion with Joanna Macrae and Nicholas Stockton.

[4] See Mark Duffield, *Global Governance and the New Wars: The Merging of Development and Security* (New York: Zed Books, 2001).

[5] Previously in Afghanistan, the fragmentation of humanitarian interventions was perceived as inadvertently lending an element of legitimacy to the Taliban regime, which in turn was able to exploit the gaps in the nature and types of responses to further its consolidation of control and other aims. Similar concerns regarding the potential of spoilers to exploit the gaps in the implementation of peace processes have also been leveled against incoherent peace implementation strategies (see Bruce D. Jones, "The Challenges of Strategic Coordination," in Stedman, Rothchild, and Cousens, *Ending Civil Wars*).

[6] The instrumentalization or politicization of humanitarian aid refers to at least three distinct but often intertwined ways in which political imperatives can implicitly or explicitly seek to synchronize the planning and delivery of relief with political objectives. The first is the use of humanitarian assets to affect political dynamics in the area of intervention (such as aid conditionality to effect compliance); the second, and related, is the use of humanitarian assets in support of a domestic political agenda (such as legitimizing military intervention abroad); and the third is the use of humanitarian assets as a substitute for political (in)action such as many argued was the case in Rwanda in 1994 (see John Ericksson, et al., *The International Response to Conflict and Genocide: Lessons from the Rwanda Experience—Synthesis Report"* [Copenhagen: Steering Committee of the Joint Evaluation of Emergency Assistance to Rwanda, 1996]).

2

Afghanistan, War, Aid, and International Order

NICHOLAS STOCKTON

Here is where humanitarian need and the priorities of relief agencies all but offer themselves up as a rationale for the new twenty-first century interventionism that in many ways recapitulates the "new imperialism" of the 1870s, when Europeans justified their takeover of Africa on humanitarian and anti-slavery grounds.

—DAVID RIEFF, *A BED FOR THE NIGHT*

Afghanistan has always exerted influence beyond its very porous borders, and likewise the outside world, through force of ideas, force of arms, or just through dismal economics, has also made its impact upon Afghanistan. Therefore, there is no obvious reason to suppose that the restoration in December 2001 of international respect for Afghanistan's sovereignty will seal the country off from external influence in the future. Political change and development in Afghanistan need to be viewed not as a *sui generis* narrative, in spite of the many particularities of the country, but rather as a complex interplay among ideas, power, and organizational practices played out in a global context.

The purpose of this chapter is to describe how the role of international aid has evolved in Afghanistan, primarily as an occasional and flexible instrument in the international relations toolbox of the major powers. In the closing years of the Cold War, international aid played a lead part in US policy toward Afghanistan. In the immediate post–September 11 period it has played a subordinate supporting role to the dominant part played by the US-led Coalition forces. In between these periods, with the attention of the major powers focused elsewhere, international aid agencies operated with greater bureaucratic autonomy, with aid policies and practices being driven by a combination of donor preferences and organizational interests. Business principles then tended to dominate the behavior of the international aid agencies, each one trying to establish the case for its continued existence in highly competitive markets. However, while the two forces of realpolitik and organizational economics explain much about the shape and behavior of the international aid system, its formal raison d'être is steeped in "humanitarian" and "development" discourse, rich in references to ethics, principles, and rights. Nevertheless, on closer examination, this ethical framework appears to enjoy significant influence over the practices of the international aid system only during those times when big powers are preoccupied with other matters and in those places where "principles" happen to coincide with the economic interests of the host organization.

During the 1990s, within the framework provided by realpolitik and the demands of organizational economics, the international aid system has had to contend with events that have generated the greatest-ever crisis of confidence in its political, economic, and social utility. Brought into question has been its capacity to transform war into peace, to overcome social disorder through the application of justice and the rule of law, and to generate wealth for the poor. In the face of the difficulties it has encountered in pursuit of these challenges, the response of the aid system has been to close ranks, largely through vertical and horizontal integration, controlling messaging to external audiences, and sanctifying a culture of risk-aversion, sometimes perhaps at a significant cost to those most urgently in need of assistance. However, while these adaptations may have enabled the aid system to survive the ten-year recession in public and private aid financing of the 1990s, the events of September 11 have generated new and perhaps far more onerous demands on it.

As a counterpart to US military power, the international aid system has been tasked to deliver the political and security utilities that its protagonists claim can be produced from the practice of peace-building, a peculiar developmental phenomenon invented in the 1990s. Even a skeptical US Republican administration has been persuaded by a combination of events, and the lack of obvious alternatives, to increase international aid resources for these purposes. Under unprecedented scrutiny, the aid system is now expected to bring about a prosperous, law-abiding, and peaceful future for Afghanistan, primarily to enhance the domestic security of the United States. So far, the aid bounty generated by September 11 has unleashed an orgy of bureaucratic expansion by the UN agencies and NGOs operating in Afghanistan. Some early signs suggest that one lesson being taken from Afghanistan to Iraq is that the conventional international aid system has failed to deliver on its promises. With the security of the United States and other Western nations under threat, the tenuousness of evidence for the ability of the international aid system to convert conflict to peace, disorder to the rule of law, and poverty into wealth is driving Western political leaders toward other prospective solutions. The oft-argued case that peace-building is a long-term process is an indigestible excuse for politicians operating within a four-year election cycle. In Afghanistan the urgent search for peace and quick economic growth explains the move toward replacing civil by military capacities in "humanitarian space," and for the growing competition between conventional aid agencies and new for-profit corporate contractors in the development zone.

This return to Marshall Plan–style pacification and development methods, however, is proceeding only incrementally. Private donors continue to provide some NGOs with a significant amount of income, giving them a strong comparative advantage over commercial businesses. From the point of view of Western governments, their sometimes-annoying claim of independence is tolerated, given their propensity to socialize, in part, the costs and the risks of the humanitarian duties that should properly attach to belligerent and occupying powers. Furthermore, while the production of peace, order, and affluence may have confounded the best efforts of the United Nations and bilateral and nongovernmental development agencies, the new "peace-building" players—the military and the commercial contractors—so far appear devoid of genuinely innovative ideas. Instead, they seem to mimic the discredited paradigms of the conventional aid system. If the newcomers also turn out to be ineffective, their disadvantageous cost base will militate in favor of aid resources flowing back to conventional aid agencies or, more likely, may result in increased dependence upon coercive methods of peace enforcement. This is likely to mean that international aid will slump back into recession until it can demonstrate that it can deploy more effective policy instruments for the pacific prevention of poverty, warfare, and terrorism. Relatively small shifts in public opinion in the United States could determine which pathway is followed. The longer-term consequences of the perceived failure of the policy and practice of aid-induced pacification in Afghanistan are likely therefore to be considerable.

THE COLD WAR:
REALPOLITIK, INSURGENCY,
AND "HUMANITARIAN SOLIDARITY"

Told as a short story, the history of international peace and security since the founding of the United Nations in 1945 has just two chapters. The first chapter contains the story of the bipolar world of the Cold War up to 1989, followed by the second, as yet unfinished chapter concerned with globalization, in which liberal capitalism was rolled out under the economic and military hegemony of the United States. While both chapters contain many verses, the post–Cold War era, for our purposes, is most obviously subdivided into the periods before and after September 11, the events of which propelled the "Bush doctrine" into the vacuum left by the more laissez-faire tendencies of the Clinton years.

Still smarting from its defeat in the Vietnam War, the Carter doctrine of Cold War by proxy deliberately provoked the Soviet invasion of Afghanistan in 1979 by financing the Islamic mujahedin uprising.[1] Intent on creating an unsustainable military and economic burden upon the Soviet occupying forces, the United States provided copious "humanitarian" support for the mujahedin-controlled refugee camps in Pakistan. This strategy depended heavily upon the cooperation of international NGOs and the UN system, as well as the "freedom fighters" themselves.[2] The international organizations that flocked to Peshawar enhanced the legitimacy of the mujahedin insurgency and provided a crucial and impenetrable web of actors that allowed the United States to enjoy the spectacle of a Vietnam-style defeat for the Soviet Union without the risk of GIs coming home in body bags. Furthermore, the genuine popularity of the mujahedin cause helped to spread the costs of the US strategy of support for the mujahedin insurgency. The war by proxy also provided the US government with "plausible deniability" for any direct responsibility for the human consequences of the war in Afghanistan. As reported, most war atrocities were committed by the Soviets or their Afghan clients, thus allowing the West to win the propaganda war too.

The strategic "success" of this period of Western "civil society solidarity" with the mujahedin following the Soviet invasion had considerable impact upon the conduct of the international aid system elsewhere.[3] Arguably, the strategic potential of the "soft power" of nongovernmental agencies, multiplied by Western official aid funds, private donations, and voluntary effort, and coordinated by the United Nations, was first fully demonstrated in the Afghanistan refugee camps in Pakistan.[4] When combined with the "hard power" of the mujahedin "freedom fighters," international "civil society" showed that it had the flexibility to partner with local insurgents, inflicting the most grievous defeat experienced by the Soviet Union throughout the Cold War. This politically low risk and relatively cheap winning formula was already well established as an important tool for advancing US strategic interests by the time of the ignominious Soviet withdrawal from Afghanistan in 1989, so successful had it been during the final years of the Cold War, when US public opinion was still averse to any foreign military adventures. It was not the last time that humanitarian assistance might be described as being a "force multiplier"[5] on behalf of the United States.

Although the scale of the Afghanistan cross-border operation probably makes it unique, lessons derived from it were certainly exported elsewhere. The most obvious parallel was the pressure exerted upon the Heng Samrin regime of Cambodia through the Thai border camps. Certain aspects of Western support for the cross-border operations into Ethiopia in solidarity with the Eritrea Peoples Liberation Front and the Tigray Peoples Liberation Front, cross-border support for the Sudan Peoples Liberation Army, and "humanitarian aid" for the Contras against the Sandinistas in Nicaragua also illustrate other variants of proxy wars fought against "hostile" regimes. These have the essential ingredients of an Afghan-style partnership between the soft and legitimizing power of Western NGOs, loosely shepherded within a UN co-ordination system, blended with covert military support to so-called freedom or resistance fighters.

For the international NGOs, and latterly the United Nations agencies too, humanitarian space in Afghanistan during the cross-border years was defined by the mujahedin, the Pakistan government, and the US government's Bureau of Population, Refugees, and Migrants.[6] Little was heard about humanitarian principles from the NGOs and the UN system during these years.

THE "END OF HISTORY": THE ERA OF AID-DRIVEN PEACE-BUILDING

In mid 1992 the newly appointed UN secretary-general Boutros Boutros-Ghali presented an ambitious plan for the global eradication of warfare through the provision of a universal guarantee of human security. The *Agenda for Peace*[7] set out to take full advantage of the depoliticization of warfare and development, the result, according to Francis Fukuyama, of the "end of history."[8] Consistent with this vision of the triumph of liberal capitalism over totalitarian socialism, the secretary-general blamed any ongoing violent conflict upon underdevelopment and historical misunderstandings about identities. The remedy was not, therefore, a matter of seeking diplomatic and political formulas. It needed also to enter the realms of economic and social transformation. The *Agenda for Peace* identified "fierce new assertions of nationalism and sovereignty" and threats to the cohesion of states from "brutal ethnic, religious, social, cultural or linguistic strife" (para. 11). The document continues:

> Social peace is challenged on the one hand by new assertions of discrimination and exclusion and, on the other, by acts of terrorism seeking to undermine evolution and change through democratic means (para. 11).

To this Boutros-Ghali added:

> Poverty, disease, famine, oppression and despair abound, joining to produce 17 million refugees, 20 million displaced persons and massive migrations of peoples within and beyond national borders. These are both the sources and the consequences of conflict that require the ceaseless attention and the highest priority in the efforts of the United Nations (para. 13).

To address these challenges, the secretary-general identified four key policy instruments: preventive diplomacy, peace-making, peace-keeping, and post-conflict peace-building.

> Taken together, and carried out with the backing of all Members, [these] offer a coherent contribution towards securing peace in the spirit of the Charter (para. 22).

Significantly, humanitarian assistance was cast as a player in the first three of these policy instruments. The secretary-general suggested that "humanitarian assistance, impartially provided, could be of critical importance" as part of a conflict prevention effort (para. 29). Similarly, he argued that humanitarian assistance could play an important role in ameliorating the circumstances that generated conflict, for example, in assisting displaced persons and in the belief that effective relief aid might also encourage social and political reconciliation. In peace-keeping operations the secretary-general argued that "civilian political officers, human rights monitors, electoral officials, refugee and humanitarian aid specialists and police play as central a role as the military" (para. 52). It seems that Boutros-Ghali did not anticipate that the integration of humanitarian action into the UN-led international peace-building system would threaten the perceived neutrality and independence of humanitarian action. This assumption held good even though the *Agenda for Peace* envisaged the use of more robust means of providing security than was traditionally understood to be acceptable under, for example, the Red Cross Movement's humanitarian principles:

> When United Nations personnel are deployed in conditions of strife, whether for preventive diplomacy, peacemaking, peacekeeping, peace-building or humanitarian purposes, the need arises to ensure their safety. . . . Before deployment takes place, the [Security] Council should keep open the option of considering in advance collective measures, possibly including those under Chapter VII when a threat to international peace and security is also involved, to come into effect should the purpose of the United Nations operation systematically be frustrated and hostilities occur (paras. 66, 68).

All this pointed to the implicit assumption that there was no ideological or political content in the directives of the Security Council, a view consistent with the "end of history" thesis. The new role for humanitarian actors was thus to be a partner to the technical capacity of the UN system, working together for international peace. The *Agenda for Peace* thus provided the opportunity for humanitarian organizations to convert from their cross-border role as partners in insurgency to a new era as partners in peace-building, even though sometimes this might require international peace-keepers, instead of armed insurgents, to ride shotgun for humanitarian operations.

While militarized "humanitarian" intervention has since become a more familiar phenomenon, it is worth recalling that it was impatience with the more conventional interpretations of independence and neutrality that caused the founders of Médecins sans Frontières (MSF) to break away from the International Committee of the Red Cross during the Nigerian civil war of the late 1960s. The fundamental principles of the Red Cross, as adopted by the 1956 International Red Cross Conference, require that "the Movement may not take sides in hostilities or engage at any time in controversies of a political, racial, religious or ideological nature." In accordance with most readings of the 1949 Geneva Conventions and 1977 Additional Protocols, humanitarian intervention is allowed only with the consent of the "high contracting parties" or "controlling authorities." Thus, without ever acknowledging support for MSF's notion of "le droit d'ingérence" (literally, the right to interfere), this challenge to the fundamental principle of national sovereignty was implicitly endorsed by the *Agenda for Peace*. It effectively amplified the ambiguity of the wording of General Assembly Resolution 46/182, which established the UN Department of Humanitarian Affairs (DHA, now OCHA), which states, "humanitarian assistance *should* be provided with the consent of the affected country and, *in principle*, on the basis of an appeal by that country" (para. 30, emphasis added). This implies that neither consent nor an appeal by a state is absolutely necessary. For the humanitarian system, the *Agenda for Peace* predicated incorporation into, or at the very least, close partnership with, an ambitious and expansive political project: the global pursuit of what Mark Duffield has called "liberal peace."[9] In other words, the imposition, by force where necessary, of the "end of history."

The secretary-general thus proposed first to resolve wars, either through peaceful negotiation or under the enforcement provisions of Chapter VII of the UN Charter, and second, to bring together the combined resources of the UN system, donor nations, and international civil society to establish sustainable "human security" as the necessary precondition for peaceful development. Boutros-Ghali announced that, in pursuit of democracy, human rights and "the empowerment of the unorganized, the poor [and] the marginalized," he had begun "taking steps to rationalise and in certain cases *integrate* the various programmes and agencies of the United Nations within specific countries" (para. 81, emphasis added). UN mission integration, and its weaker cousin "strategic coordination," subsequently became the key tools adopted to achieve greater interagency policy coherence, the outcome of UN reform deemed most necessary for the system to be capable of assuming a lead role in the delivery of the post–Cold War peace dividend.

The end of absolute sovereignty tacitly endorsed by the *Agenda for Peace* (with one eye on the air-exclusion zones in Iraq) thus gave license to the use of coercive action to end gross violations of human rights, where these could be argued to constitute a threat to international peace and security. While this option of enforcement in support of human rights and humanitarian considerations may have since been used very selectively, by establishing the principle that it could, the secretary-general implicitly lent credence to the concept of "humanitarian" war. Although born out of the hubris immediately following the collapse of the Soviet Union and the ignominious defeat of socialism, the *Agenda for Peace* has left a legacy that has survived the naiveté of that period. As Joanna Macrae and Nicholas Leader observe, the watchwords *coherence* and *integration* continue to provide the normative framework for the coordination of international aid.[10] However, in 1993 the *Agenda for Peace* was given its first serious practical trial as the international community squared up to deal with the growing crisis in Somalia.

AFTER SOMALIA: "PEACE-BUILDING LITE"

The new international peace-building enterprise was soon to encounter the "dangerous circumstances" envisaged by Boutros-Ghali. Frustrated by the intractability of Somali warlords, US NGOs used their considerable leverage with the outgoing Bush Administration (credit in no small part earned by the part they played in the US policy of support for the mujahedin during the Reagan years) to seek the deployment of a US military force to protect the humanitarian operation in Somalia. With US forces at that time still searching for a new post–Cold War raison d'être, it perhaps seemed timely to oblige, but the actual dangers and resource requirements of the integrated policies of the *Agenda for Peace* soon became apparent. Nation-building, even without the complexity of ideological debates, turned out to be a potentially lethal undertaking. Ironically, having brought down the Soviet Union's occupation of Afghanistan without any US military casualties, Operation Restore Hope was to end with America mourning the body bags of returning Marines killed in their first post–Cold War humanitarian intervention.

After the disastrous failure of the operation to capture General Aideed, US troops were withdrawn from Somalia and the American commitment to the *Agenda for Peace* contracted into a new period of relative disinterest in the affairs of the nonstrategic areas of the Third World. The deaths of US troops in Somalia did much to persuade American public opinion that an ungrateful and savage Third World might be best left to its own devices. Much better the burden-shifting formula of African solutions for African problems, which enjoyed the merits of being cheap, safe for Western soldiers, and politically correct too. Implemented through the multilateral channels of regional organizations, such as the Organization of African Unity, with support provided by the UN system, the policy of local solutions for local problems also had the advantage of distancing Western powers from any immediate responsibility for protracted failures of governance in the South. This was especially important at a time when expensive crises with critical implications for Western Europe were being played out under conditions of NATO military and OECD aid "overstretch." The tensile strength of US political disenchantment with multilateral peace-building in the South was to be exposed within a year by the refusal to even name, let alone respond to the first ever real-time televised genocide, which took place in Rwanda in 1994. While the experience of Somalia was to usher in the period of peace-building lite, Rwanda demonstrated how determinedly attached the US and Western powers were to this "aid alone" form of peace-building.

AFTER RWANDA: MEAN TIMES

Arguably, the international community's quiescence in the face of the growing domination of the Taliban in Afghanistan was in no small part due to the stultifying effect of the fiasco of Operation Restore

Hope, which not even the low-tech genocide in Rwanda was able to disturb. From 1994 to 1997 humanitarian aid spending dropped dramatically, from US$5.6 billion to US$3.8 billion. While this fall coincided with a decline in the global caseload of refugees and asylum seekers from a high point of 16.3 million in 1994 to 13.6 million in 1997,[11] the simultaneous rise in internally displaced persons during the same period[12] would suggest it was not a simple matter of reduced humanitarian demand. Actual humanitarian needs were probably redistributed rather than reduced, and the new mean times were reflected both in declining humanitarian spending and in a rapidly growing list of countries turning asylum seekers away. It is true that 1997 did produce only ten UN consolidated appeals for humanitarian assistance to countries in crisis (against an average over the decade of 14.6), but the fifteen appeals made in 1998 produced the lowest ever donor response as a percentage of assessed needs.[13] This suggests that the 1997–98 period taken as a whole represents the nadir of humanitarian response during the decade, independently, it would seem, of any calculus of human need.[14]

Two "big ideas" emerged during this period that, though perhaps inadvertently, supported the downsizing and reshaping of the humanitarian enterprise. The first was an influential essay written in the immediate aftermath of the 1994 genocide in Rwanda in which Alex de Waal castigated what he saw as the irresponsible use of the growing power of humanitarian agencies operating in post–Cold War Africa.[15] De Waal's case for "humanitarianism unbound," as he called it, was made on the apparent influence of humanitarian agencies, especially NGOs, over the foreign polices and aid budgets of rich nations. He claimed that they were able to provoke international military intervention in support of humanitarian objectives. It now seems clear that de Waal had mistakenly assumed that Operation Restore Hope was to typify the international response to humanitarian crises. In fact, the weak international response to the killings in Rwanda actually marked the onset of the "mean times" associated with post–Operation Restore Hope inertia in international affairs.[16] It is true that several major NGOs had urged military intervention to stop the genocide in Rwanda in 1994, although unsuccessfully. Nevertheless, de Waal felt justified in asking whether the humanitarian NGOs were only accountable to a "fawning and forgetful press?"[17] In fact, de Waal's own polemic was taken up by influential sections of the international media. In 1996 many journalists seemed to take delight in the "spontaneous" return of many Rwandese from the camps in Zaire after aid agencies had called (unsuccessfully again) for another military intervention to protect bona fide refugees caught up in Rwanda's assault upon the rear bases of the re-grouped *génocidaires* in Zaire.

If one thought that humanitarian agencies, NGOs in particular, had ever enjoyed much influence over the behavior of the major powers, the events of 1996 and 1997 illustrated otherwise. A further 200,000 Rwandese and Zairois were murdered under the noses of frustrated aid workers as they sought refuge in Zaire's jungles.[18] It became clear that humanitarian leverage over the political realm was a mirage that had evaporated on the beaches of Mogadishu. This analysis is supported by the principal conclusion of the seminal Joint Evaluation of Emergency Assistance to Rwanda, which concluded that "humanitarian action cannot substitute for political action."[19] Ironically, this was to be widely reinterpreted as a call for the politicization of humanitarian assistance rather than the "humanitarianization" of international politics, the latter being the approach actually recommended by its authors.

While Alex de Waal was leading the attack upon humanitarianism, Mary B. Anderson was proffering an instant solution. Instead of "undermining local strengths, promoting dependency and allowing aid resources to be misused in the pursuit of war," Anderson announced that

> aid agencies have a new and profound opportunity to shape their relief and development work so it accomplishes its intended goals of alleviating human suffering and supporting the pursuit of sustainable economic and social systems and at the same time promotes durable and just peace. The opportunity is new because the situations in which aid workers find themselves are often different today from those in even the very recent past. The opportunity is profound because in the face of these differences the role for grassroots action in relation to high-level diplomatic efforts to resolve conflict is as great as ever in our history. Non-governmental organisations—the primary operational arm of the large relief and development enterprise—are and can be positioned to support peace and negate war as never before.[20]

Taken more literally than its author perhaps intended, "do no harm" was probably a significant factor in explaining the decline of humanitarian aid funding during the 1994–97 period, when aid workers traumatized and fatigued by their experiences in Africa, converted en masse to Anderson's beguiling promise of peace, justice, and development through the simple expedient of "building local capacities for peace."[21] Widely adopted by donors as well as international NGOs as a convenient moral case for ending both the expense and the risks associated with large scale material relief distributions in war-zones and as a means to starve the war economy, Anderson's abiding legacy has been the promise of peace-building on the cheap.

The second "big" idea that contributed to the deflation of humanitarianism built upon an observation made by Alex de Waal that international relief plays only a small part in people's survival strategies.[22] Also taking inspiration from the smart bombs deployed against Baghdad in 1991, Paul Richards coined the idea of a minimalist form of "smart relief." This was to deliver "knowledge intensive assistance" and "relief multipliers," such as new high-yielding seed varieties and technical and peace-orientated information via radio broadcasting, as a substitute for the bulk delivery of easily misused conventional relief supplies.[23] Smart relief instantly appealed to donors and international NGOs because it also promised greater humanitarian impact at lower cost and with reduced risk.

Doing no harm, building local capacities for peace, and smart relief together exemplify what Mark Duffield has called the "new humanitarianism."[24] Although there are many variations of new humanitarianism, they have two basic features in common: They promote relief "minimalism" in acknowledgment of the potential for aid to fuel warfare, and they seek to promote peace from within "humanitarian space." War is treated as a local pathogen. Of course, the integration of a political objective into the humanitarian system was not new, as the era of the Afghanistan cross-border operation well demonstrates. The new humanitarianism, however, was different from the earlier form of "humanitarian solidarity" practiced during the Cold War in its assumption that it could use "principled humanitarianism" to bring an end to conflict through negotiation, rather than acting as an ally in the quest for a military and political triumph of good over evil. Peace, for the new humanitarians, is an apolitical good, a commodity that is opposed only by the ignorant and the ill-informed, and by unscrupulous warlords profiteering from the war economy.[25] By ensuring that the warlords could no longer use relief agencies as quartermaster for their own nefarious military ends, the perverse incentives for war provided by humanitarian assistance would be ended. Thus, in a potentially deadly version of "being cruel to be kind," the new humanitarianism consciously prejudices the future over the present. By withholding aid that might fuel conflict today, warfare will consume itself more quickly for the benefit of everyone tomorrow. With additional pressure from "capacities for peace" in civil society, the self-evident benefits of peace and the prospects of sustainable development would surely then prevail.

Not surprisingly, in a comprehensive study of financing trends during this period, Margie Buchanan-Smith and Judith Randel conclude:

> The allocation of humanitarian assistance is not impartial. The major destinations of official humanitarian aid funds tend to be high-profile emergencies, and emergencies in countries or regions that the donors consider politically or strategically important.[26]

However, the demand side of the equation has been equally complicit in the form of politicization of humanitarian assistance that followed the Somali episode. While donors may have become meaner during these years, operational humanitarian delivery agencies also asked for less. Many relief agencies recoiled from undertaking mass relief distributions in war zones, in part, at least, from fear of being exposed to further media attacks of the sort that characterized the coverage of humanitarian affairs during this period[27] and that drove many agencies to projects which purportedly tackled root causes rather than risk being accused of doing more harm than good. But as Randel and German point out, this shift in the quality of humanitarian response was also reinforced by the growing donor habit of earmarking and the trend toward "bilateralization."[28] This tends to confirm that the observed changes in the quality of humanitarian assistance were deliberate rather than contingent or accidental. Events, such as the genocide in Rwanda and its aftermath in Zaire/Congo, were especially formative, and the lessons were soon applied to the aid effort in Afghanistan.

THE HUMANITARIAN CONSEQUENCES OF "PEACE-BUILDING LITE"

As Afghanistan had provided the venue for crucial events linked to the end of the Cold War, it would have been reasonable to expect it to have been a principal beneficiary of the post–Cold War peace dividend too. Instead, reinforced by the Somalia debacle, interest leached away as the increasingly catastrophic battle for Kabul intensified after the collapse of the Soviet-backed regime in 1992. For the international community it came as something of a relief when the Taliban finally took the capital in 1996. The Taliban ended the mayhem of the mujahedin years and consequently received an initial welcome from the West, where interest in far-flung crises had greatly diminished with the failed promise of the "end of history."

Just as Afghanistan has bequeathed "lessons" about the malleability of nongovernmental relief and development policies and practices to the rest of the world, so too has it been subjected to lessons learned elsewhere. Perhaps the most celebrated case during the era of "mean times" was the 1997 Strategic Framework initiative. The SF was conceived originally as a means to address the "disconnect" between the diplomatic/political and the international assistance realms, the key issue identified by the Joint Evaluation of the 1994 Rwanda crisis. However, as the deeply entrenched post-Somalia practice of "peace-building lite" was premised upon the continuing disengagement of Western military power in the Third World, in practice the SF for Afghanistan became an exercise in constructing closer integration among the UN assistance agencies and seeking greater coherence in the aid policies of the bilateral donors and NGOs.

In essence, the SF represented an experimental form of remedial action pursued by the United Nations in reaction to the charges that it had been "feeding the killers in the camps" in Goma.[29] The practice by NGOs of "feeding the killers in the camps" had been all but invented in the Afghan mujahedin settlements in Pakistan and then exported to Latin America and Africa. The irony was certainly not lost on many of the veterans of the mujahedin cross-border era. Many of them were puzzled that resistance to the Taliban was not pursued through the same channels and with the same cast of warlords who had so effectively resisted the Soviet-backed regime. Thus, although Afghanistan was in 1997 experiencing a crisis of governance that was subsequently globalized by the actions of Al Qaeda in Kenya, Tanzania, and Yemen, before finally hitting the United States itself, the application of the SF was conducted under the twin pieties of do no harm, on the one hand, and local solutions to local problems, on the other.

The SF initiative had it roots in the soil of the *Agenda for Peace* but was subject to the austere top dressing of smart relief and building local capacities for peace. Thus, while Afghanistan had experienced years of "unprincipled" international neglect before 1997, after the SF it was subjected to a regime of "principled" neglect instead. Arguably, it was a period when humanitarian agencies made a virtue of necessity, cutting their coats according to the cloth available and in a style that corresponded with the trends of the times.

Though it is difficult to assess whether Afghanistan was better off as a consequence of the SF, the experience of the Democratic Republic of the Congo (DRC), subjected to almost identical aid policies that characterized the "mean times" of the pre–September 11 era, has been researched more thoroughly and may be illustrative. In 2001 the International Rescue Committee estimated that 2.5 million civilian deaths could be attributed to the preceding two years of warfare in the DRC. More recently, a UN enquiry into the DRC's war economy has estimated that "excess mortality" in the eastern DRC totals 3.5 million.[30] A simple extrapolation to the end of 2002 would imply a death toll now in excess of 4 million. A study by MSF covering parts of the country not surveyed by the International Rescue Committee implies that the figure for the whole of the DRC is yet higher still.[31] As the IRC correctly pointed out, if these figures are accurate, "they indicate that more people have died in the war since 1998 than have died in all of the other wars combined over this period."[32] In fact, it is possible to go much further than this. If the IRC figures are accepted, then four times as many people have died as a consequence of the war in the DRC between 1998 and 2001 than the global total of all *recorded* fatalities caused by all natural and technological disasters for the period from 1992 to 2001.[33]

The reasons for such an extraordinary death toll are complex, but there is evidence that "new humanitarianism" had a significant impact upon aid planning, with fears of aid dependency and the risks of relief supplies being diverted into the war economy uppermost in the minds of those participating in the annual relief aid planning sessions. This is perhaps most clearly illustrated in the huge gap between observed needs and planned response in every UN Consolidated Inter-Agency Appeal for the DRC since 1999. For example, 16 million people were reported by the World Food Programme to be critically food insecure and surviving on 20 cents per day in 2001.[34] The planned response was to provide food aid for just 1.29 million people.[35]

Unfortunately, Afghanistan, like many other war zones, has not yielded any accessible comparative mortality data that could provide an estimate of the numbers of deaths that have occurred due to the combination of war and the meanness of the international aid regime in the late 1990s. However, the 1999, 2000, and 2001 United Nations Appeals for Afghanistan reveal a set of objectives that are almost identical to those pursued in the DRC.[36] While each appeal points to ever deteriorating life chances for Afghans as a consequence of drought and prolonged war, no estimates are ever offered of the number who might have died as a result, for example, of the habitual failure of the appeal to achieve income of more than 40 to 50 percent of the requested amount.[37] Furthermore, while malevolent warlords and mean donors are routinely blamed for Afghanistan's dreadful public health indicators, as in the DRC case, there exists a huge gap between reported emergency relief needs and planned response. For example, in mid 2000 the United Nations described the drought in Afghanistan in the following manner:

Afghanistan is currently in the grip of the worst drought since 1971. . . . The people most affected are rain-fed wheat producers whose crop, normally harvested between May and July 2000, has almost totally failed. These include 2.3 million rain-fed wheat farmers in northern Afghanistan. A preliminary estimate suggests that between now and June 2001 at least half of the population of Afghanistan may be affected by drought, three to four million severely and another eight to twelve million moderately.[38]

From this assessment, it would be reasonable to expect that the UN appeal would have sought to procure food aid for between 3 and 12 million people. In fact, and in spite of an estimated cereal deficit of over 2.3 million tons, the UN-led international humanitarian aid system patted itself on the back for planning an operation to distribute 120,000 tons of wheat to 1.5 million people. Actual distributions only reached 1.13 million in 2000.[39] In this context, as in the DRC, the

United Nations also reported that "food may be better appreciated when it is earned."[40] It did not explain why this might be the case, nor did it speculate upon the eventual fate of the unassisted population. Yet, embedded in this gap between reported needs and planned response, there is the implication of the cruellest form of humanitarian triage: deciding by some rationale or other who gets the food and who does not. When based on humanitarian principles, such decisions should be made, as with medical triage, on the criteria of urgency and need. In Afghanistan, as in the DRC, the decision seems to have been determined by the availability of NGOs to distribute food and, in turn, their access to populations in need.

While it is true that the humanitarian agencies in the DRC, as in Afghanistan, faced serious problems of access, it is also likely that this resulted in part from a widespread distrust of aid agencies. While Afghanistan, like Central Africa, has a long history of feeling neglected and sometimes betrayed by the international community, the "principled" denunciations by the new humanitarians of human rights violations, the misuse or diversion of relief aid by local authorities, and warlords profiteering from the criminalized war economy have exacerbated such suspicions. Public condemnation of human rights abuses and war racketeering plays straight into the "hearts and minds" propaganda war in circumstances where objectivity is virtually impossible to achieve. Such concerns have been compounded by fears associated with the actual consequences of local capacity building in these murderous environments. Local capacities for peace are invariably connected to one political faction or another and are often purposefully set up to tap international aid funds. Such projects may avoid directly fueling the shooting war, but they are just as prone to fanning the propaganda war. Likewise, the brokering of a local peace deal by an international humanitarian agency can also appear to be a hostile political act for other belligerents engaged in the maintenance and development of complex military alliances. Yet the operating assumption of the aid agencies that their peace-building mantle confers legitimacy on their actions and produces only good political utility from their work has proven to be a powerful tool of self-delusion. Thus, "insecurity" is frequently cited by humanitarian agencies as the cause of the inaccessibility of populations in need. In reality, this lack of access derives as much from a failure of consent, itself a manifestation of the distrust of the humanitarian system that many ordinary people, as well as fighters and politicians, in war zones will openly express on the all too rare occasions when their opinions are sought. In the meantime the provision of practical assistance to help poor people survive the depredations of war has become a victim of the "new humanitarian" fashion.

As such, while drought relief assistance in Afghanistan was increased during the SF period, it is not apparent that it was expanded in a manner commensurate with assessed needs. Rather, the scale of the relief program seems to correspond more with funding and distribution opportunities. To qualify for food aid, the latter had to comply with the SF principles, which included the requirement that "assistance shall be provided as part of an overall effort to achieve peace."[41] While the international aid system's formula for peace in Afghanistan was never fully explained, it clearly excluded activities that might enhance the legitimacy of the Taliban and thus made distribution of food through international or local NGOs more or less mandatory. Thus, while the UN drought-response strategy for Afghanistan stated that "the goal remains to reach the most vulnerable in as many locations as possible," the constraint to this in some drought-affected areas was reported as the absence of "aid agencies or national implementing partners."[42] Although the United Nations itself claimed that "at the national level, Afghanistan's humanitarian problems continue to break world records,"[43] access to life-saving food aid was made conditional upon an NGO being available to organize the distribution. As in the DRC, the UN appeals for Afghanistan are at pains to point out that "the proposals . . . have been designed . . . to ensure that no project contributes to further conflict and illicit activities."[44]

A byproduct of the approach to humanitarian action pursued in Afghanistan under the SF banner was to complicate the always difficult relationship between humanitarian principles and human rights. Under the SF, while being required to ensure that aid projects did no harm, UN agencies and NGOs were also encumbered with responsibility for "mainstreaming" human rights and gender policies. Even more than in the DRC, in Afghanistan both policies involved highly complex and often controversial confrontations between human rights and gender practices deemed essential to upholding Afghanistan's particular Islamic traditions and those deemed necessary as a precondition for receiving international assistance. This led David Rieff to suggest that "what Afghanistan under Taliban rule seemed to demonstrate was the degree to which upholding human rights norms got in the way of humanitarian work and vice versa."[45] What Rieff had encountered in Afghanistan was a variant of the DRC insecurity syndrome, a phenomenon assumed by most international aid agencies to be entirely independent of themselves.[46] Insecurity is typically blamed for their lack of unimpeded access to civilians in war zones. For example, the 2001 Afghanistan appeal states that "insecurity continues to be a major constraint to the provision of assistance."[47] However, what the United Nations and aid agencies failed to acknowledge was that their lack of access to populations in need was also due to the absence of a meaningful pact of humanitarian access with the belligerents, which, under international humanitarian law, would require the strict adherence of the relief agencies to the principle of neutrality. Reaching such an agreement was in the DRC (and perhaps doubly so in Afghanistan) made almost impossible by the mandatory integration of human rights and gender-equity conditionalities into the negotiations. This is not to suggest that it would have been good to ignore human rights violations committed by the Taliban or other presumptive authorities in Afghanistan. However, given the total intractability of some of the regional and provincial leaders on human rights and gender-equity issues in Afghanistan, it is arguably the case that it might have been less bad to have selectively avoided such controversies, at least from the point of view of gaining access to populations in urgent need of humanitarian assistance.[48] In the integrated and coherent world of principled common programming in Afghanistan, this option was not available for consideration.

In sum, given the principled austerity associated with international aid policies before September 2001, it is possible that the new humanitarianism ushered in with the SF and "principled" common programming may have reduced the diversion and misuse of relief aid, and it may have taught the Taliban and the warlords some lessons about human rights, gender equity, and international law. However, it is equally clear that the SF and the principled common program did not stop or resolve the war in Afghanistan, nor did they persuade the Taliban to embrace Western standards of justice and gender equity and to close down Al Qaeda's training facilities. Further, new humanitarianism may well have made the task of surviving the drought as difficult, if not more difficult, especially for those populations to which access was deemed too difficult or impossible, than it might have been in the absence of the SF and principled common programming.

As happens throughout the humanitarian system, background life-chance indicators are usually described in considerable detail, yet figures of excess mortality, that is, lives lost as a consequence of a specific event such as a war or an earthquake, are rarely produced. Significantly, neither the United Nations nor the Red Cross systematically maintains records of the numbers of deaths arising from war-related humanitarian disasters. Thus, in spite of the drama of the 2001 famine-relief race in Afghanistan to beat the snows and dodge the bullets and bombs, it is quite in character that the system produced no comparative mortality data. Thus, it is impossible to calculate the number of lives lost over and above Afghanistan's normal, and quite appalling, winter death toll. Instead, the judgment over the contested efficacy of the relief effort rests entirely upon anecdote and typical expatriate conjecture about "plucky and resilient" Afghans. However, in view of the enormous gap between reported food shortages and actual aid deliveries, combined with a background of some of the worst public health indicators in the world, it seems certain that either many Afghans must have succumbed in the absence of adequate international relief or the relief agencies had exaggerated the severity of the situation. We are unlikely ever to know. To understand the actual consequences of its policies, the humanitarian system would, as in the DRC, risk being confronted with the hard evidence of either its own dereliction or its duplicity. The awful implications of both are probably sufficient reason not to look.

There are other ethical and practical questions associated with the mean times of contemporary "peace-building lite" practices. The trend toward capacity building and away from the provision of basic relief also suggests a significant change in the characteristics of international aid beneficiaries away from very poor or destitute people and toward those employed either directly or indirectly by the aid system itself. Furthermore, compassion fatigue seems to be a genuine threat to the welfare of people affected by protracted emergencies. The practical question is how to determine when aid dependency is acceptable and when it is not. The normative question is when to betray the immediate interests of today's victims of war in the interests of a better future. While the humanitarian system makes much of its post-Goma ability to make such choices, it defends them in abstract terms rather than in real-time, concrete cases. In reality, it seems deliberately to avoid laying down a clear audit trail of decisions that can be subsequently linked to actual outcomes. Transparency and accountability are aspirations of the principled programming that have never been achieved. How often have do-no-harm policy choices that require sacrifice now on the basis of assurances of a better future complied with the principle of informed consent? Where is the professional association of humanitarians who can review the complaints of those whose sacrifices have been in vain?

TOUGH TIMES:
PAX AMERICANA
AND HUMANITARIAN REGIME CHANGE

While it is true that the era of post–Cold War peace-building announced by Boutros Boutros-Ghali's *Agenda for Peace* in 1992 suffered many setbacks, most dramatically in central Africa (Rwanda, Burundi, and Zaire/Congo), the former Yugoslavia, and the former Soviet Union (in particular, the Caucasus region), the original peace-building paradigm remained generally intact for most war-torn nations until September 2001. In its essentials this consisted of a sequence beginning with a negotiated settlement, followed by the deployment of impartial UN Chapter VI peace-keepers,[49] internationally supervised elections, and international aid-driven demobilization, resettlement, reconstruction, and development.

But after September 11, it was the "counter factual" lessons drawn from the less conventional peace support operations in Haiti, Kosovo, Sierra Leone, and East Timor that were to prove formative. Experience from these suggests that deep foreign-policy traction in war-torn nations is best achieved by taking sides, picking local allies, and then going in with overwhelming military force. In these operations international aid agencies played a subordinate support role. The negative experiences of peace-support operations in Afghanistan (in the 1990s), Sudan, the DRC, Angola, Rwanda, and many other African conflicts lend further support for this approach. In these cases international aid-led peace-building, whether or not supported by weak Chapter VI peace-keepers, took a very long time to achieve very little.

Although the events of September 11 caused these lessons to be generalized beyond the group of relatively small nations where coercive peace enforcement had been employed, some of these arguments had previously been articulated both in the Rwanda Joint Evaluation and more explicitly in what has become known as the "Brahimi report."[50] In reviewing the UN's experience in peace-support operations, the panel of experts led by Lakhdar Brahimi argued forcefully that "for peace-keeping to accomplish its mission . . . no amount of good intentions can substitute for the fundamental ability to project credible force."[51]

For Brahimi's panel of experts, the main reason for failure in peace-support operations stemmed from the lack of member states' political will to back peace-keeping mandates with sufficient coercive capacity, often leaving an exposed and fatally under-resourced UN system as the scapegoat for ill-conceived peace-support missions.[52]

In the post–September 11 era, the political will of the United States can no longer be in doubt, at least in the short term. But rather than entering the theater claiming to be an impartial broker in helping to resolve some local political squabble, the United States and its allies in Afghanistan have taken charge of the peace-building system while also being engaged as belligerents. Therefore, instead of supporting persecuted minorities to achieve autonomy or independence, as in Kosovo and East Timor, the exercise of regime-change undertaken in Afghanistan from October 7, 2001, was fought in the name of the people of the United States for the purposes of preventing future terrorist attacks upon the homeland. The means adopted, however, owed much to the experience of NATO's bombing campaign in Kosovo. Local proxy forces, supported by overwhelming US air power and logistics, removed the offending regime, with the international aid system set up to provide a tangible peace dividend to legitimize, or more accurately, to lend popularity to, the new political dispensation. However, as the Brahimi panel observed:

Force alone can not create peace; it can only create a space in which peace can be built. . . . The key conditions for the success of future complex operations are political support, rapid deployment with a robust force posture and a sound peace-building strategy.[53]

In principle, at least, this argument seems to have informed, or since described, US policymaking. Shortly after the military intervention in Afghanistan, President Bush announced a major increase in the US foreign-aid budget, justified in the following way:

As the civilized world mobilizes against the forces of terror, we must also embrace the forces of good. By offering hope where there is none, by relieving suffering and hunger where there is too much, we will make the world not only safer, but better.[54]

However, as the Brahimi report argued, a "sound peace-building strategy" is also required in practice, and this appears—almost two years after the events of September 11—to be as elusive as ever, a point not lost upon the Bush administration. It is clear that the long-standing US Republican Party skepticism about the ability of the international aid establishment to design and deliver a sound peace-building strategy remains undiminished. The urgent and demanding task of enhancing Western domestic security threw down an even more complex challenge for an aid establishment still chronically unable to confront the reasons for its own failures and hitherto declining fortunes.[55] Other delivery channels—for example, those provided by the private sector or the military—were therefore tested, taking market share away from the established international aid agencies. This shift is likely to represent a long-term trend in international aid financing, particularly if the new peace-support actors can demonstrate greater impact and efficiency than that found within the existing international aid establishment.

However, the new players in the peace-building marketplace will be expected to bring with them some fresh ideas about inducing social, economic, and political change in war-torn nations. One of the great conundrums of the modern international aid system is that it lionizes strategic planning, coordination, cooperation, and collaboration, and frowns upon overt expressions of independence and organizational competitiveness. Yet paradoxically, "developmentalism," in theory at least, is the champion of diversity, innovation, tolerance, economic competitiveness, and political, social, and cultural pluralism. Indeed, contemporary civil society is supposed to be a manifestation, even a celebration of the triumph of these liberal societal values over the stultifying hand of state socialism with its overblown five-year strategic plans, and "development" dealt out project by inefficient project, a simulacrum of which is oddly still adhered to by the international aid system.

In post-Taliban Afghanistan these tendencies have been displayed in an especially exaggerated manner, fueled by the aid bonanza prompted by the signing of the Bonn Agreement of December 2001. In spite of the UN commitment to a "light footprint," it was reported in early 2003 that there were approximately seven hundred international staff employed by the United Nations in Afghanistan, probably costing somewhere in the region of US$200 million a year in salary and support costs alone. The costs of the numerous expatriate NGO staff probably are in excess of US$100 million. As public expectations of the anticipated post-Taliban regime-change dividend have been confounded, Afghanistan has become rife with anti–aid agency sentiment. Indeed, were opinion polls to be undertaken to ascertain the popularity of the international aid system among those whom it purports to serve, it is probable that these would record ratings comparable with the nadir of state socialism in its most self-serving, corrupt, and decadent form. Early signs from Iraq suggest that US disappointment in the performance of the aid establishment in Afghanistan has resulted in the US administration channeling the majority of its peace-support funding through the military establishment and commercial contractors.

Yet as aid agencies in Afghanistan often point out, the work of the new players, such as the Coalition Joint Civil-Military Operations Task Force (CJCMOTF), is all too easily confused with their own projects.[56] Likewise, the World Bank's experiment with a new community-empowerment approach, symbolized in its National Solidarity Program, sounds and looks remarkably like old-fashioned NGO community-development work.[57] It seems that the new actors are simply copying worn-out developmental paradigms from the aid establishment. As a consequence, patience with the post-Taliban international aid operation has continuously declined, whether delivered through the old or the new institutions. Indeed, the regime-change strategy in Afghanistan may yet fail if it is unable to meet the Brahimi report's criterion of soundness in its peace-building strategy. Given Brahimi's position at the head of the UN mission for Afghanistan, this would prove to be deeply ironic. What might be going wrong?

In spite of the predisposition of the international aid system to treat peace and development as apolitical products created from a set of discrete technical tasks, actual peace and development can follow radically different pathways and arrive at very different destinations, each of which will generate alternate sets of winners and losers. In this sense, the "end of history" is not yet with us, as the events of September 11 illustrated. Thus, the internal and external opponents of Afghanistan's UN-led peace process are not only against certain particularities of the version of peace and development on offer from the international aid system but are also actively in favor of, and some are clearly even willing to die for, their preferred and alternate forms of peace and development. In the case of Afghanistan the resilience of the warlords is almost certainly linked to their patronage of the two most profitable of all rural enterprises in Afghanistan: poppy growing and trafficking in international contraband. These are what Mark Duffield would describe as "actually existing development."[58] Although the warlord domains may be abusive of "universal" civil and political rights, they are also supportive of these profitable livelihoods. Most crucially, opium production and international smuggling are maintained in a politico-military framework that also provides a form of security and protection rooted in the durable affinities of shared cultures and ethnicities, each of which struggles to survive in a shell of a state that is unable to provide such guarantees. Furthermore, the new regime installed in Kabul threatens to eradicate poppy production and to dismantle the tribal security system. There is a lot at stake in giving these things up in favor of the uncertainties surrounding the new state on offer, itself heavily dependent upon the notoriously fickle (from an Afghan point of view) international community.

Thus, what may appear as a self-evidently attractive, modern, and uncontroversial design to international peace-builders may seem far less attractive than the status quo in the eyes of many Afghans. While largely unseen and unheard, political opposition to UN-led peace-building is real and presumably perceived as legitimate from the perspective of the millions in Afghanistan who find shelter and make some sort of living within these alternate forms of development, justice, and security. The challenge of persuading the people of Afghanistan to opt for a state designed under the supervision of the new and coercive version of post–September 11 *Pax Americana* is not therefore simply about a choice between democracy and autocracy, or between secularism and theocracy. It is also about abandoning existing forms of working alternative development in favor of a Western development chimera that has perceivably failed Afghanistan since the 1950s. Although the forces ranged against the particular form of peace being pursued by the international community under the hawkish eyes of the B-52s remain hidden, the very fact that they survive in spite of the perceived omnipotence of US force suggests that they continue to exert a potent influence over public opinion and private behavior in Afghanistan and beyond. Yet the international aid establishment seems incapable of seeing anything beyond the pejorative label of "warlord." The typical aid narrative in Afghanistan concerns itself with fictional concerns about aid dependency and deprecatory references to the war economy. It fails to recognize the tenuous nature of its own weak influence upon economic life in Afghanistan, and it is willfully amnesiac about all those who live or die in Afghanistan as members of an indigenous political economy largely untouched by the squeamishness of an international aid system grown risk averse and defensive in its obsession with doing no harm.

For the humanitarian system, the "war on terrorism" in Afghanistan has also meant becoming accustomed to sharing humanitarian space with some less familiar actors, for whom the principles of neutrality, impartiality, and independence are completely alien. If the experience of Afghanistan in late 2001 is anything to go by, partners in the war against terrorism will also have to get used to an arbitrary approach to international law. The war against the Taliban and Al Qaeda involved the tactical closure of Afghanistan's international frontiers to potential asylum seekers wishing to seek refuge from the war. The essence of the 1951 Refugee Convention, the principle of *non-refoulement*, was comprehensively violated in order that the "guilty" could not escape from the pressure cooker that the B-52 bombing campaign was designed to produce. Participants in the emerging peace-building doctrine of *Pax Americana* may have to make their own accommodation with such practices if they wish to remain in business. So far, their behavior in Afghanistan since the US-Coalition intervention suggests that they will. However, what the war on terrorism may also signal is a growing disparity of US and Coalition engagement between those countries where terrorist cells are believed to reside and those in which terrorists have not yet been identified.[59] While UN Security Council Resolution 1401 pressed the entire UN system into contributing to regime change and regime legitimation in Afghanistan,[60] its claim to be able to provide neutral or impartial humanitarian assistance and coordination is surely unlikely to be believed by those other regimes that the US-led Coalition against terrorism seeks to replace, or by those groups, communities, societies, or sects that are the unwilling targets for enforced "modernization" by the international aid system. For the time being, perhaps, the peace-building system in Afghanistan is relatively safe under the protection of patrolling B-52s and the ISAF's (International Security Assistance Force's) security blanket in Kabul. But it remains to be seen how far such military protection can stretch and whether the opening of another front in Iraq might affect the Coalition military assets in Afghanistan. Certainly, if a genuinely globalized anti-US/Coalition terrorist capacity does exist, aid agencies that have been closely associated with the expansion of the aid effort in post-Taliban Afghanistan may find that they are now soft targets for anti-US networked groups seeking revenge for their losses in Afghanistan, Pakistan, Iraq, Yemen, Somalia, Indonesia, Colombia, the Philippines, Georgia, Uzbekistan, Tajikistan, and anywhere else where the war on terrorism is waged. Indeed, it may yet prove to be the case that the Taliban, and the values they stood for, simply opted for a temporary retreat until it is safe to come out again. After all, this could be as soon as the next US presidential election.

NOTES

[1] Andrew Hartman, "'The Red Template': US policy in Soviet-occupied Afghanistan," *Third World Quarterly* 2/3 (2002), 467–89.

[2] Helga Baitenmann, "NGOs and the Afghan War: The Politicization of Humanitarian Aid," *Third World Quarterly* 12/1 (1990), 62.

[3] All language is loaded. Russian commentaries often see this period as one of self-sacrificial trusteeship. The empire in charge has now changed, but the language is similar, and it is unclear how different it looks from every Afghan perspective.

[4] The UN High Commissioner for Refugees (UNHCR) coordinated the Pakistan refugee camp operation from the early 1980s.

[5] Remarks to the National Foreign Policy Conference for Leaders of Non-governmental Organizations by Secretary Colin L. Powell, US Department of State, Washington D.C. (October 26, 2001). Available online.

[6] Baitenmann, "NGOs and the Afghan War."

[7] Boutros Boutros-Ghali, *An Agenda for Peace 1995: With the New Supplement and Related UN Documents*, 2d ed. (New York: United Nations, 1995).

[8] Francis Fukuyama, *The End of History and the Last Man* (New York: Penguin, 1992).

[9] Mark Duffield, *Global Governance and the New Wars: The Merging of Development and Security* (New York: Zed Books, 2001).

[10] Joanna Macrae and Nicholas Leader, *Shifting Sands: The Search for 'Coherence' Between Political and Humanitarian Responses to Complex Emergencies*, HPG Report 8 (London: ODI, 2000).

[11] US Committee for Refugees, *World Refugee Survey 2002*, Table 3.

[12] R. Cohen and F. Deng, *Masses in Flight: The Global Challenge of Internal Displacement* (Washington D.C.: Brookings Institution, 1998).

[13] ReliefWeb, accessed online.

[14] According to the International Federation of Red Cross and Red Crescent's *World Disasters Report 2002* (distributed by Kumarian Press), 1997 and 1998 saw respectively the lowest and highest numbers of persons affected by disasters during the decade, although these years ranked respectively fourth and second worst in terms of numbers of disaster fatalities during the decade.

[15] Alex de Waal, *Humanitarianism Unbound* (London: African Rights, 1995). Available online.

[16] Michael Bryans, Bruce D. Jones, and Janice Gross Stein, "Mean Times: Humanitarian Action in Complex Political Emergencies—Stark Choices, Cruel Dilemmas," *Coming to Terms* 1/3 (Toronto: University of Toronto Program on Conflict Management and Negotiation, 1999). Available online.

[17] De Waal, *Humanitarianism Unbound.*

[18] Fiona Terry, *Condemned to Repeat: The Paradox of Humanitarian Action* (Ithaca, N.Y.: Cornell University Press, 2002).

[19] John Eriksson, et al., *The International Response to Conflict and Genocide: Lessons from the Rwanda Experience—Synthesis Report*, Steering Committee of the Joint Evaluation of Emergency Assistance to Rwanda (Copenhagen, 1996).

[20] Mary B. Anderson, *Do No Harm: How Aid Can Support Peace or War* (Boulder, Colo.: Lynne Reinner Publishers, 1999), 2.

[21] During this period the UK's Disaster Emergency Committee went for almost three years without making a public appeal, so nervous were UK agencies of the various accusations made by Alex de Waal, Clare Short, Lindsay Hilsum, John Ryle, and others.

[22] Alex de Waal, *The Famine That Kills: Darfur, Sudan, 1984–1985* (London: Oxford University Press, 1989).

[23] Paul Richards, *Fighting for the Rainforest: War, Youth and Resources in Sierra Leone* (Oxford: James Currey, 1999), 157.

[24] Duffield, *Global Governance and the New Wars.*

[25] New humanitarianism and contemporary peace-building discourse has an alarming resonance with a Kiplingesque view of the world, where without Western enlightenment and tutelage, the "natives have a tendency to take leave of their senses" (Mark Duffield, "Mud-Splattered Men Hack Down Tangled Grass and Scoop up Handfuls of Muck" [AP, March 1998], available online; Duffield is referring to the underlying rationale for Mary B. Anderson's *Do No Harm.*)

[26] Margie Buchanan-Smith and Judith Randel, *Financing International Action: A Review of Key Trends*, HPG Briefing 4 (London: ODI, 2002).

[27] See, for example, Alex de Waal, "No Bloodless Miracle," *The Guardian* (London), November 15, 1996.

[28] Judith Randel and Tony German, "Trends in the Financing of Humanitarian Assistance," in *The New Humanitarianisms: A Review of Trends in Global Humanitarian Action,* ed. Joanna Macrae, HPG Report 11 (London: ODI, 2002), 19-28.

[29] In 1994, soon after conducting the genocide of some 800,000 predominantly Tutsi Rwandans, the *génocidaires* fled along with several hundred thousand refugees to the Kivu region of Zaire. Goma, the capital of North Kivu, subsequently lent its name to the Rwandan refugee camps where the United Nations allegedly housed and fed many members of the former Rwanda Army and the Interahamwe militia, responsible for the genocide. These camps were attacked and forcibly closed by the Rwanda Patriotic Army in October 1996.

[30] United Nations, *The UN Experts Panel on the Illegal Exploitation of Natural Resources and Other Forms of Wealth of the DR Congo*, UNSC S/2002/1146, para. 96.

[31] Michel Van Herp et al., *Mortality, Violence, and Lack of Access to Health Care in the Democratic Republic of Congo* (London: ODI, forthcoming).

[32] International Rescue Committee, *Mortality in Eastern Democratic Republic of the Congo—Results from Eleven Mortality Surveys,* final draft (2001), 19.

[33] *World Disasters Report 2002* offers the figure of 622,363 for all natural and technological disaster deaths for the period from 1992 to 2001.

[34] It would perhaps have been more appropriate to describe people as "dying" rather than surviving on 20 cents per day.

[35] OCHA, *Democratic Republic of the Congo, Consolidated Inter-Agency Appeal 2002* (New York/Geneva: OCHA, 2002).

[36] The "Principles for Assistance Provision" of the Strategic Framework for Afghanistan include the statements that "assistance shall be provided as part of an overall effort to achieve peace," "institution and capacity-building activities must advance human rights," and "assistance activities must be designed

to ensure increasing indigenous ownership at the village, community and national levels and to build the country as a whole."

[37] The donor response to the UN appeal for Afghanistan did increase gradually in 1999, 2000, and 2001, although not in a manner commensurate with observed humanitarian needs. Senior UN officials claim that the amounts requested were shaped to a large extent by realistic anticipated donor response, based on levels of funding provided in previous years.

[38] OCHA, *Strategy of the Assistance Community in Response to the Drought in Afghanistan (1 June 2000—31 May 2001)* (Geneva: OCHA, June 1, 2000). Available online.

[39] OCHA, *Consolidated Inter-Agency Appeal for Afghanistan 2001,* (Geneva: OCHA, November 17, 2000). Available online.

[40] OCHA, *Strategy of the Assistance Community in Response to the Drought in Afghanistan (1 June 2000—31 May 2001).*

[41] OCHA, *Consolidated Inter-Agency Appeal for Afghanistan 2001.*

[42] OCHA, *Strategy of the Assistance Community in Response to the Drought in Afghanistan (1 June 2000—31 May 2001).*

[43] OCHA, *Consolidated Inter-Agency Appeal for Afghanistan 1999* (Geneva: OCHA, December 16, 1998). Available online.

[44] Ibid.

[45] Rieff , *A Bed for the Night: Humanitarianism in Crisis* (London: Vintage, 2002), 246.

[46] The major exception being the International Committee of the Red Cross, which routinely involves itself in disseminating international humanitarian law to belligerents and other relevant parties.

[47] OCHA, *Consolidated Inter-Agency Appeal for Afghanistan 2001.*

[48] The Red Cross Movement's 1956 fundamental humanitarian principles describe neutrality as the avoidance of "controversies of a political, racial, religious or ideological nature."

[49] Peace-keeping with the consent of the state, as envisaged under UN Charter Chapter VI, "Pacific Settlement of Disputes."

[50] United Nations, *Report of the Panel on United Nations Peace Operations,* A/55/305 S/2000/809 (New York: United Nations, August 21, 2000).

[51] Ibid., 1.

[52] While the Joint Evaluation and the "Brahimi report" both highlighted the key issue as the lack of major power political will to engage in nonstrategic regions, both documents are often cited in relation to their recommendations concerning aid agency coordination. Paradoxically, both reports, by repute rather than by intent, have reinforced the view that assistance policies rather than foreign policies are the main problem confronting peace-support operations.

[53] United Nations, *Report of the Panel on United Nations Peace Operations.*

[54] President George Bush (March 14, 2002). Available online.

[55] In 2001, fourteen of the twenty-two OECD countries were giving less international aid in absolute terms than they were in 1992. The OECD total has fallen by 14 percent since 1992 (OECD website).

[56] CJCMOTF is the branch of the US military deployed in Afghanistan that undertook small-scale relief and community-development projects, in part for

purposes of force protection and in part for "winning hearts and minds" over to the new post-Taliban political dispensation.

[57] Community development (like *animation rurale* in the French colonies) was an invention of the colonial authorities designed to lend credibility to local indigenous leaders by providing them with small amounts of state resources for local development projects, such as improved water supplies or schools. As well as being part of the system of indirect rule, community development also had the merit of giving a source of patronage to local leaders, and, through "voluntary" community participation, socialized the costs of state infrastructure such as schools, clinics, and roads. In the post-colonial period, NGOs have adopted an almost entirely unchanged development paradigm which, perhaps unsurprisingly, meets with about the same level of community enthusiasm as it did during the colonial period.

[58] Duffield, *Global Governance and the New Wars,* chap. 6.

[59] For example, in 2002 USAID transferred funds from its DRC budget to its Afghanistan budget.

[60] UN Security Council, Resolution 1401 (March 28, 2002): "[The Security Council] . . . *stresses* that the provision of focussed recovery and reconstruction assistance can greatly assist in the implementation of the Bonn Agreement and, to this end, *urges* bilateral and multi-lateral donors to coordinate very closely with the SRSG, the Afghanistan Interim Administration and its successors." The resolution is available online.

Part One

GOVERNING THE PERIPHERY WITH AID, PEACE, AND JUSTICE

3

The Politics
of Peace-building

Year One: From Bonn to Kabul

J. ALEXANDER THIER

Afghanistan is in the midst of a radical political transformation. In the fall of 2001 the fundamentalist Taliban regime and its Al Qaeda backers were dislodged from the seat of power in Afghanistan by a US-led international military coalition and a hodgepodge of Afghan opposition factions. Those factions—many of which had been responsible for a devastating civil war in the early 1990s—were swept into power throughout the country, dividing Afghanistan into regions under the control of various commanders and "warlords." The international community and the United Nations acted remarkably quickly to bring these factions and diaspora Afghan political leadership together to agree to interim power-sharing arrangements, culminating in the Bonn Agreement in December 2001.[1] Meanwhile, however, the international military coalition continued to arm, fund, and train independent militias to aid them in their fight against the Taliban and Al Qaeda.[2] These independent factions have reignited old conflicts, vying for power and the spoils associated with control of territory and trade. These intertwined strands of intervention and entropy—the (re)creation of a central state, the continuing "war on terrorism," and a relapse into division and conflict in the countryside—are the story of Afghanistan's first year of post-Taliban political transformation.[3]

The results of efforts to give effect to the Bonn Agreement throughout 2002 were decidedly mixed. On the positive side of the ledger, Afghanistan was largely peaceful. There were outbreaks of factional fighting throughout the country, but nothing that triggered a wider conflict or seriously threatened to end the process agreed to in Bonn. Those outside the Bonn framework who were opposed to the nascent Afghan government and the presence of foreign troops engaged in continual sniping at international military forces in the south and east and in Kabul. Although these attacks caused more symbolic than actual harm, an upsurge in these attacks combined with other failures could tip the balance, creating a serious menace to long-term stability. Reconstruction programs were getting under way, with substantial, albeit insufficient, external pledges for continued funding over the next five years. The Afghan interim administration weathered a broadly representative but flawed national assembly, a Loya Jirga (a traditional Afghan "grand council") and emerged largely intact as the Afghan transitional administration with a twenty-four-month life span. And its leader, Chairman Hamid Karzai, narrowly escaped an assassination attempt. Finally, some two million Afghan refugees, far more than expected, showed a ray of confidence by returning to Afghanistan in 2002.

Many of these successes were mirrored by failures that portended continued trouble and hardship for Afghanistan. A fragile peace held between the armed factions within the Bonn framework. While factional fighting was kept in check, the factions themselves hardly diminished. The Afghan National Army had but a few thousand newly trained troops, while militia armies under the command of regional warlords and local commanders had an estimated 200,000 men in arms. As a result, the entire country outside the confines of Kabul was controlled by these militia armies, and the success of the overall peace process lay on the shoulders of leaders with questionable motives and problematic records. Disarmament programs remained mostly conceptual through the year, and efforts to reduce income flows to warlords from opium, stolen customs revenues, and outside support foundered. As ever, interference by and competition among Afghanistan's neighbors also threatened to disrupt the delicate balance. Similarly, there was a twenty-nation, 4,800 strong International Security Assistance Force (ISAF) in Kabul, but the key nations in the US-led international military coalition and ISAF continued to refuse entreaties by the Afghan government, the Afghan people, and the international aid community to expand international security forces beyond the capital.[4] The threat from the remnants of Al Qaeda, the Taliban, and others opposed to the Afghan government and the international military forces remained. Reports indicate that these forces were active in the Afghanistan-Pakistan border regions, regrouping, recruiting, and training.[5] These forces launched scores of attacks on foreign military and civilian personnel, a major car-bomb attack in Kabul, and an assassination attempt on Chairman Karzai that was inches from success.

Progress on reconstruction was also hindered by insecurity, slow delivery on donor pledges, lack of capacity within the government, and an overall insufficiency of resources. The US$5 billion over five years pledged for Afghanistan's reconstruction in Tokyo in January 2002 provides Afghans with only one-eighth of the funding Bosnians received on a per capita annual basis between 1996 and 1999.[6] Finally, life in Afghanistan remained, to paraphrase Hobbes, poor, brutish, and short. With some of the world's highest infant and maternal mortality rates, a destroyed health care and education infrastructure, years of drought, and a plague of landmines, Afghanistan continued to have one of the lowest life expectancies in the world. The joy of long-delayed refugee return had for many become a struggle to survive.

This picture is at once unique and depressingly familiar. The cause of peace in Afghanistan brought an intensity of purpose unseen in other recent peace-building arenas. Afghanistan has been shrouded in the notion that failure to make it secure could mean that once again it would become a haven for terrorists and a threat to nations far beyond its borders.

Yet despite this new intensity, the politics of peace-building in Afghanistan suffered from many of the same hurdles as the postwar efforts of the last decade from Bosnia to Sierra Leone to East Timor. Intervention followed years if not decades of war, ethnic tension, disintegration of state institutions and civil society, human rights abuses, and the development of entrenched war-time economies reliant upon drugs, guns, and the looting of cultural artifacts. These peace-building missions entered extremely complex situations with a poor understanding of the needs, insufficient resources to address those needs, and sometimes lack of patience to see long processes through.

THE CLEAVAGES

For much of the world, having been introduced to Afghanistan in the late 1990s, the need for peace-building, in addition to reconstruction, may be confusing. The Taliban's harboring of Osama bin Laden and record of human rights abuses against women and ethnic minorities was widely known for years. Indeed, the United States sent a barrage of cruise missiles against Al Qaeda camps in Taliban-controlled Afghanistan in August 1998 in response to the bombings of the US embassies in Kenya and Tanzania earlier that summer.[7] Afghanistan came under UN Security Council sanctions in 1999.[8] Following September 11, the menace to the Afghans and the world that these avatars of militant-fundamentalism posed reached unacceptable levels. However, once the Taliban and Al Qaeda were dislodged by the overwhelming force of the US-led international military coalition and its Afghan allies, what remained to forestall the leap into post-conflict reconstruction?

The answer to this question is complex, combining simmering historical tensions in Afghanistan and the region with expedient decisions made in the heat of war. There are numerous cleavages in Afghan society and in the region, including urban-rural, modern-traditional, the role of Islam and politics, and ethnicity. These cleavages have fueled and have been further exacerbated by recent conflicts. In the course of these thirty years Afghanistan went from being a constitutional monarchy, to a republic, to a communist dictatorship under Soviet occupation, to a failed and fractured state engaged in total civil war, to the home of a uniquely fundamentalist and obscurantist theocracy that thrived, in part, upon the largess of the leadership of a global terrorist confederation and the world's largest opium crop. These cleavages continue to manifest themselves in the ongoing peace-building process.

Afghanistan has had a troubled history, serving as a buffer between encroaching and receding empires for most of its history. The territory of modern Afghanistan was consolidated in the late nineteenth century through a series of brutal campaigns. Establishing central government control over a tribal, independent-minded, and geographically isolated patchwork of peoples was an ongoing project through much of the twentieth century, yet the country remained mostly peaceful, albeit exceedingly poor, between 1931 and 1973. Control of the state apparatus remained largely in the hands of a unrepresentative elite, but a new constitution in 1964 promised democratic reforms. However, the tension between a modernizing urban elite and a traditional rural majority had been, and would continue to be, a critical cleavage in Afghan society.[9]

Afghanistan's slow trajectory of political and economic reform changed abruptly in 1973. A coup by Sardar Daoud, the former prime minister and cousin of the constitutional monarch, was the first watershed in what became three decades of turmoil.[10] President Daoud's attempt to play both ends against the middle in the intense Cold War rivalry between the United States and the Soviet Union as well as the enormous gulf between Afghanistan's urban elite and its traditional rural majority led to political upheaval, a series of coups, and the 1979 Soviet invasion. This invasion galvanized a rural resistance movement that, with the assistance of foreign military support,[11] morphed into a series of guerilla militias, or mujahedin parties, that fought a devastating and ultimately successful ten-year war of attrition against the Soviets. Many of the mujahedin parties, and some of their backers, were organized around the ideology that this was not merely a war to repel a foreign invasion but an Islamic holy war against an aggressive and expansionist infidel. These holy warriors wanted not only to liberate Afghanistan but to create a state based on Islam as a political and legal organizing principle. This Islamist ideology was spread to hundreds of thousands of Afghans through recruitment of mujahedin and through education programs run by the mujahedin parties in the refugee camps of Pakistan. With the Soviets in the cities and the mujahedin in the countryside and refugee camps, a new ideological facet of the old urban-rural conflict emerged between radicalized cadres. Rifts also grew between the traditional pro-monarchy mujahedin and the more radical devotees of political Islam.

The Soviet invasion and Afghanistan's descent into war unavoidably drew its other neighbors into the conflict. Iran and Pakistan became home to some 5.5 million refugees, the largest such crisis since World War II. They also became the home base and armory to the mujahedin parties, who organized, raised money, and received arms from their bases there. For its part, the United States saw an opportunity to fight Soviet expansion, the spread of communism, and to give "the USSR its Vietnam war."[12] Regional and great power rivalry along with the dependence of Afghan antagonists on foreign support have made foreign intervention a mainstay of conflict perpetuation in Afghanistan.

The collapse of the Soviet Union presaged the collapse of the Soviet-backed government in Afghanistan, and in 1992 a series of negotiations and defections left Afghanistan with an interim government of mujahedin parties and former government militias. Longstanding rivalries between these parties, exacerbated by ideology, hunger for power, foreign designs, and the limited attention of the international community, placed a country already devastated by thirteen years of brutal conflict in the hands of radicals and opportunists. A new civil war quickly escalated between these groups, destroying Kabul, the remaining infrastructure, and the hopes of the Afghan people. The mujahedin parties had largely formed along regional and therefore ethnic lines in the Soviet-era due to their limited geographic areas of operation. Once full-blown civil war commenced between these groups, the country became divided into six or seven semi-autonomous regions with fighting within and between each region. As the conflict dragged on, it also began to take on an ethnic character. While ethnic tensions were not new to this diverse country, ethnicity began to be associated with parties and the atrocities committed by those parties, thus deepening another fundamental cleavage.

OPERATION ENDURING FREEDOM AND THE LEAD-UP TO BONN

Prior to the advent of Operation Enduring Freedom, the Taliban controlled at least 90 percent of Afghanistan's territory. Since they emerged in 1994, amid the darkest days of the civil war, the Taliban slowly took over the country. By 1998 they controlled most of Afghanistan, unable to dislodge the remaining resistance from their redoubts in the mountainous northeast of the country. Officially known as the United National and Islamic Front for the Salvation of Afghanistan, the Northern Alliance was composed of the remainder of several once powerful military/political parties who were brought together in their common struggle against Taliban rule in Afghanistan.[13] Most of the territory and soldiers in the Northern Alliance belonged to the Shura-i-Nazar, the wing of Jamiat-i-Islami controlled by Ahmad Shah Massoud.[14] Other groups held small pockets of land. There was very little practical coordination among these parties, all of which had faced one another on the battlefield between 1992 and 1996.

The decision to launch Operation Enduring Freedom was made soon after September 11. After unsuccessfully demanding the handover of Osama bin Laden, Coalition military operations against Afghanistan commenced on October 7, 2001, with the chief aim of destroying Al Qaeda and ousting its Taliban supporters.[15] A massive infusion of cash, arms, and communications equipment was provided to the Northern Alliance forces, and US military and intelligence personnel accompanied them on the ground to provide guidance and air support for military operations. From a short-term military perspective, the collaboration was a remarkable success, leading to the collapse of the Taliban within five weeks.[16]

From a longer-term political and military perspective, the choices made at the start of Operation Enduring Freedom have proved extremely costly. Many voices warned early on that failure of the Coalition to impose political constraints on its Afghan allies could result in instability and a return to the warlordism of the early 1990s:

> Military operations carried out by US and its allied force may cause the fall of the Taleban regime any time, which will create a political vacuum. If that vacuum were filled by a particular group through military operation, it would turn to a new phase of bloodshed and disorder and would afflict our nation with new misfortunes.[17]

The Coalition and the United Nations were aware of these concerns and were making some efforts in Afghanistan, Pakistan, and Rome to create a broader-based Afghan political coalition that could take over the government once the Taliban collapsed. Given the central importance of the capital, there was also reportedly specific pressure placed on the Northern Alliance not to take Kabul.[18] However, events on the ground proceeded rapidly. As the Taliban disintegrated, the newly reinvigorated factional armies rolled into their old domains, one after the other. On November 13, despite repeated assurances that it would respect international calls to the contrary, the Northern Alliance marched into Kabul.[19] Throughout the next several weeks, Operation Enduring Freedom effectively handed control of Afghanistan to an array of regional commanders who had spent the early 1990s fighting each other in a vicious civil war.

THE BONN PROCESS

The alacrity with which the military campaign proceeded in Afghanistan was matched by a diplomatic scramble to get Afghanistan's non-Taliban political leadership together. To shepherd the negotiations, UN Secretary-General Kofi Annan reappointed Lakhdar Brahimi, on October 3, as his special representative (SRSG) to Afghanistan. Brahimi, the former Algerian foreign minister, had served as the SRSG to Afghanistan from 1997 to 1999.

Representatives of the Northern Alliance and the former king held talks in Rome and on October 1 agreed to form a Supreme Council of National Unity of Afghanistan. The non-Taliban Pashtun mujahedin felt excluded by this agreement and by heavy Coalition reliance on the Northern Alliance. In response, some fifteen hundred Pashtun tribal and religious leaders met in Peshawar, Pakistan, on October 24–25 to formulate a role for themselves. The meeting was led by the head of the National Islamic Front of Afghanistan, Pir Syeed Gailani, a former mujahedin leader and religious figure. This meeting reiterated the call for a Loya Jirga to establish the next government.

Events on the ground moved quickly, buffeting negotiations to determine the political shape of post-Taliban Afghanistan. Kabul changed hands on November 13, prompting UN Security Council Resolution 1378 the following day. The resolution affirmed the UN's central role in supporting political transition efforts and called for a new government that would be "broad-based, multi-ethnic and fully representative of all the Afghan people."[20] The resolution also encouraged UN member states to ensure the safety and security of the capital and an eventual transitional authority. This final appeal appeared to be a call to create an international security force that could provide the essential "political space" needed in Kabul to create a broad-based government.[21] However, the Northern Alliance quickly rejected proposals for a security force, arguing that it would provide security.

As the noose began to close on the Taliban in their home base of Kandahar, the intense diplomacy of the United Nations and the United States got key parties to agree to a conference to name an interim administration and chart the future political transition. The meeting began in Bonn on November 27 and included representatives from four main Afghan groupings: the various factions of the Northern Alliance; the Rome group, composed of the family and supporters of the former King Zahir Shah; the Peshawar group, Pashtun mujahedin, tribal and religious leaders based in Pakistan; and the Cyprus group, a mixture of factions with close ties to Iran. Numerous Afghan civil society groups from inside and outside Afghanistan felt that those meeting in Germany did not represent the Afghan people and participated in a civil society forum near Bonn, in tandem with the political negotiations, in an attempt to inject alternative voices into the process. The Bonn Agreement acknowledges in its preamble that many groups were not adequately represented at the talks.

The Bonn meeting evoked the failed peace talks from 1992 to 1994 in places like Islamabad and Ashkabad. Many of these same representatives had come together, with UN mediation, inked flowery agreements, and swore on the Qur'an to abide by them. Each of these efforts had dissolved almost instantly, subjecting Afghanistan to new rounds of internecine bloodshed. In his opening remarks at Bonn, SRSG Lakhdar Brahimi warned the delegates: "You must not allow the mistakes of the past to be repeated, particularly those of 1992."[22] However, a critical difference between 1992 and 2001 was Washington's newfound interest in Afghanistan and its willingness to twist arms to secure agreement on contentious issues.

Shura-i-Nazar, the Panjshiri Tajik faction of the Northern Alliance, played a dominant role at the Bonn talks. With undisputed control of the capital, the strongest military, a honed leadership, and a robust battlefield alliance with the United States, there was little to oppose its insistence on retaining the lion's share of the key positions in the new government. In exchange, the Shura-i-Nazar agreed to a relatively unaffiliated Pashtun tribal leader, Hamid Karzai, to head the interim administration; a limited international security force in Kabul; and a transition process designed to lead to the creation of a new constitution and elections in just thirty months.

The Bonn Agreement

The Bonn Agreement was a framework for the transformation of the Afghan political system. Although extraordinarily ambitious in scope, it provided little detail on how its most essential aspects could or should be accomplished. Despite its weaknesses, the agreement was a cause for rejoicing in Afghanistan. A unique and unexpected moment had arrived—a *deus ex machina*—that swept seemingly insurmountable obstacles aside and created a new chance for peace. It was widely perceived, however, that to squander this chance could mean many more years of darkness and regression. The Bonn Agreement was an Atlas, bearing the burden of all Afghans' hopes upon its shoulders.

The Agreement laid out the powers of an interim administration and then transitional administration intended to shepherd Afghanistan through reconstruction and the unification of Afghanistan's military power in a central government. It provided guidance on the laws and institutions that should control these decisions. The agreement did not, however, provide details on how its provisions should be enforced, such as how and when disarmament and integration of military forces were to occur, or what the powers of the emergency and constitutional Loya Jirgas were to be. Nor did it clearly lay out, or guarantee, penalties for transgressions.

The lack of detail is understandable in an agreement produced in a short time under intense pressure. The agreement represented a decision to push difficult questions into the transition process rather than resolve them up front. Instead, the agreement established a series of milestones that the parties could be held to when the time came. Thus the Bonn Agreement set two simultaneous processes in motion: a state-building process and a peace-consolidation process. The state-building process was intended to be the engine for reconstruction, formation of long-term security arrangements, and a return to national unity. The peace-consolidation process was meant to maintain order among factions, allowing them to lessen their enmity while acknowledging, if implicitly, their de facto control of the country. The Bonn Agreement envisioned that state and political institutions, such as constitutional reform and elections, would draw sovereign authority back to the government and people, and away from the rule of the gun.

Due to objections that the signatories at Bonn were not fully representative of the Afghan people, the agreement created an interim authority with a life span of only six months.[23] An independent commission was responsible for organizing an emergency Loya Jirga—a national assembly—to choose a transitional authority that would "lead Afghanistan until such time as a fully representative government can be elected through free and fair elections to be held no later than two years from the date of the convening of the Emergency Loya Jirga."[24]

The Bonn Agreement also provided for the drafting of a new constitution, to be approved by a constitutional Loya Jirga that was to convene within eighteen months after the establishment of the transitional administration, or just two years after the Bonn Agreement.[25] Until the adoption of a new constitution, the 1964 constitution would be in force, except with regard to the executive and legislature,[26] thus excluding a substantial portion of the meaningful provisions of that instrument. The agreement also allowed for the operation of existing laws that did not contradict the provisions of the 1964 constitution. While sensible, this provision was unenforceable due to the enormous task of sorting through the laws of multiple and antithetical regimes over thirty years, as well as a general inability to enforce laws throughout the country.

The chairman of the interim and transitional administrations had the power to make law by decree with the agreement of his cabinet, which simplified pressing legal issues.[27]

The Bonn Agreement also attempted to address the fractious security situation in four ways. First, the agreement requires that "upon the official transfer of power, all mujahedin, Afghan armed forces and armed groups in the country shall come under the command and control of the Interim Authority, and be reorganized according to the requirements of the new Afghan security and armed forces."[28] Second, the agreement asks the international community for assistance in establishing and training a new Afghan army.[29] Third, the agreement requests the UN Security Council to establish a force to "assist in the maintenance of security for Kabul and its surrounding areas," and possibly in other areas.[30] Fourth, the Bonn participants pledged to remove all military units from Kabul and other areas where the UN-sanctioned force was deployed.[31]

In comparison to the process of political transition established by the agreement, the security provisions were demonstrably weak from the start, and critical aspects, as a result, have not been enforced. The provision putting all armed forces under the control of the Afghanistan interim authority (AIA) proved unrealistic. While the Bonn Agreement established the important principle that armed forces should obey the AIA, this provision undermined the overall agreement by papering over a critical issue with empty platitudes. Indeed, a significant security requirement that all Afghan military units withdraw from Kabul was not enforced. The ISAF deployed to Kabul and was successful at infusing a sense of security among citizens there. However, the refusal of the key Western military powers to expand ISAF to other areas left the rest of the country considerably less secure in physical and psychological terms. At the same time, training for an Afghan national military began in earnest, although by December 2002 only a few thousand soldiers had been trained, and military sources estimated that a serious force would be nearly a decade in coming. The short-term security needs of Afghanistan will, therefore, not be met by this emerging force.

The final critical aspect of the Bonn Agreement was the selection of the AIA cabinet. In Afghanistan, confidence in peaceful transitions of power is understandably low, and thus the composition of the AIA to many meant the future of the Afghan government. The distribution of posts was widely viewed to be extremely lopsided, with the Panjshiri faction of the Shura-i-Nazar claiming the three most powerful ministries: defense, interior, and foreign affairs. The selection of Hamid Karzai, head of the Pashtun Popalzai tribe as chairman, and the agreement to allow the return of the former king were attempts to reduce Pashtun concerns. However, the idea of potential power in the chairmanship of the interim government and the return of the former king was far less concrete than the very real power that the Shura-i-Nazar triumvirate exerted over Kabul and Afghanistan's foreign relations. It was not only the less-well-represented non-Northern Alliance groups that complained that "injustices have been committed in the distribution of ministries."[32] Powerful members of the Northern Alliance, such as Rashid Dostum and Ismael Khan, decried the outcome as unfair and even humiliating.[33]

THE POST-TALIBAN SECURITY ENVIRONMENT

Much of Afghanistan remained insecure, and active conflict throughout 2002 in almost every region underscored that the "post-conflict" label was not yet applicable to the Afghan situation. Insecurity in Afghanistan ran along two intersecting axes. The remnants of the Taliban, Al Qaeda, and their sympathizers remained a threat in the south and east, while other military factions within the Bonn process continued to compete for power and resources throughout Afghanistan. These dangers intersected in the Pashtun heartland, where many leaders felt disaffected by their perception that the political and military changes in the year after September 11 left the Pashtuns disenfranchised and under siege. There was growing resentment against, rather than a sense of liberation by, the Coalition forces that remained in the Pashtun heartland searching for enemies and their weapons caches. As the Pashtun-controlled Taliban fell from grace, they were replaced by a US-backed, Tajik-controlled government. Many Pashtuns complained that they were labeled Taliban, terrorists, and drug lords, and were harassed by the defense minister's Shura-i-Nazar soldiers upon entering Kabul. Their fears were compounded by documented reports of attacks against Pashtun minorities in the north.[34]

With the return of antagonistic and unaccountable armed factions throughout the country, Afghanistan remains a fractured state, with geographic, linguistic, sectarian, and cultural fault lines. Poor transport and communication networks have kept populations isolated from each other. Rural village culture is largely conservative, with little patience for interference from outside authorities, including the central government. The last twenty-three years of war have exacerbated these fault lines. Fighting and neglect destroyed roads and bridges, and front lines created real boundaries between regions. Ethnically identified factions engaged in ruthless combat, often stirring sectarian hatreds that spiraled into reprisals and spates of ethnic cleansing. In many parts of the country the central governments of the Communist and Taliban eras were seen as foreign-supported occupation forces.

The militias that once again dominate much of the country are controlled at the local level by commanders with regional affiliations. These local commanders are generally loyal to a mid-level commander, who may control a substantial portion of a province and, in turn, is usually affiliated with a regional entity, party, or organization led by a recognized personality. Maintaining the loyalty of mid-level commanders is a fundamental occupation of regional leaders, requiring significant and sustained patronage.

Military power remains very dispersed, with rivalries posing both short-term and long-term challenges to stability. Afghan government authority extends little beyond Kabul, and control of the regions has reverted virtually to the status quo of the period before 1992. The predominantly Tajik Jamiat-i-Islami forces control the northeast and compete for power in the north with the mostly Uzbek militia Jumbish-i-Milli and the predominantly Hazara Hezb-i-Wahadat. Ismail Khan, the nominally Jamiat but fiercely independent commander in Herat, is strong in the west and draws considerable resources from his control over trade with Iran. Hezb-i-Wahadat factions control the central region, and power in the east is split between the family of Haji Din Mohammad, the Pashtun governor of Nangahar, and the forces of Hazrat Ali, the Pashai military commander loyal to Jamiat in Jalalabad. In the south, Governor Gul Agha of Qandahar, a Pashtun, presides over a weak alliance of tribal leaders. Throughout the south and east the Pashtun tribes remain powerful and independent in the areas they control. Throughout 2002 there were clashes between these factions in the southeast, north, west, and center of the country.

As ever, Afghanistan remains subject to extensive foreign involvement in its internal affairs. Neighboring powers, especially Iran and Pakistan, remain fearful that loss of influence in Afghanistan will lead to insecurity and domination by rival powers. Although Western engagement has momentarily dwarfed and partially displaced the regional influences, both state and non-state actors in neighboring countries provide support to favored factions in Afghanistan. The enormous tensions in the region, between Pakistan and India, the United States and Iraq, and internal struggles in Iran, Pakistan, and the Central Asian states ensure that Afghanistan will remain an aspect of everyone's designs for promoting security or insecurity.

THE TOOLS OF PEACE-BUILDING

A substantial gulf remains between the goals of the Bonn Agreement and the reality on the ground in Afghanistan. A legitimate government must take form and expand its reach throughout the country, spreading security and economic resources. This cannot be accomplished primarily by force, as the government has neither the strength nor the legitimacy to do so. Instead, the government, with the help of the international community, must initially reestablish itself by rebuilding the institutions of state, which draw in the support of the people and the resources of the factions.

SECURITY

Positive changes in the security sector have been very slow in coming. The initial months after the Bonn summit were dominated by the continued fight against the Taliban and Al Qaeda. Instead of taking steps to begin disarming factional militias and to create a national army, the Coalition continued to distribute arms and money to militia armies to assist them in this battle. Despite the high costs of this policy to long-term security, it is also questionable whether short-term security was enhanced. Evidently, the groups that were supposed to be aiding the Coalition allowed the Taliban and Al Qaeda to escape through the mountains into Pakistan. The most significant long-term security issues are those concerning heavily armed factions who, with new weapons and funds from the United States and other backers, quickly moved into the security vacuum to retake their old fiefs. These factions are not representative of much of the Afghan population, and the dominance of the Northern Alliance factions has engendered a growing feeling of disenfranchisement among the Pashtuns. Inter-factional skirmishes, and the threat of return to civil war has reemerged as the greatest threat to stability in Afghanistan.

But what role do the international military forces have in keeping a lid on tensions between the resurgent factions? In Kabul, ISAF has been critical in maintaining a sense of security in the city. However, despite the nearly universal calls for the expansion of ISAF from Afghans and the international community, the Coalition blocked its expansion into other areas. Fearful that an expanded ISAF would require substantial Coalition support and get in the way of its primary military objectives, the US military at first blocked the expansion outright, then dropped their overt objection later in the year once they were certain that ISAF would not expand without their cooperation.

Without ISAF in the countryside, the US military has played an important but ambiguous role keeping factional fighting in check. Washington claims that it does not intervene in instances of "green on green" fighting (fighting between non-Taliban factions), although they do play a "mediation" role. US Special Forces teams are scattered throughout the country and they regularly interact with military commanders. Although perhaps more implicit than explicit, the presence of US military clearly represent a threat to commanders should they cross an unclear line. These US forces are small but they carry the threat of immediate, massive, and overwhelming firepower from the air. "B-52" has entered common parlance in Afghanistan as air power is seen as the dominant factor in the rapid collapse of the Taliban and the redrawing of Afghanistan's political map.

The US military seems to be engaged in a form of strategic ambiguity with the warlords. The United States supports the Karzai government and wants to see stability emerge in Afghanistan, but it is not willing to disarm its Afghan allies. Meanwhile, the United States relies on the factions to help with the war on terrorism and to remain within the Bonn process, wherein the factions will eventually have to cede their power to the central government. What keeps the warlords in the game is partially the fear that pulling out will incur the wrath of the US military. Do they know how far they can push—for instance by attacking rivals—before they've crossed the line? Probably not.

This situation was illustrated by an incident in December 2002 in western Afghanistan. A significant battle broke out between Ismael Khan and his rival, Amanullah Khan, in southern Herat province. Amid the fighting, several US bombs were dropped on the opposing forces. The US military claims that several US soldiers on patrol were caught in the crossfire, and that the bombs were dropped simply to extricate the soldiers. The effect of this action, whether intended or not, was both to end the fighting, and to make the rival commanders believe that they were bombed because they were fighting.

A strategy, however, is not a policy. The long-term security policy of the United States and the international community in Afghanistan was laid out at Bonn: subordinate the factional armies to the central authority, create a national army, and integrate or disarm the remaining soldiers. However, the pursuit of Washington's immediate objective essentially means thwarting efforts needed to nurture the political transformation set out in the Bonn Agreement.

Creating a central government and restoring a monopoly on the use of force requires a program that simultaneously draws authority away from Afghan regional commanders and gives them incentives to integrate into the evolving political and social context. The role of military commanders has deep roots in Afghanistan and includes complex interplay between economics and social structures. For years, many communities have relied on militias for survival, seeing them as the source of largess and the target of their petitions. This patronage culture must be supplanted, preferably by government institutions that offer support and services to the community. However, it will take time for institutions to form and take over this function.

Disarmament, demobilization, and reintegration programs (commonly referred to as DDR) are a critical element of the peace-building process, as the sheer inertia of up to 200,000 armed men, otherwise jobless, can wreak havoc upon any peace process. The first year saw substantial planning for an eventual DDR process, but funding and implementation lagged. Demobilization programs elsewhere, such as those in Angola, suggest that there must be a tight fit between community development and local demobilization programs. But economic-pull factors alone will not be strong enough to dismantle the current patronage system, as substantial incentives remain for those who control regional trade and other resources.

The other long-term goal is to create a national military force that can integrate the atomized military commands and eventually be a bedrock national institution that can challenge recalcitrant actors. On December 1, 2002, at the anniversary meeting of the Bonn conference, President Karzai signed a decree calling for the establishment of a seventy thousand person national army.[35] Training of Afghan national army and guard units by United States, French, and ISAF contingents was ongoing throughout 2002. By the end of the year an estimated three thousand soldiers had been through basic training, but reports indicated that up to *50 percent* of the soldiers trained had already left the service. Original estimates that the full army could be trained by 2009 were downgraded by a French general, who said that, realistically, perhaps twenty thousand professional soldiers could be trained by 2009. Creating a military is not simply a question of training soldiers—the greatest obstacles are creating a professional officer corps that is fully subordinate to civilian rule and puts national interests above local ties.

POLITICAL RECONSTRUCTION

The most intensive peace-building efforts in 2002 were undertaken in the political sphere, including the organization of an emergency Loya Jirga and initiation of constitutional and judicial-reform commissions. The ability to accept and direct massive amounts of foreign aid created intense pressure to set up a viable government in Kabul. While the Kabul administration had little reach into the provinces, the highly centralized unitary state model envisioned in Kabul was intended to bring the provinces, politically, administratively, and financially, firmly under Kabul's control.

The emergency Loya Jirga

The emergency Loya Jirga held June 10–21, 2002, in Kabul was a small but critical step in Afghanistan's political development. It was an opportunity to accord national legitimacy to the peace process initiated in Bonn, but it produced mixed results. From a narrow perspective, it was a success. Representatives from across Afghanistan came together to elect, or rather anoint, a head of state, and the major armed factions kept their hats in the political ring rather than resorting to armed violence. Given the last three decades of war and turmoil, this is significant.

However, the Loya Jirga failed in important respects as well. The opportunity to assert civilian leadership, promote democratic expression, and draw authority away from the warlords was squandered. An all-consuming concern for short-term stability prompted key Afghan and international decision-makers to bow to undemocratic sectarian demands.

The Loya Jirga is an Afghan tradition with an august but vague history. The concept was extrapolated from the model of the tribal *jirga* or *shura*, an ad hoc, village-based institution that allows broad representation and, nominally, consensual decision-making. A Loya Jirga is intended to be a national manifestation of community decision-making. The Loya Jirga has been used on average every twenty years to confirm the succession of monarchs, to pass constitutions, and to approve government policy. The last Loya Jirga deemed broadly legitimate was held in 1964 to approve a new reformist constitution.

The greatest success of the Loya Jirga may have been the selection process for the delegates. Although subject to significant intimidation in certain areas, the overall exercise brought together communities to discuss issues and peacefully choose representatives. A two-phase local indirect election system combining consensus-based selection of local leaders with a secret ballot in the second round chose 1051 representatives from up to 390 electoral districts in 32 provinces. An additional 500 delegates were appointed by the independent Loya Jirga commission in consultation with various organizations, civil society groups, nomads, and refugees. The overall delegate selection process was intended to create balance: on a regional and rural/urban basis by allowing at least one representative for each administrative district *(uluswali)*; on an ethnic basis primarily by relying upon geographic concentrations; on a gender basis by reserving 160 appointed seats for women; and on a social-cultural basis by providing seats for religious figures, refugees, nomads, and traders. The geographical, ethnic, and ideological diversity under the tent was a testament to the success of the system—and critical to the ability of Afghans to choose representatives.

Just before the Loya Jirga, however, a crack in the facade of fair selection of representatives appeared, when up to one hundred extra "political" delegates were summarily added to the rolls. These delegates, mostly provincial governors and other political-military figures unwilling or unable to stand for election, constituted a blanket of intimidation upon the delegates. Although able to act independently in the "Kabul-free-zone" under the watchful eyes of ISAF and the international media, the delegates and their families would have to deal with local power brokers once they arrived back home.

The key expectation for the Loya Jirga on the part of the assembled delegates, most Afghans, and the international community was that it would correct the ethnic/factional imbalance produced at the Bonn conference. No matter how fair the selection process for delegates was, the legitimacy of the Loya Jirga would ultimately rely on the names and positions that emerged. In the end, although the delegate selection process went better than expected, the opportunity for real participation and reconciliation at the Loya Jirga was squandered.

The Loya Jirga was mandated to choose the head of state, the structure of the transitional authority, and its key personnel.[36] Many delegates came armed with plans and speeches outlining the powers and functions of a new parliament, cabinet ministries, and independent commissions. Ultimately, delegates were given little opportunity to address any of these tasks seriously. This was largely due to behind-the-scenes orchestration, exacerbated by procedural confusion and poor chairmanship. The exact substance of decisions to be made had been vague since Bonn, most likely because many of the power struggles that were evident at that conference were still unresolved. This lack of clarity was exploited by those wanting to expand or contract the agenda to suit their needs. The result was several agenda-less days, chaotic speakers' lists, and delegates frustrated at not knowing what, when, or how they were to decide issues.

One day before the Loya Jirga began, Zaher Shah's nomination for consideration for the position of head of state was withdrawn, apparently under significant pressure from the Shura-i-Nazar and the United States. The US special envoy to Afghanistan, Zalmay Khalilzad, an Afghan by birth, played a direct, visible role as "king unmaker." On the eve of the Loya Jirga, Khalilzad called a press conference at the US embassy to announce that the king would not seek office at the Loya Jirga. In a staged press conference two hours later, the king sat impassively flanked by Khalilzad and Foreign Minister Abdullah as a statement to the same effect was read on his behalf. This overt orchestration set a cynical tone for the gathering, and significant Pashtun discontent erupted at the outright exclusion of Zahir Shah.

Once the Loya Jirga began, another crucial error was made in allowing the National Security Directorate, Kabul's Panjshiri-controlled secret police, into the Loya Jirga grounds. With the combination of warlords and governors occupying the front rows while National Security Directorate agents scurried around the adjacent consultation tents, an air of repression and intimidation filled the Loya Jirga tent. Many delegates complained of threatening phone calls and the minister of defense, General Fahim, threatened the husband of Masooda Jalal, the female candidate for president, in front of a large group. The discontent among delegates was compounded by the failure to redistribute the power of the key security ministries of defense, interior, and foreign affairs away from the Shura-i-Nazar.

To many delegates who had come great distances from inside and outside the country to participate in the selection of their government for the first time in decades, the last-minute deal-making outside the tent was disappointing. There were no illusions inside the tent that the Loya Jirga could be a fully democratic process. Compromise between and with those still prepared to use force to achieve their political ends remains unavoidable in today's Afghanistan. However, the orchestration of outcomes throughout the process set a heavy-handed and disappointing tone.

The Afghan transitional administration

The Kabul government has become increasingly split between two facets. On the security side, the government remains divided, itself a factional entity among factions, unable to rise above the field. On the administrative side, however, President Karzai, with the backing of the international donor community, has managed to insert a small but powerful band of technocrats into positions of authority. This cabal of talented, forward-looking, and above all, politically unaffiliated Afghans are working on extending the authority and capacity of the Kabul government to the provinces. Their mission is to provide an alternative to warlordism—a responsive and representative government that provides services and respects human rights.

This is a relatively new concept for Afghanistan. Although the centralized state did manage to reach into most parts of the country after nearly a century of state-building that began in the 1880s, the state was never particularly representative or focused on rights protection and service delivery. The remnants of the Afghan civil service remain in the provinces and are surprisingly functional despite more than two decades of state collapse.[37] Rather than disappear, the administrative units simply stopped reporting to Kabul and instead survived under local and regional political arrangements. Now this cadre of civil servants, still loyal to the concept of a centralized state, is being reinvigorated and reintegrated in the effort to re-nationalize the government. Tying the government bureaucracy back into the center is a key means of undermining the capacity and attractiveness of alternative sources of power. It will be increasingly difficult for the regional power-brokers to maintain loyalty with the center providing salaries, program resources, and a compelling vision of the future.

PEACE AND DEMOCRATIZATION?

Despite considerable uncertainty and the continuing domination of Afghan politics by the *tofangdar*, or gun-holders, there are signs that some political actors, warlords among them, are preparing for a transition from rule of the gun to the rule of law. Although by the end of

2002 there were no formal preparations for eventual elections, and work on the constitutional process had only barely begun, some political actors had started organizing for a political future off the battlefield. Apart from the Loya Jirga, the sanctioned means for pursuing political agendas have been through government commissions, especially the constitutional commission, the judicial-reform commission, the human rights commission, and the national assembly commission, as well as through semi-sanctioned political party development.

The constitutional commission was to be appointed within two months after the emergency Loya Jirga.[38] Political concerns delayed its creation and only a drafting committee was appointed in November 2002, with the full thirty-five-member commission finally appointed April 26, 2003, just five months before the constitutional Loya Jirga was scheduled to begin. No presidential decree was issued assigning the duties or time line of the commission, and thus in practice nothing was accomplished in the first year after the Bonn consultation. Several civil society groups, however, made early preparations to ensure that they would have input into the constitutional development process. Their early organization came in response to fears that the constitutional process, like the emergency Loya Jirga, would be undermined by backroom deals among unrepresentative power brokers. There were also broader fears that enormous pressure and expectations would be placed on the constitutional process to sort out the underlying issues around which the potential for conflict still loomed large.

The human rights, judicial, and national assembly commissions all started with significant mandates for change, but all have been bogged down due to lack of funding, lack of operational capacity, and political infighting. The judicial commission, first formed in June 2002, was disbanded in September, having accomplished nothing; it was not re-constituted until November 2002. The national assembly commission, an unwanted stepchild of the government agreed to at the emergency Loya Jirga, remained hampered by uncertain membership and mandate. Finally, the human rights commission, given the enormous mandate of human rights policy, investigation, education, and transitional justice, struggled to prioritize its work and to deal with the very real security threats facing its members. Its capacity to work throughout the country has been very limited, and capacity building support, as with all the commissions, has been slow.

One area of more rapid, albeit unregulated development has been in the area of political parties. Although Afghanistan has no law allowing for the creation or regulation of parties, such political entities are emerging in a variety of ways. Key power brokers, such as Younus Qanooni, the powerful former interior minister, Wali Massoud, the brother of assassinated leader Ahmad Shah Massoud, and Karim Khalili, the Hazara leader who heads the Hezb-i-Wahadat party, have been working aggressively to create strong party structures. Although there is no formal party, a religious coalition of conservative mujahedin leaders such as former president Rabbani and Rasool Sayyaf also seems imminent.

There is also a budding democratic movement, boosted by the formation of a coalition of small groups, called the National Council of Peace and Democracy of Afghanistan. It comprises students, university professors, liberal republicans, and Afghan NGO workers. This coalition has put forward a basic democratic platform and is in the early stages of organization. Although not very powerful in the current Afghan context, there were numerous sympathetic delegates at the Loya Jirga.

Development of a party system in Afghanistan will be needed both for civic participation in the political process and for elections. Support for development of democratic institutions and parties in the next few years must be a top priority of the government and the international community.

Demobilization and reconstruction programs, even if successful, will be slow and incomplete. There is a pressing need to wrest control of the fruits of the warlord economy—opium production, smuggling, and illicit taxation of trade—away from the regional power brokers, while at the same time producing the economic incentives of stability. The ultimate safeguard against a return to conflict in Afghanistan, however, will be political stability. Afghanistan's future lies in the ability of its people to forge a political community that resolves disputes pacifically and democratically.

NOTES

[1] The UN-sponsored talks on Afghanistan took place from November 27, 2001, to December 5, 2001, outside Bonn, Germany and resulted in the Agreement on Provisional Arrangements in Afghanistan Pending the Re-Establishment of Permanent Government Institutions, otherwise known as the Bonn Agreement.

[2] As recently as November 2002, nearly one year after Bonn, the US military admitted to continuing support to "regional leaders" (David Zucchino, "General Values Alliance with Afghan Warlords," *Los Angeles Times*, November 4, 2002).

[3] The author witnessed much of this process firsthand, including the emergency Loya Jirga, as an analyst for the International Crisis Group in 2002. Significant aspects of the information for this chapter were gathered during this period, some of which appeared in two International Crisis Group (ICG) reports: *The Loya Jirga: One Small Step Forward?* Kabul/Brussels, May 16, 2002; and *The Afghan Transitional Administration: Prospects and Perils,* July 30, 2002.

[4] The Coalition embarked in late December 2002 on a program of deploying provincial reconstruction teams to seven to ten locations in Afghanistan

outside of Kabul. The first three teams were deployed in spring 2003 to Gardez, Bamiyan, and Kunduz. The first British-led team was deployed to Mazar in July 2003, and others are currently being planned. These teams consist of security forces for protection and civil affairs teams to undertake specific reconstruction projects. The approach is experimental, and the security function of the forces, outside of protecting themselves, is not yet determined.

[5] See "Third Report of the Monitoring Group Established Pursuant to Security Council Resolution 1363 (2001) and Extended by 1390 (2002)," UN doc. S/2002/1338; and David Rhode, "Threats and Responses: Pakistan Tribal Region; An Anti-US Haven for Al Qaeda," *New York Times*, December 26, 2002.

[6] CARE International Policy Brief, "Rebuilding Afghanistan: A Little Less Talk, A Lot More Action" (October 1, 2002). Per capita annual giving by the international community for Bosnia was US$326, Kosovo was US$288, and East Timor was US$195, in comparison to a projected US$42 per person per year in Afghanistan.

[7] Richard J. Newman, "America Fights Back: Clinton Raises the Stakes in the War Against Terrorism," *U.S. News & World Report* (August 31, 1998).

[8] UN Security Council Resolution 1267 (1999), UN doc. S/1999/1267.

[9] Based on the best estimates of the time, in 1969 less than 5 percent of the Afghan population lived in cities (population estimates taken from Louis Dupree, *Afghanistan* [Princeton, N.J.: Princeton University Press, 1980]).

[10] Sardar Daoud deposed his cousin, King Mohammad Zahir, on July 17, 1973, declaring Afghanistan a republic and himself president and prime minister (Dupree, *Afghanistan*, 753).

[11] The mujahedin parties received billions of dollars in military aid between 1980 and 1989, with the lion's share coming from the United States, Saudi Arabia, and other Arab sources and channeled through Pakistan's military intelligence wing, the Inter-Services Intelligence (ISI).

[12] Interview with Zbigniew Brzezinski, *Le Nouvel Observateur* (France), January 15–21, 1998.

[13] The Northern Alliance primarily consisted of Jamiat-i-Islami, Jumbish-i-Milli, Hezbe-i-Wahdat, and Harakat-i-Islami, and included other more marginal participants, such as Haji Qadeer's Eastern Shura, and Ittihad-i-Islami. It is significant to note that the Northern Alliance was devoid of significant Pashtun representation.

[14] The Shura-i-Nazar (Supervisory Council) was formed by the late Ahmad Shah Massoud within the predominately Tajik Jamiat-i-Islami party nominally headed by former president Burhanuddin Rabbani. Much of its strength was located in the Panjshir Valley, Massoud's redoubt. This wing of Jamiat, in which the military and administrative power of the party became concentrated, was controlled by Defense Minister Muhammad Qassem Fahim; former-interior minister, now Education Minister Yunus Qanooni; and Foreign Minister Abdullah Abdullah.

[15] "Letter from Stewart Eldon, Chargé d'Affaires, UK Mission to the UN in New York, to the President of the Security Council," S/2001/947 (October 7, 2001).

[16] As of October 31, 2001, in addition to the US and UK forces, the Coalition included direct military support from seventeen nations ("Operation Enduring

Freedom: Foreign Pledges of Military and Intelligence Support," *Congressional Research Service* [October 17, 2001]).

[17] "Final Resolution, Conference for Peace and National Unity, Peshawar, Pakistan, October 25, 2001," *Afghan Islamic Press*, October 25, 2001, from *SWB Asia-Pacific*, October 27, 2001. This conference was a meeting of mainly Pashtun former-mujahedin, tribal, and religious leaders.

[18] House of Commons Library, "Operation Enduring Freedom and the Conflict in Afghanistan: An Update," Research paper 01/81 (October 31, 2001), 34–35.

[19] Kathy Gannon, "Taliban Desert Kabul, Northern Alliance Moves In," *Chicago Tribune*, November 13, 2001; see also, House of Commons Library, "The Campaign Against International Terrorism: Prospects After the Fall of the Taliban," Research paper 01/112 (December 11, 2001).

[20] United Nations Security Council Resolution 1378 (2001). UN doc. S/2001/1378.

[21] Jarat Chopra, Jim McCallum, and Alexander Thier, "Planning Considerations for International Involvement in Post-Taliban Afghanistan," *Brown Journal of World Affairs* 8/2 (winter 2002). Available online.

[22] Ahmed Rashid, *Far Eastern Economic Review* (December 6, 2001).

[23] Bonn Agreement, Art. I(4). Available online.

[24] Ibid.

[25] Ibid., Art. I(6).

[26] Ibid., Art. II(1).

[27] The power of decree was granted to the interim administration in the Bonn Agreement, Art III.C.(1), but was never explicitly granted to the Afghanistan transitional authority (ATA) through the Bonn Agreement or the emergency Loya Jirga. The ATA has, however, continued to exercise this power. As of December 2002, Chairman Karzai had issued over 150 decrees.

[28] Bonn Agreement, Art. V(1).

[29] Ibid., Annex I(2).

[30] Ibid., Annex I(3).

[31] Ibid., Annex I(4).

[32] Pir Sayeed Gailani, quoted in "Uzbek Warlord Rejects Afghan Accord," *Reuters* (December 6, 2001).

[33] Rashid Dostum, quoted in ibid.

[34] Human Rights Watch, "Paying for the Taliban's Crimes: Abuses Against Ethnic Pashtuns in Northern Afghanistan" (April 2002).

[35] Decree of the Islamic Transitional State of Afghanistan on the Afghan National Army (December 1, 2002). The decree states that the ANA will not exceed seventy thousand persons, including "soldiers, officers, all air and ground forces, civilian employees, student cadets, and other specialized units." This suggests a relatively small number of actual soldiers.

[36] The emergency Loya Jirga was to choose a "Head of the State for the Transitional Administration and . . . approve proposals for the structure and key personnel of the Transitional Administration" (Bonn Agreement, Art. IV(5)).

[37] World Bank/AREU report, "Assessing Subnational Administration in Afghanistan." Working draft available online.

[38] Bonn Agreement, Art. I(6).

4

Justice Postponed

The Marginalization of Human Rights in Afghanistan

Norah Niland

Post-Taliban Afghanistan has seen many welcome changes for the Afghan people including renewed hope in the prospect of real peace and accountable governance. Unfortunately, happy images of a land free from the turmoil of the past are overshadowed by a continuing reluctance on the part of the international community to face up to the challenges inherent in a long tradition of contempt for fundamental human rights. Over one year after the signing of the Bonn Agreement in December 2001, a fragile peace is threatened by warlords who enjoy power thanks primarily to the United States and its Coalition partners. The Bonn process is also threatened by growing disenchantment in the Pashtun belt, where resurgent Taliban are able to exploit concerns about the dominant role of the Shura-i-Nazar Tajik faction ensconced in Kabul courtesy of US firepower.

Respect for human rights is fundamental to peace, justice, and a modicum of human security. However, Afghans have never had much opportunity to enjoy these basic entitlements that are the right of all human beings. This chapter examines why non-Afghan actors have chosen to ignore or instrumentalize the human rights crisis in Afghanistan. It discusses the general ineffectiveness of UN human rights machinery and the preference for rhetoric over meaningful interventions and support that would nurture sustainable improvements in the human rights situation. It examines the changes that occurred in the wake of the events of September 11, 2001, when Washington equated peace with the departure of the Taliban, and human rights issues were relegated to the back burner. This chapter argues that a peace strategy that marginalizes human rights and issues of justice is a betrayal of the wishes of the Afghan people. It is also unethical and imprudent, and it runs counter to the overall goal of ending armed conflict in Afghanistan and creating the conditions for a durable peace.

HUMAN RIGHTS AND THE STATE: THE RURAL-URBAN DIVIDE

The Afghan state that developed in the twentieth century was centralized and weak, with little direct bearing on the lives of most of its citizens. Afghanistan, a feudal, land-locked, and impoverished state, suffered from a number of debilitating features and a pitiful human rights record. This included profound underdevelopment and a political culture that concentrated power and influence in the hands of tribal elders in the provinces and the ruling monarchial elite in Kabul. Coopting local leaders and patronage were the principal means for maintaining stability and control beyond the confines of the capital and a few other urban centers.

Statistics from the 1970s attest to the rural-urban divide, which became more pronounced as development and modernization efforts served to undermine traditional patterns of social organization. Less than 15 percent of registered primary school children in 1975 were girls, and the majority of these were from Kabul and other urban areas.[1] There were thirty-six hundred hospital beds in 1975, but 60 percent of these, and 83 percent of all Afghan doctors, were concentrated in the capital.[2] Meanwhile, 85 percent of the population lived in rural areas much as it does today.

Tensions between tradition and modernization initiatives came to a head in 1973 when King Zaher Shah was deposed by his cousin, Daoud, a former prime minister. Daoud's coup signaled a break with the past; he declared Afghanistan a republic and opened the prospect of an end to the politics of palace intrigues and patronage. But Daoud was not a popular figure. He was overthrown by the Saur Revolution of April 1978, which brought to power the People's Democratic Party of Afghanistan (PDPA). It had strong links with Moscow, ruled by decree, had little capacity to relate to rural Afghan realities, and pursued a modernist agenda that was perceived as antagonistic to Islam. The PDPA was greatly resented and was soon confronted with incipient guerrilla activity in rural areas and the emergence of *jihadi* groups with training camps in Pakistan.

HUMAN RIGHTS AND COLD WAR POLITICS

Growing instability on the Soviet Union's southern flank, combined with other geo-strategic Cold War concerns, including Washington's support for the mujahedin, prompted Moscow's decision to invade Afghanistan in December 1979. The arrival of the Red Army in Afghanistan led to the announcement of the "Carter Doctrine" (January 1980), which set out US government policy and commitment to resist Soviet expansion. Shortly thereafter, significant amounts of military support began to flow to Afghan resistance groups with the help of the authorities in Pakistan.

The war against the Soviets, with its high cost in lives and massive refugee flows, had a profound impact on Afghan society and its politics. Arms flowed into the country, contributing to the emergence of commanders as the new power holders and diminishing the role of the *khans*, the traditional landed elite, and that of the urban intelligentsia. The emergence of new political parties linked to armed factions contributed to the politicization of Islam and undermined nascent efforts to liberate females from centuries of tradition that limited their role in public life and opportunities for employment outside the home environment.

From the beginning, both sets of military actors showed scant respect for the laws of war and the rights of civilians who bore the brunt of the fighting. An estimated one million Afghans were killed during the 1980s. The war, and related atrocities, triggered one of the largest population upheavals, including refugees, internally displaced, and migration flows, in contemporary times.[3] An International Committee of the Red Cross (ICRC) study in 1999 found that a "remarkable 83 percent of Afghan respondents say that the war forced them to leave their homes."[4] The same study found that more than half of the respondents (53 percent) reported that a member of their immediate family was killed during the conflict, and 16 percent reported knowing someone who was raped.

The Soviets used their military might indiscriminately as they bombed villages and valleys in a vain attempt to suppress insurrection in the countryside. An early feature of the jihad against the Soviets and the PDPA regime included the deliberate killing of teachers and destruction of schools and administrative buildings in rural areas. These were presented as "symbols of Communism" that were antithetical to traditional rural values and Islam.

Throughout much of the Cold War, discussion and debate on human rights violations in intergovernmental forums were often used as a political football to score points within the context of East-West tensions. The situation concerning Afghanistan was no exception. In 1984 a UN special rapporteur was appointed to examine the human rights situation in Afghanistan and to submit reports to the UN Human Rights Commission and General Assembly.[5] Much of the human rights reporting on Afghanistan focused on violations that occurred at the hands of the Soviets; there was little interest in documenting or addressing abuses committed by the mujahedin. Various advocacy NGOs, operating under a humanitarian banner, concentrated on drumming up support for the resistance and nurturing an atmosphere of "unconditional sympathy for the 'freedom fighters' in which anyone criticizing the rebels for their human rights violations . . . [was] automatically seen as an apologist for the Soviet and Afghan armies."[6] Some NGOs were also vocal in chastising the government side for human rights violations but "remained largely silent about the atrocities committed by the mujahedin."[7] The United Nations was no less partisan, lacking in leadership on human rights matters and demonstrating "a striking example of Cold War tunnel vision."[8]

In November 1987, a few months before the conclusion of the UN-sponsored Geneva Accords that spelled the departure of the Soviets from Afghanistan, Dr. Najibullah, a longtime stalwart of the moderate wing of the PDPA, took over as president in Kabul. Najibullah was able to hold onto power, with Soviet financial backing, until 1992, by which point different mujahedin factions had captured large parts of the country and significant numbers of government troops had defected.[9]

MUJAHEDIN LAWLESSNESS
AND CONTEMPT FOR HUMAN RIGHTS

Najibullah's announcement that he would leave office in March 1992 led to the collapse of the PDPA and intensified factional rivalries. By this time the Cold War had ended, the Soviet threat had disappeared, and the United States and the West had disengaged from Afghanistan and its accumulation of unresolved problems. The departure of the Soviets negated the rationale for jihad and obliged Afghans to question the role of the mujahedin groups as they fought for control of Kabul and ruled with impunity in their individual spheres of influence. The willingness of different commanders to raze much of the capital city, and the lawlessness of mujahedin who killed, pillaged, and raped with abandon, marked a new phase in the war. It also exposed the mujahedin to greater scrutiny than before on their human rights record, particularly in relation to women.

In a report to the UN General Assembly in February 1994, the UN special rapporteur referred to massive numbers of civilians killed indiscriminately in Kabul as a result of rocket and air attacks, including the use of cluster bombs. A few months later the special rapporteur noted that the Rabbani-led government had introduced a decree stipulating various restrictions on female dress and mobility and noting that women should not wear "sound-producing garments" or go outside their homes "without their husband's permission."[10] As this was still the pre-Taliban era, discrimination and violence against women did not generate much interest or concern beyond Afghanistan's frontiers, although human rights violations were highlighted in various reports. A 1995 report by Amnesty International concluded that armed groups "have massacred defenseless women in their homes, or have brutally beaten and raped them. Scores of young women have been abducted and then raped, taken as wives by commanders or sold into prostitution. Some have committed suicide to avoid such a fate. Scores of women have reportedly 'disappeared' and several have been stoned to death."[11] In mid 1995 the Rabbani government canceled the participation of its own representatives to the Fourth World Conference on Women in Beijing on the grounds that the prepared statement of the delegation was not in line with Islamic principles.

Widespread disgust with factional fighting and human rights violations, in particular the abuse of women, was a significant factor in the Taliban rise to power and the extent to which they were tolerated, if not welcomed, in their early years as they rid much of the country of the lawlessness and predatory activities associated with mujahedin rule. The Taliban were largely an unknown quantity beyond Afghanistan's borders when they arrived in Kabul in September 1996, but they had the ironic effect of making the world wake up to the human rights crisis in Afghanistan.

TALIBAN YEARS:
HUMAN RIGHTS AND POLITICAL WARFARE

The Taliban were a harsh and brutal collection of religious "purists" who were intent on imposing their fundamentalist interpretation of Islam and Sharia law; the latter included executions, flogging, and amputations, public events normally reserved for Friday afternoons. The Taliban came to power with the backing of Pakistan and the promise of ridding the country of the lawlessness, killing, and abuse of women that had characterized the mujahedin era. The Taliban were products of the war, their Pashtun culture, and a *madrassa* education while refugees in Pakistan; they were schooled in the Deobandi tradition, a conservative and orthodox view of religious ritual and responsibility. In Kandahar and the Pashtun southern belt that was the heartland of the Taliban inner leadership, there was little adverse reaction to Taliban strictures, which had much in common with prevailing local norms. Elsewhere, the situation was quite different. Herat, a city of learning with longstanding trading links with its Shia neighbors in Iran, bristled under the imposition of Taliban rule. The same was true of other urban centers which the Taliban tended to see as dens of iniquity. Women and girls were forced into a twilight existence with their access to the limited health, education, and job opportunities that were available severely curtailed.

The "pious student" image of the Taliban took a beating when they proved themselves to be no less cruel and bloody than their predecessors upon capturing Mazar in August 1998 after a failed attempt the previous year. In 1998 the Taliban also captured the Central Highlands, the traditional home of the Hazara community, after a two-year economic blockade. Hazarajat and front-line areas in the northeast of the country, where the Northern Alliance tried to maintain defensive positions, were the scene of much brutal repression in the latter Taliban years. Indeed, it soon became a hallmark of Taliban seasonal offensives that civilians in contested areas were most often treated as "the enemy"; they were subjected to summary executions, arbitrary detention, forced displacement, and a scorched-earth policy that included the destruction of homes and agricultural assets—including irrigation systems—essential for survival and a means of livelihood.

RHETORIC OVER SUBSTANCE ON HUMAN RIGHTS

The arrival of the Taliban generated reams of newsprint about the human rights situation in Afghanistan, but much of the debate in international circles had more to do with demonizing Mullah Omar and his band of religious zealots than supporting interventions geared to bringing about actual improvements in the lives of Afghan citizens. Much of the attention was focused on issues such as the mandatory requirement for women to wear the *burqa* or for men to grow beards of a certain length. Issues of more concern to Afghans, including the direct and indirect threats to their right to life resulting from the war, the way it was prosecuted, and appalling levels of poverty and underdevelopment, received only nominal attention.

The campaign against the Taliban took precedence over the rights and well-being of Afghans who had been at the receiving end of abusive regimes, and the policies of those who backed them, since the 1970s.[12] Aid agencies received only a fraction of the amount required for vital humanitarian work. For example, there was very little funding for education in refugee camps that, in theory, should have been an opportunity to counter the discrimination that worked against the participation of girls in primary schooling inside the country. There was very little financial or technical support for the efforts of Afghan and other NGOs working to address the deliberate abuse of civilians, including work focused on documenting and analyzing particular events or patterns of human rights violations. For the most part the international community, whether the Security Council or the UN Human Rights Commission, was content with resolutions that periodically denounced the Taliban while ignoring the Northern Alliance and a long history of impunity that fostered an environment of no-holds-barred warfare and contempt for the rights of civilians.

A notable exception was a UN investigation into massacres in 1997–98 in Mazar-e-Sharif, a key northern stronghold and the last remaining city of significance to be held by the Northern Alliance. When the Taliban were obliged to retreat from a failed bid to capture the city in May 1997, an estimated two thousand of their prisoners of war were summarily executed by anti-Taliban forces under the command of General Malik, the deputy of General Rashid Dostum, the most influential Uzbek warlord; Dostum was loosely associated with the Northern Alliance. When the Taliban succeeded in taking Mazar in August 1998, they focused their revenge on Hazara neighborhoods; Human Rights Watch (HRW) estimated that at least two thousand and possibly more civilians were killed.[13] Both the UN Security Council and the General Assembly requested the United Nations to investigate, as did the Taliban, immediately after the 1997 killings. The UN Office of the High Commissioner for Human Rights (OHCHR), however, was unable to deliver. It had little experience in investigating massacres, and when it finally fielded a team in mid 1999, the outcome was less than helpful. The investigation team did not add to information that was already available and was unable to reach definitive conclusions concerning the role of alleged perpetrators, notwithstanding the availability of detailed eyewitness accounts. The latter included a HRW report that documented the role of General Malik in the 1997 killings. HRW also recounted the pursuit and killing of Hazara males in methodical house-to-house searches by the Taliban when they took control of Mazar in 1998. The failure of the United Nations to expose what happened in Mazar sent the wrong message to perpetrators and was widely seen as a lost opportunity to counter the prevailing climate of impunity. It also dampened hopes that after two decades of war and wide-scale slaughter of civilians the United Nations and the wider international community would take meaningful action to bring the bloodshed to an end.[14]

Aid actors working with front-line communities pushed for measures that would help protect civilians. They were acutely aware that relief efforts, however effective, were inadequate in terms of preempting avoidable loss of life. Aid agency efforts to reach the most vulnerable, to safeguard humanitarian space, and to operate in a manner that helped enhance the protection of at-risk groups, were greatly influenced by the ethos and parameters of the Strategic Framework (SF) and commitment to principled common programming, processes aimed at maximizing synergies between assistance, peace-making, and human rights activities in Afghanistan.[15] Although the SF has been subjected to much negative criticism and stereotyping as a subjugation of humanitarian values and responsibilities to partisan political agendas, it opened the door to greater awareness of the human rights dimension of the crisis; the SF also mobilized aid workers to push for more concerted and effective action to protect civilians. The Consultative Group on Human Rights, developed with the support of the UN Coordinator's Office, allowed NGO and UN personnel to review issues, define strategies, develop policy, and provide advice to the wider aid community on factors affecting the protection of civilians and related human rights concerns. It also nurtured networks that allowed for discreet fact finding and sharing of sensitive information with entities willing and able to advocate for measures needed to protect noncombatant civilians, including their right to asylum.

For the most part field personnel were unimpressed with the general lack of commitment by external actors to bring about meaningful change in a human rights situation that was loudly and routinely condemned as abysmal in international forums. Concern of the rhetorical type was particularly apparent in relation to the problems faced by women and girls who suffered from centuries of discriminatory practices and beliefs. The marginalization of women was compounded by, but not solely the result of, repressive Taliban edicts. Aid agencies sought to find ways and means to work with rural and urban women within the strict confines of Taliban legislation and prevailing mores. However, there was very limited external support for the kind of longer-term programming needed to build local capacity, whether in health, education, or other sectors that provided opportunities for women and men to tackle the many manifestations and sources of discrimination that marginalized one-half of the population.

Aid actors were equally unimpressed with the rather lackluster response of the Security Council to the constant stream of information it received about the killing of civilians and other human rights violations. Beyond its preoccupation with the internationally renowned Al Qaeda terrorist network presumed to be operating in Afghanistan under Osama bin Laden and the sanction measures adopted in an effort to curb it, the Security Council was largely content with ritual expressions of concern and denunciation of the Taliban.[16] Deliberations in the UN Commission on Human Rights echoed those of the Security Council. Debate on the human rights situation in Afghanistan was less than profound and appeared driven by political rather than human rights considerations.[17] Like the Security Council, the commission was essentially content with the issuance of annual resolutions devoid of operational content.

SANCTIONS: NEITHER SMART NOR PRODUCTIVE

The Security Council, at the behest of Washington, introduced sanctions at the end of 1999 to compel the Taliban to hand over Osama bin Laden in connection with deadly attacks on US embassies in Kenya and Tanzania in August 1998. At the end of 2000 the Security Council adopted additional sanctions that included a one-sided arms embargo. Aid workers were truly appalled that the United Nations could adopt a "more war" strategy at a time when Afghans were already dying in alarming numbers and were fleeing towns and villages to escape the combined effects of armed conflict and drought. For some time UN and NGO humanitarian field personnel had called for an end to the supply of arms to warring parties. They also urged the UN to involve a cross-section of Afghan civil society representatives, including women, in peace-making efforts and not rely exclusively on the usual cast of gun-toting characters.

Sanctions represented a form of collective punishment in a situation where there was little possibility that international coercion could be translated into domestic pressure for policy change in Kabul. Taliban hard-liners were seen to benefit the most from hard-knuckle policies that treated Afghanistan as a pariah state, the citizens of which had no capacity to exert influence on the foreign policy of the Islamic Emirate. But political considerations took precedence over the rights and well-being of the Afghan people. Even UN special rapporteurs came out in favor of sanctions and a halt to assistance beyond short-term relief. In a heated Security Council exchange in December 2000, Moscow and Washington dismissed the concerns of humanitarian actors and other Security Council members about the humanitarian and peace-making implications of a one-sided arms embargo. However, as noted by UN Secretary-General Kofi Annan at the time, the nature of the sanctions would not "facilitate our peace efforts nor is it going to facilitate our humanitarian work."[18]

IMPUNITY AND SLAUGHTER OF CIVILIANS

By the end of 1999 the deliberate targeting of civilians had become a routine feature of Taliban military offensives.[19] Afghans often risked their lives to document, and to keep the world informed, of the vicissitudes of life in their war-torn country. Information on atrocities was routinely brought to the attention of the Security Council and UN human rights mechanisms, but with little useful effect. Given the absence of meaningful initiatives by international level mechanisms to protect civilians, the Consultative Group on Human Rights began to lobby for action on impunity and the non-stop supply of arms to both warring parties.

By 2000, aid actors were increasingly strident that reporting on human rights violations should not be seen as an end in itself but rather a means to achieving the larger objective of halting the killing and abuse of civilians. Early in the year some eighty village elders were killed by Taliban forces in Gosfandi near Dar-e-Souf in central Afghanistan when they tried to broker a local ceasefire. In May, shortly after both warring parties had agreed to a POW exchange at an Organization of Islamic Conference meeting in Jeddah, eyewitness reports began to emerge of the killing of 190 detainees from Shibergan, Mazar, and Samangan jails. These men had earlier been rounded up after fighting in the Central Highlands. They were taken from jail in the middle of the night, executed, and left in plain view on the roadside, presumably as a warning and to terrorize the population into greater compliance with Taliban rule.

A lot of pressure was put on the United Nations to take prompt action. When Francesc Vendrell, the personal representative of the secretary-general and head of the UN Special Mission in Afghanistan (UNSMA), discussed reports of the killings with Taliban Foreign Minister Mullah Muttawakil, the latter denied the allegations and suggested that UNSMA conduct an investigation. However, even though its civil affairs team had come into being to deter mass killings, UNSMA concluded that any formal participation in an investigation would be counterproductive to its impartial role as a peace negotiator. The Taliban objected to an investigation by the special rapporteur, citing biased reporting on such issues as the trafficking of women. The Taliban were also unenthused about the involvement of the OHCHR, citing lack of effective action in response to the 1997 killing of Taliban POWs in Mazar. In the end, a formal investigation into these killings was never conducted. The United Nations was still debating and trying to determine how to deal with gross violations, including the role of UNSMA civil affairs officers in relation to the work and responsibilities of the OHCHR, when news of yet another massacre, this time in Yakawlang in the Central Highlands, began to emerge in January 2001.

The Yakawlang massacre came at a low point in aid agency interactions with the Taliban; never an easy relationship, a packed agenda of contentious issues made dialogue and efforts to safeguard humanitarian space a fraught experience. The Yakawlang killings happened within the context of a fast-accelerating crisis of war, drought, and persistent human rights violations that contributed to a rising death toll and growing population movements. These problems were exacerbated by the reality of closed borders to Afghan asylum seekers and the forced return of refugees by both the Iranian and Pakistani governments.

Reliable eyewitness accounts of the Yakawlang killings became available through trusted networks shortly after the massacre. Eyewitnesses provided detailed accounts that included photographic and videotape evidence of the methodical and targeted killing of 170 men, including ten Afghan aid workers. "The men were herded to assembly points in the center of the district and several outlying areas and then shot by firing squad in public view."[20] HRW stressed that a "prompt and thorough investigation could deter further killings of Afghan civilians," noting that the "UN so far has failed to systematically document and pursue accountability for abuses in Afghanistan."[21] The UN secretary-general, UN High Commissioner for Human Rights Mary Robinson, and special rapporteur Kamal Hossain condemned the killings and underlined the need for a prompt investigation so that those responsible could be brought to justice.

At the time it seemed that past efforts to mobilize the UN's human rights machinery were finally paying off. There was consensus on the need to move rapidly to gather available evidence and to promote a process of accountability. In March 2001 the OHCHR sent a two-person feasibility team to Pakistan together with the special rapporteur to ascertain the quality of available data. This led to a followup mission in June of that year, which included interviews with a handful of eyewitnesses who had fled the Central Highlands. Changes in Afghanistan after the events of September 11 allowed for site visits in December when ground realities, including access, had changed substantially in Afghanistan. However, just as the United Nations was finally pulling together a policy, strategy, and capacity to deal with impunity in Afghanistan, the routing of the Taliban and the return of the former mujahedin commanders at the end of 2001 brought into play a new set of questions, opportunities, and constraints that torpedoed forward movement on the development of an accountability process and related human rights issues.

HUMAN RIGHTS IN POST-TALIBAN AFGHANISTAN: ORPHANED AGAIN

The downtown skyscrapers of Manhattan and the rubble that makes up much of Kabul are worlds apart. However, on the evening of September 11, 2001, aid workers in Afghanistan were instantly alert to the potential connections between the two cities as they watched in disbelief the collapse of the World Trade Center towers. Shortly thereafter, Osama bin Laden became widely touted as the evil genius who plotted and/or funded the lethal attacks on New York and Washington. Within forty-eight hours all expatriate staff had been withdrawn from Afghanistan, given the high probability of US retaliation. A few days later the Taliban cut aid agency communication networks with the outside world, with the exception of a few monitored radio links, severely inhibiting humanitarian efforts. Aid workers were acutely aware of the extraordinary changes then unfolding but were unsure what this might mean for Afghans.

In August, on the basis of an extensive contingency-planning exercise, the UN coordinator's office had alerted the world to the catastrophic situation in Afghanistan. It underlined the need to *scale up* assistance dramatically prior to the onset of winter and a new fighting season to meet the food and other requirements of an estimated 5.5 million vulnerable Afghans affected by drought, conflict, and human rights violations. By mid-September aid agencies were confronted with a significant *reduction* in their ability to reach vulnerable groups dependent on humanitarian support for survival.

The US-led Coalition bombing that began on October 7 heralded a sea change in attitudes at the headquarters of UN humanitarian agencies to reports of problems that affected the protection of civilians. A central tenet of Washington's political stance was that it could bomb to its advantage from a secure height in the skies without significant cost to civilians. Anyone who questioned this perspective, whatever the realities on the ground, was at odds with the world's one and only superpower.[22] Suddenly, it was problematic for UN field personnel to express concern about the use of cluster bombs, the destruction of residential areas, new population flows, and the dire situation of hungry Afghans. It was deemed equally impolitic to draw attention to the inability of Afghans to seek international protection, including refugee status. Prior to September 11, neighboring countries had closed their borders to Afghan asylum seekers. After September 11, this problem was exacerbated by the sealing of Afghanistan's borders to block potential escape by Al Qaeda members. Washington declined to use its leverage to get the borders open, even though it had achieved a complete U-turn in Pakistan's foreign policy when Islamabad agreed to support Coalition objectives in Afghanistan.

The fast-paced military events of October and November 2001 deflected attention from frenzied behind-the-scenes negotiations to pull together a "broad-based Afghan government," the long-sought goal of peace-makers since the departure of the Soviets in 1989. Unfortunately for Afghans, the "war on terrorism" took precedence over other considerations, such as the ingredients needed to make peace viable in their battered land. The return of warlords, notorious for their heinous crimes in the early 1990s, with the backing of the US military and as part of a grand design for post-Taliban Afghanistan, left little room to maneuver in the lead-up to Bonn.[23] Aid personnel and human rights groups argued for the participation of a strong female delegation and representatives of civil society groups, and for the exclusion of those with blood on their hands. But it was not to be. Bonn was the outcome of American firepower and Washington-style diplomacy, which dictated who would enjoy the spoils of war. US arm-twisting shaped events in Bonn but did not extend to measures that would hold to account those responsible for war crimes and crimes against humanity.[24]

The Bonn Agreement signed in the early hours of December 5 was a milestone in Afghanistan's modern political history. Relieved to be free of the Taliban, most Afghans welcomed it as an opportunity to turn a corner on Afghanistan's violent past. Afghans remained watchful and concerned about the resurgent and refurbished mujahedin commanders but were hopeful that with a strong international presence, the warlords would be kept in check. They hoped in vain.

THE POST-BONN FORMULA

Even a cursory examination of post-Taliban Afghanistan reveals a troubling cocktail of glossed-over problems that constantly threaten the edifice of *Pax Americana*. Before the ink was dry in Bonn, Afghans from all walks of life were vocal in explaining that their top three priorities were security, security, and security, an issue intimately linked to the use and abuse of power and respect for the rights of civilians. The weakness of a power-sharing arrangement that was mostly devoid of "sharing" was obvious, as was the limited ability of the administration in Kabul to shape events beyond the confines of the capital. The Kabul-provincial disconnect, with its echoes of the past, raised doubts about the viability of the Bonn formula and Washington's commitment beyond the realization of its immediate objectives in Afghanistan.

Hamid Karzai, Washington's chosen cheerleader to head the interim administration that emerged from the Bonn talks, faced a tough task steering Afghanistan out of its turbulent past. Abroad, he is known for his eloquence and elegance. At home, he enjoys much popular support. Speaking on national radio at the beginning of 2002 he pushed all the right buttons when he outlined a long list of priorities from reopening schools to just and accountable governance. He has tried to bridge conflicting agendas as he has struggled to tame or coopt the warlords while simultaneously trying to reassure the population that he understands their fears and grievances. Opening a workshop in the capital on March 9, 2002, on the occasion of a visit by UN High Commissioner for Human Rights Mary Robinson, he said that "severe violations have taken place in Afghanistan" and proposed the creation of a fact-finding commission "so that people would feel there is a judicial entity to listen to their voices and take care of them."[25] However, he also promoted General Dostum, the ranking warlord in the north, to deputy defense minister a short while later. In addition, in a BBC "Hard Talk" interview during the Loya Jirga, he said that "justice is a luxury for now; we must not lose peace for justice."[26]

Karzai is clearly hamstrung by continued Coalition bombing and the tendency of the US military to operate as a sovereign entity in its latest protégé enterprise. Bombing mistakes took a toll in Afghan lives throughout 2002. In one incident, shortly after Karzai was inaugurated, fifty villagers were killed in Paktika province on the basis of erroneous information concerning the presence of abandoned military hardware. When villagers fled for cover after the first bombing sortie, helicopters with searchlights pursued them, resulting in the deaths of additional civilians. However, while US B-52s are a problem, Karzai's biggest headache is US financial and military support, which engineered the return of former mujahedin commanders who run the territory they control as individual fiefdoms.

JUSTICE AS LUXURY: IMPLICATIONS FOR PEACE-BUILDING

The ousting of the Taliban left a power vacuum that was quickly filled by a motley bunch of characters. Many of them are notorious for the bloodshed and mayhem that was a crucial factor in the rise to power of Mullah Omar and his brand of fundamentalist Islam in the mid 1990s. It is too early to determine if the peace-building strategy to nurture a transition from war to democratic and accountable governance will succeed, but it is already clear that sacrificing justice and respect for human rights in a vain attempt to achieve short-term stability is an unwise proposition, particularly in the Afghanistan context.

In Kabul, the UN-sanctioned ISAF offered a stabilizing presence in and around Kabul throughout 2002 but was nonetheless unable to stop attacks on civilians and government installations. Beyond the capital a combination of human rights violations and lawlessness linked to warlordism and the resurgence of the poppy industry underscored fears that Afghanistan was on the road back to the type of chaos and abuse of civilians that characterized mujahedin rule in the early 1990s. Numerous examples highlight the danger of not taking assertive action on the issue of impunity and ongoing human rights violations and support the view that absence of deterrence contributes to a climate of contempt for the rule of law and respect for civilians.

Ismail Khan, the self-declared emir in the west, brooks no opposition to his autocratic ways, including stringent limitations on females that echo Taliban rule.[27] An HRW report concluded that Ismail Khan "is operating an independent mini-state in which there is no political freedom, no freedom of speech, and a pattern of physical abuse and torture at the hands of local police and army forces."[28] From the moment Dostum and his erstwhile Northern Alliance allies took over in Mazar in November 2001 there have been well-documented reports of targeted attacks on Pashtun homes and communities, arming and abuse of IDPs, inter-factional fighting, and exploitation of tensions among groups for individual gain.

The Coalition priority in Afghanistan was the defeat of Al Qaeda, and it pursued this goal with the help of local warlords. Given Washington's agenda, UNAMA, which was established in early 2002 to support the implementation of the Bonn Agreement, was reluctant to subject human rights violations to public scrutiny or aggressively to pursue measures aimed at deterring further violations. For instance, though an independent Afghanistan Human Rights Commission (AHRC) was established just before the emergency Loya Jirga in June 2002 and following the provisions of the Bonn Agreement, it was clear from the outset that the AHRC was handed a "poisoned chalice." It was given the task of dealing with a very problematic human rights situation—without any of the requisite resources or political support—that the United Nations, the Afghan administrations, and the Coalition had all declined to address. As in any other country, it is the national government that is responsible for ensuring that the rights of civilians are respected. Deflecting this responsibility to the AHRC raises questions about the commitment of the successive Afghan interim and transitional administrations and that of their backers to remedying the human rights situation in Afghanistan.

Karzai, to his credit, did attempt to stop attacks on civilians. He sent a three-person delegation, led by Minister Noorzai, to Mazar in March 2002. However, Karzai soon found that he had little room to maneuver when it came to confronting abusive commanders, and the delegation's report was never released. Top-level government officials, familiar with events in the north, did ask senior UNAMA personnel to speak out on human rights violations and to send a warning to perpetrators that the age of warlordism and impunity had to end, a message that was deemed particularly important in the lead up to the Loya Jirga.[29] But UNAMA was allergic to assertive or overt action on human rights and tended to lob the ball back into the Afghan court. Indeed, maintaining the line that Afghans were in charge, when it was all too apparent that Washington was calling the shots, was little more than a convenient fiction to camouflage inaction and lack of commitment to address human rights issues.

Giving a green light to warlords is a questionable practice at any time but was truly alarming in the evolving Afghan context of 2002. Some allowance was made for Karzai, given his wedged-in position, but it was difficult to understand why Lakhdar Brahimi, the SRSG and head of UNAMA, needed to proclaim publicly that justice was not a priority. "Politics," he said, "is the art of the possible" and "choices have to be made." He added that "our responsibility to the living has to take precedence" over accountability for the dead.[30]

His comments were made during a press conference in which journalists questioned what the United Nations was planning to do about mass graves associated with the move of POWs from Kunduz to

Shibergan after the last pitched battle with the Taliban in the north in November 2001. From the outset, the graves at Dasht-i-Laili were an embarrassing find. There were allegations that up to three thousand Taliban fighters who had surrendered were suffocated as they were transported in airless containers or killed as the containers were sprayed with gunfire. Dasht-i-Laili and other grave sites are in Dostum-controlled territory, and according to various press reports, the killings allegedly happened under the eyes, or with the knowledge of US Special Forces. A graphic account by *Newsweek* (August 26, 2002) questioned whether the United Nations had any serious intention of investigating what happened at Shibergan. Though the SRSG made it clear that the fledgling Afghan administration "did not have the capacity to carry out an investigation," a well-known fact that no one disputed, it subsequently became equally clear that there would be little followup by the United Nations.[31] By the end of 2002 no substantial efforts had been made to protect the sites or to develop a witness protection program, though the OHCHR was developing plans to study the graves in the spring of 2003.[32] However, as one Kabul-based journalist, referring to UN sources noted, given "the delicate political climate, the United Nations will not press the Afghan government to launch a truth commission or war crimes tribunal even if a wealth of evidence indicating atrocities is found."[33] In sum, concrete and concerted action on the issue of impunity is unlikely unless Washington and its Coalition partners rethink their approach to peace and justice in Afghanistan.

CONCLUSION

Repressive rule and the deliberate abuse of civilians are not the only human rights issues of concern in Afghanistan. After so many years of war, and with some of the worst socio-economic indicators in the world, Afghans are truly anxious for a peace that allows them to live with a modicum of dignity and human security. They want their children to go to school—and the dramatic upsurge in school attendance in 2002 is testimony to this—and they want access to health care and other fundamentals such as food, shelter, and a decent means of livelihood that are the rights of all human beings.

Afghan citizens are the strongest believers in the need for a peaceful future, but their confidence in the Bonn formula diminished throughout 2002. Afghans resented the reimposition of warlord rule and had difficulty understanding why the United Nations and the United States did not take a more active and assertive role on human rights issues. As noted by one villager in Nangahar when interviewed in January 2002, "If the United States can defeat the Taliban why can't they disarm the warlords? If the United States believes in democracy, why support these warlords in Kabul?"[34] Karzai himself noted in July 2002 that in meetings with fellow Afghans, they "first asked for security and peace and to get rid of guns and then they asked for an improvement in education."[35]

At a minimum it was assumed that the United Nations would use its leverage to convince Washington to rein in the men with guns; it was all too clear in Mazar, for example, that the United States and its Special Forces had a special relationship with the local authorities.[36] The fact that the United Nations was reluctant to address human rights problems and was willing to give a veneer of respectability to US action further undermined confidence in the Bonn process. Politics may well indeed be the art of the possible, but it is also "the area where conscience and power meet."[37] As noted in one study, ruthless individuals with blood on their hands have been accorded "a legitimacy that many Afghans find offensive."[38] In a meeting in Kabul in April 2002 with a senior government official who is now a minister in the transitional administration, this author was told that the United Nations no longer had any moral authority in Afghanistan, and it was best if Afghans did not expect action from the United Nations on human rights matters.

Confidence is critical to the success of any peace process and is closely linked to an improved security environment and the ability of the average citizen to participate in, and benefit from, the peace dividend that, in principle, should include greater economic as well as greater physical security. With practically all the regional power holders controlling and exploiting licit and illicit trade in their particular sphere of influence, there is very limited opportunity for transparent and accountable governance at the local level or for any genuine rural development.

The politicization and marginalization of human rights, coupled with the ineffectiveness of UN human rights machinery throughout the conflict in Afghanistan, meant that Afghans were at a disadvantage and unable to exploit opportunities for peace with justice upon the demise of the Taliban regime. The unwillingness and inability of the United Nations to draw a line in the sand to demarcate an end to past practices and attitudes in relation to human rights—both on the part of perpetrators and UN mechanisms responsible for the promotion and protection of human rights—was a powerful and troubling signal that hobbled the peace process from the outset.

Human rights field personnel at the end of 2001 argued for a strong human rights capacity as an integral part of UNAMA and for a separate human rights investigative and analysis unit that would report directly to the UN high commissioner for human rights. This would have allowed the SRSG to be free to dialogue and negotiate with abusive commanders without the stigma of being directly responsible for human rights reports. Instead, UNAMA insisted on an extremely limited human rights capacity and has been reluctant to address critical human rights problems. UNAMA's argument that it wishes to take a different and more constructive approach to human rights in Afghanistan than in other settings does not hold water. During the Taliban, for example, the focus of the UN coordinator's office was on strengthening indigenous human rights capabilities.[39] Simultaneously, it pursued measures geared to protecting civilians and realization of their fundamental rights. In other words, principled and constructive approaches are not mutually exclusive.

No one expected miracles, or the emergence of transparent judicial processes and capacities to implement them, overnight. But ignoring the rights and aspirations of Afghans is not a formula for peace or the political basis needed to build just and democratic governance. Neither is it a formula that has a good record in the history books of Afghanistan. History also shows that backing one group of Afghans against another has proved disastrous for peace and for human rights. At a minimum, Afghans expected the peace-builders to distinguish between power that is legitimate and based on the will of the people, and power that comes from the barrel of a gun, terror tactics, and the ruthless exploitation of minority groups.

There is a strong and symbiotic relationship between building peace and addressing the demands of a people who want justice. UNAMA should have ensured the availability of prompt and meaningful support for above-board judicial processes. It should have pursued a strong UN communications strategy so that Afghans were adequately informed and their viewpoints well understood as part of an overall approach to marginalize those with a history of contempt for the rights of their fellow Afghans. This opportunity was squandered before and during the emergency Loya Jirga, even though the Bonn Agreement required the exclusion of war criminals.

From an early point in 2002 the Consultative Group on Human Rights advocated that UNAMA support the organization of a survey and a national dialogue on the issue of transitional justice. It was apparent that a large proportion of Afghans did not want the warlords back; a reliable survey that captured this perspective would have given leverage to those interested in marginalizing war criminals and holding them to account. Opportunities were also lost at the beginning of 2002 to initiate the collection of evidence in a discrete but structured manner before abusive authorities became entrenched. When the United Nations was challenged to take a more active role in relation to evidence pertaining to mass graves in the north, it claimed that the absence of a witness protection program precluded action. It is worth recalling, however, that it proved possible to ensure the protection of witnesses during the time of the repressive Taliban regime. Clearly, the absence of political commitment within United Nations and Coalition circles has been a critical factor in sustaining the prevailing climate of impunity in Afghanistan.

Securing a just and viable peace after two decades of war also necessitated a recovery process and development strategy geared to undoing
structural injustices and systemic inequalities that have marginalized
women and minority groups and ensnared millions in a vicious cycle of
poverty and deprivation that works against the realization of human
rights. The first Karzai administration highlighted the importance of
prioritizing support to communities harmed by human rights violations and discrimination in the past. To date, no special efforts have
been made to analyze or define the harm inflicted on particular groups
or to identify interventions that would provide a measure of rectificatory
justice, namely, a process of reckoning that will allow individuals and
society to deal with past wrongs. Instead, the rhetoric has focused on
the technical aspects of peace-building, as if past abuses and the reality
of warlords, lawlessness, and repressive authorities are immaterial to
the stated goal of democratic and accountable governance.

Transforming the human rights situation in Afghanistan was des-
tined to be a laborious and uncertain process, given the country's history and political culture. Afghans must be on the front lines of securing respect for human rights. But it is the responsibility of the
international community—the United Nations, aid agencies, human
rights groups, and donors—to help indigenous efforts give effect to
international standards and obligations. Given Washington's Cold War
and post–September 11 role in strengthening the hand of well-known
systematic violators of human rights in Afghanistan, the United States
has particular responsibilities, even as it has limited credibility when it
comes to issues of peace and justice.

Afghanistan's post-Bonn experience illustrates the immorality and
short-sightedness of expedient politics. Vociferous concern about the
rights of Afghan women when the Bush administration was mobilizing
support for its bombing campaign was paralleled by military, financial, and political support for lawless factions that have again killed
and raped women and girls with impunity in Afghanistan. Such cyni-
cism exposes the contradictions in Washington's stated policy of making the world safe for Americans and liberating the rest of humankind
from terror, tyrants, and foes of human rights. When US issues of strategic concern, narrowly defined, trump global human rights values,
the world is a more dangerous place for Americans and for all peoples
at the receiving end of unjust and brutal regimes.

NOTES

[1] Hafizullah Emadi, *Politics of Development and Women in Afghanistan*
(New York: Paragon Press, 1993).

[2] Government of Republic of Afghanistan, *First Seven-Year Economic and
Social Development Plan, 1976–1983* (Kabul, 1976).

³ Between 1979 and 1992, an estimated six million—more than one-fifth of the population—fled their places of origin. Fighting for the control of Kabul (1992–94) led to further refugee and internally displaced person (IDP) flows, as did the Taliban era. A significant number of Afghans have suffered involuntary displacement on more than one occasion.

⁴ ICRC, *People on War: Country Report on Afghanistan, ICRC Worldwide Consultation on the Rules of War* (Geneva: ICRC, 1999).

⁵ The special rapporteur was appointed by the chairman of the UN Commission on Human Rights, having been requested to do so by the UN Economic and Social Council. The mandate of the special rapporteur has been renewed annually by the commission and endorsed by the council. Special rapporteurs are independent experts and not UN staff members.

⁶ Helga Baitenmann, "NGOs and the Afghan War: The Politicization of Humanitarian Aid," *Third World Quarterly* 12/1 (1990), 78.

⁷ Antonio Donini, *The Policies of Mercy: UN Coordination in Afghanistan, Mozambique, and Rwanda* (Providence, R.I.: Watson Institute, Brown University, 1996), 56.

⁸ Ibid.

⁹ Defectors included Uzbek General Abdul Rashid Dostum, who was Najibullah's general in Mazar before he joined forces with the mujahedin in the north.

¹⁰ UN doc. A/49/650 (November 1994).

¹¹ Amnesty International, *Women in Afghanistan: A Human Rights Catastrophe* (London, May 1995).

¹² Russia, Iran, and India provided military and other support to the Northern Alliance. The United States and the UK spearheaded efforts to demonize and isolate the Taliban.

¹³ HRW, *The Massacre in Mazar-i-Sharif* (New York, November 1998).

¹⁴ The deployment of a team of eight civil affairs officers at the end of 1999 in UNSMA, the political arm of the United Nations, as a result of a December 1998 Security Council resolution to deter mass killings, also failed to meet expectations due to their inability and unwillingness to operate as human rights investigators. The political mission was concerned that overt involvement in highlighting human rights violations could jeopardize peace-making efforts.

¹⁵ For further elaboration on the SF, see Chapter 7 in this volume.

¹⁶ It was not lost on Afghans that Osama bin Laden had enjoyed sanctuary in Afghanistan prior to the arrival of the Taliban or that he had benefited from the backing of Washington for the mujahedin in an earlier phase of the war.

¹⁷ The Consultative Group on Human Rights advocated that special rapporteurs' reports reflect rigorous fact finding and analysis of patterns and circumstances pertaining to particular human rights issues, such as discrimination, as well as individual incidents of abuse. The group argued that the human rights problems emanating from *all* parties to the conflict be addressed in special rapporteurs' reports. Anything less was considered counterproductive and unhelpful in terms of efforts to foster a dialogue on human rights with both sets of authorities.

¹⁸ Xinhua (news agency), "UN Chief Criticizes Proposed Sanctions Against Taliban" (New York, December 19, 2000).

[19] In 1999 this included offensives in Bamyan in February and March, in Shomali in July and August, in Kunduz and Takhar in September and October, and intermittent fighting for the control of Dar-e-Souf throughout the latter part of the year.

[20] HRW, "Massacres of Hazaras in Afghanistan" (New York, February 19, 2001).

[21] The HRW report also covered the killings in Samangan at the Robotak Pass and other locations in May 2000 and noted that the failure of the Taliban to hold perpetrators accountable for previous attacks on civilians "made it critical that the UN itself investigate" both Samangan and Yakawlang. It indicated that the UN "should not repeat the mistakes that resulted in an inconclusive 1999 field investigation . . . into the 1997 killings of Taliban prisoners by United Front forces in Mazar-i-Sharif and the reprisal massacre of Hazara civilians by Taliban forces the following year" (see ibid.).

[22] For the first time in the history of annual national immunization days, the United Nations Children's Fund (UNICEF) did not call for a ceasefire in November 2001 as it had done in previous years.

[23] The supply of arms and cash to different warlords continued well after the Taliban were routed, so that Afghanistan is once again awash with weapons.

[24] Afghans were quick to point out that the Northern Alliance "walked in on American legs" when it took control of Kabul. At Bonn, in "a bow to political realities, it [the Northern Alliance] agreed that the top spot in the interim administration should go to a Pashtun. With the Americans pushing for Hamid Karzai, the alliance accepted his selection as chairman" (Michael Massing, "Losing the Peace," *The Nation* [New York], May 13, 2002).

[25] AFP (news agency), "No Amnesty for rights violators in Afghanistan: Mary Robinson" (March 9, 2002).

[26] Lyse Doucet, "Hard Talk," BBC World interview, Kabul, June 14, 2002.

[27] A HRW report concludes that under the rule of Ismail Khan "women's and girls' freedom of expression, association, movement, and rights to equality, work, education and bodily integrity steadily deteriorated throughout 2002" (HRW, *"We Want to Live as Humans": Repression of Women and Girls in Afghanistan* [New York: HRW, December 2002]).

[28] HRW, *All Our Hopes Are Crushed: Violence and Repression in Western Afghanistan* (New York: HRW, November 2002).

[29] This perspective was shared by a wide cross-section of Afghans, including those participating in a human rights workshop that recommended a no-tolerance policy for human rights violations, no impunity for past violations, and that external backers of Afghan perpetrators be held to account. The workshop, held in Kabul in March 2002, also underlined the importance of the international community honoring its human rights responsibilities in Afghanistan.

[30] Lakhdar Brahimi, UN press conference transcript, Kabul, August 27, 2002.

[31] Ibid.

[32] Factional leaders in the north continued to operate with impunity throughout 2002. Some eyewitnesses disappeared, and UN Afghan staff who had been in touch with them were threatened and harassed.

[33] Chris Kraul, "Deaths of Taliban in Metal Containers Had Been Reported," *San Francisco Chronicle*, December 29, 2002.

[34] Center for Economic and Social Rights, *Human Rights and Reconstruction in Afghanistan* (New York: CESR, May 2002).

[35] Chris Johnson et al., *Afghanistan Political and Constitutional Development* (London: ODI, January 2003), 13.

[36] The presence of US Special Forces, with bulging muscles, weapons, and antennas, keeping a watchful eye on comings and goings, was clearly visible when this writer met with General Dostum in his compound outside Mazar in March 2002.

[37] Reinhold Niebuhr, *Moral Man and Immoral Society* (New York: Scribner and Sons, 1932/1960), 4.

[38] Johnson et al., *Afghanistan Political and Constitutional Development,* 13.

[39] Seven of the eleven original Afghan human rights commissioners hailed from the Consultative Group on Human Rights.

5

The Struggle
for Hearts and Minds
The Military, Aid, and the Media

KATE CLARK

During the Taliban era a small number of Kabul-based correspondents mainly set the news agenda for Afghanistan. After the September 11 attacks, mightier players came onto the field: the United States military and political public-relations machine, news editors back home, and, to a lesser extent, the United Nations and the aid industry. The urgency to have positive news for the American people after September 11 was also a pressure on the Bush administration, pushing it to launch a military campaign against the Taliban and Al Qaeda as swiftly as possible and without much consideration for the long-term political consequences for Afghanistan.

Since Vietnam, when some in the United States armed forces hierarchy blamed journalists for losing the war, it has been understood that getting positive reporting of a conflict is a military necessity. That becomes even more crucial when wars are not fought for national survival. The United States claimed that it launched its war on Afghanistan not just as a battle against those who had masterminded or supported the September 11 attacks but also as a humanitarian mission to liberate Afghans, particularly Afghan women, from Taliban oppression. Washington wanted to persuade other nations, particularly in the Islamic world, that this was a legitimate war and to persuade

Afghans to defect from the Taliban. It was a struggle for hearts and minds as much as a military campaign.

For the aid industry, the vast influx of journalists into the region was also an opportunity to win hearts and minds—to raise agency profiles, to impress donors into giving funds, and to get humanitarian issues onto the air. For media organizations, the war was a chance to increase audiences and readerships. The competition was fierce for scoops and exclusive access. In the era of twenty-four-hour live and continuous news coverage, it was also at times a battle to get enough decent material to broadcast. Almost lost amid all this were the voices of Afghans, particularly Afghan civilians. The whole world was talking about Afghanistan, but there was little evidence that it was listening to Afghans and their views on unfolding events.

During the Taliban era a very small band of correspondents reported from Afghanistan. The three main news agencies—Associated Press, Reuters, and Agence France Presse—all had Afghan reporters who courageously maintained independent coverage throughout the often brutal civil war and during the American campaign. The BBC—generally seen as the most trustworthy source of news by Afghans—had the only foreign correspondent stationed in Kabul. Following the 1994 murder of an Afghan stringer, Mirwais Jalil, by one of the mujahedin factions, the BBC deemed Afghanistan to be too dangerous for local reporters. Voice of America opened a part-time office briefly before shutting it down on the orders of the State Department. In 2000 Al Jazeera came to open a bureau, gaining exclusive access to Taliban front lines and Al Qaeda, but mixing very little with the rest of the press corps.

Civil wars are never easy for journalists to operate in, particularly when free speech is stifled by a heavy police and intelligence presence. There were attempts by both the Taliban and the Northern Alliance to shape the news agenda. The Northern Alliance—made up mainly of old mujahedin factions—was headed up in public-relations terms by its English-speaking spokesman, Dr. Abdullah, who is now Afghanistan's foreign minister. His faction, Shura-i-Nazar, led by Ahmad Shah Massoud until his assassination on September 9, 2001, has proved to be very canny at spinning. However, the Northern Alliance held little territory and could not get much leverage over the media.

The Taliban were in a far better position to intimidate journalists. They arrested BBC translator Abdul-Saboor Salehzai in December 2000 after he refused to be an informer for them, and they also expelled the author of this chapter after accusations of bias in March 2001. Reporting on matters that the Taliban wanted to hide was always tricky—the presence of Al Qaeda and other foreign militants, violent crime in Kabul, and abuses of civilians. Filming generally had to be clandestine, and it was always difficult to get Afghan women's voices on air without reprisal. Permission was needed to travel outside Kabul, and visiting Afghans in their homes was illegal and risky if they were not to be accused of spying.

Visiting journalists faced far more constraints: They had to stay in the Intercontinental Hotel and use foreign ministry–vetted translators/minders and official taxis. Translators who did not monitor the visiting journalists firmly enough would be dismissed and even put in jail.

Despite these constraints, in terms of spin, the Taliban were naive. They generally told the truth because they had no idea—or apparent care—how the world might view them. In terms of BBC coverage, their complaints repeatedly focused on two issues that appeared minor but reflected how they felt about their legitimacy—that the BBC should call them the Islamic Emirate rather than the Taliban, and that the Persian and Pashtu language services should use the Islamic lunar calendar made official by the Taliban instead of, or in addition to, the Persian calendar used by Afghans and the Western calendar used by most of the world. Voice of America had agreed to do this; the BBC feared it would signal that it recognized the legitimacy of the Taliban government and refused.

Despite the difficulty of reporting under the Taliban, it was in-country correspondents who shaped the news agenda in Afghanistan. We were forced to work in a way that was already old-fashioned. In other countries correspondents spend large amounts of time in their bureaus, on the telephone, receiving faxes and e-mails, and looking through the newspapers and scanning the television for news. Afghanistan was a country without television or nationwide newspapers, and few, other than military commanders and aid agencies, had telephones. There were virtually no diplomats and no in-country spokespeople for the United Nations or other aid agencies. That meant journalists had to get out of the office to report on a story and speak to people face to face, over cups of tea.

Afghanistan was then a relatively minor story—and there was little pressure from news editors back home. Any pressure that did exist was in a series of assumptions that cast the Taliban as medieval, woman-oppressing monsters and Afghans generally as passive victims of religious intolerance, war, and drought. Getting a more nuanced understanding of Afghan politics on air was difficult. The latest Taliban edict was always the surest way of grabbing international headlines. "How weird" was the attitude; "What a joke the Taliban are." In February 2001, I risked my bureau, and others, particularly UN official Michael Semple, risked their lives getting the first film/radio testimony of the Taliban massacre of civilians (when they killed 170 men and teenage boys in the town of Yakawlang in the Central Highlands of Hazarajat) out to the world. It was headline news on BBC World Service and BBC

World, but I noted wryly at the time to my domestic news editor in London that he was more interested in a Taliban ban on "foreign" haircuts than a massacre.

On September 11 the nature of reporting—like many things—changed. The Afghan war and the struggle to win hearts and minds had suddenly become an issue of global concern.

In those first days I reported how unimaginable the Twin Towers attack was for most Afghans; they had no access to television, and their experience of multistory buildings might just extend to eight or nine floors if they had ever visited Kabul. This was a time when some Americans blamed Afghans for the attack, and it seemed possible that the United States might take "revenge" on Afghanistan; it felt important to mention repeatedly that Afghans had not voted for the Taliban and that it was virtually impossible to find an Afghan who liked Osama bin Laden. Many commentators in London and Washington predicted a mass jihad on behalf of Osama bin Laden and the Taliban leader, Mullah Omar, on the grounds that Afghans had always fiercely resisted foreign invaders. For anyone who knew anything about prevailing Afghan politics, this was simply impossible to imagine. Indeed, one of the indicators of just how low Afghans have been brought by the miseries of war is that they welcomed foreign troops—particularly peace-keepers—above their own soldiers.

The historical context was also important; Islamic extremism had not appeared overnight in Afghanistan. During the 1980s, in the context of the Cold War, the United States helped fund and arm Islamist groups, giving the bulk of its aid to the most extreme factions in Afghanistan, because they were fighting the Soviet Union. Washington also funded foreign militants. It has denied ever funding Osama bin Laden, but they were clearly fighting on the same side at that time. In 1989 the Soviet army withdrew and then in 1992, under US and UN pressure, the quasi-communist government of Dr. Najibullah stood down, to be replaced by an administration of America's allies, the factions of the mujahedin. When internecine fighting broke out among these factions, Afghans were left struggling to survive, feeling completely abandoned by the world. In places like Kabul, Afghans welcomed the Taliban only as a last, desperate chance to get some sort of order out of the chaos and terror of the mujahedin era.

In the immediate aftermath of September 11 the media also affected military and political planning. The need for President Bush to have something to tell the press—and the American people—was a significant factor in starting the war in Afghanistan as quickly as was militarily possible after September 11. Domestic political expediency overruled the need to put long-term political plans in place for Afghanistan. Bombs began to drop before much thought was given to a post-Taliban government or a peace-keeping force for the capital. This media-influenced political urgency encouraged the United States to work with the Northern Alliance despite its lack of credibility with most Afghans. No mechanisms were in place—not even in Kabul—to make sure that each of the Northern Alliance's factions was not simply allowed to keep whatever territories it overran in the wake of US bombing.

Within days of September 11 the media environment itself began to change. Correspondents, camera operators, producers, and technicians from all over the world started arriving en masse in the region. The Taliban expelled all foreigners from Kabul "for their own safety" soon after the September 11 attacks, and it was left to the news agency correspondents—all of them Afghans—to maintain independent, eyewitness reporting from Taliban-controlled areas. Media organizations generally set up bases in the Pakistani capital, Islamabad, or in territory controlled by the Northern Alliance, or both. Among the correspondents arriving were veteran reporters who knew Afghanistan well, but most reporters had never been to the area before and were highly dependent on whoever briefed them. In Pakistan, that included aid workers and diplomats. In Afghanistan, translators—many of whom were linked to the Shura-i-Nazar faction of the Northern Alliance—mediated the experiences of Afghans. The inexperience of some reporters, in addition to the pressure to get a story out, contributed to eight journalists being killed during this phase of the war.

The Marriott Hotel in Islamabad swiftly became the focus for the media, which booked whole suites and set up satellite links on the roof where correspondents could report live. The advent of twenty-four-hour news programming has meant that someone—known as a "dish monkey"—has to be on standby at all times. The satellite is like a gaping maw that demands constant feeding, preferably on scoops, exclusives, and fresh interviewees. Trying to find out what is happening and filing continuously is an impossible task. The elevators and lobbies of the Marriott Hotel were filled with politicians, analysts, and aid workers—mainly foreigners or Pakistanis.

It was difficult to find Afghans who spoke English well enough to be interviewed live or who had not been frightened into silence by Taliban spies, Northern Alliance spies, or Pakistani intelligence. The future president, Hamid Karzai, was one of the few brave enough to speak. Afghans complained bitterly that many Pakistanis (often pro-Taliban and predicting a jihad) were presented as neutral commentators speaking about Afghanistan. Most Afghans blame Pakistan as the author of many of their ills—through Islamabad's support first for the mujahedin leader Gulbuddin Hekmatyar and then for the Taliban. However, for news editors back home Pakistanis gave as good a regional flavor as Afghans and were far easier to get on air.

The one Afghan group that did manage the media spectacularly was RAWA (Revolutionary Association of the Women of Afghanistan).

Through websites, focused lobbying, and the release of clandestinely made films from Taliban-controlled Afghanistan, they succeeded in becoming the spokespeople for Afghan women. RAWA is a group of brave and eloquent women, but in terms of Afghan opinion, they are completely marginal. Nevertheless, their feminist-type views were what many in the West wanted to hear; they got the ear of the media and senior opinion formers in Washington, Los Angeles, and London.

In September 2001 US bombing had not yet started, but blanket news coverage had. That gave NGO and UN aid agencies a fine opportunity to get on air. Several agencies sent dedicated spokespeople to Islamabad or encouraged their field staff to be interviewed. Humanitarian stories such as the Afghan drought—which had languished on the back pages for several years—could now get onto the air. UNHCR managed to get extensive coverage of its predictions that war would unleash a flood of Afghan refugees on Pakistan. Despite most Afghan watchers saying they thought it would be a trickle (which turned out to be the case), UNHCR wanted funding and the media needed a story in those pre-bombing days. Other non-stories, such as the relatively small Pakistani protests against the war, also made it to air. Filmed in a particular way, they could be made to look much more exciting than they actually were.

Islamabad also became the main focus of the Taliban's propaganda effort, with their ambassador, Abdul-Salaam Zaif, trying to justify his government's refusal to hand over the United States' chief suspect in the Twin Tower attacks, Osama bin Laden. Zaif called an emergency press conference on the night of September 11. "We feel America's pain," he said. "We hope the terrorists will be caught and brought to justice." Eventually, the Taliban's public-relations attempts focused on civilian casualties and efforts to persuade Muslims that this was a war on Islam, an enterprise in which they had some success.

However, there were significant currents of Afghan opinion that were not making the headlines at that time. There was a great deal of popular concern about Washington choosing the Northern Alliance as an ally. These were factions that had wrecked Kabul in internecine fighting in the early 1990s. Afghans fleeing Kabul after September 11 said they mainly feared not the US bombs but the return of the Northern Alliance. There was instead overwhelming support for the United Nations and the former king, Zahir Shah, to take leading roles. When the king made a very brief statement on the BBC Persian and Pashtu services in late September, saying efforts were under way with international support to resolve the crisis, the national currency, the Afghani, gained hugely in value.   Eventually journalists also started to get into northern Afghanistan, either trekking from Pakistan through the mountains of the Hindu Kush or flying into Tajikistan and taking the ferry across the Amu Darya, which constitutes the border. Journalists were initially funneled to Kwaja Baha-Uddin, just across the Tajik border, a small, dusty town that had become Massoud's main garrison. Again, satellite links were set up and correspondents had to deliver twenty-four-hour news. The nightmare for them was that they were several days' drive away from the main fighting. That did not stop some from describing their location merely as "north of Kabul" in an attempt to give their reports a semblance of immediacy and authority. Reporters quickly used up any possible stories from the immediate area and were then left dependent for information on Dr. Abdullah's press conferences and on news agencies (some of whose reporters, newly drafted into the region, were also on a very steep learning curve). According to one of the BBC's diplomatic editors, Bridget Kendall, coverage of the Afghan campaign on various networks descended into farce at times: "Often people were being employed to do live reports just so they could say 'that person was in Afghanistan,' when in fact quite a lot of the reports were coming in either on a laptop or from people reading Reuters copy down the phone."[1]

The Northern Alliance initially got very favorable coverage as the anti-Taliban resistance battling for human rights, including women's rights. However, being forced to pay for everything—journalist and travel permits and extortionate dollar-rates for bedding down on mattresses in multi-occupancy rooms—made many reporters question the integrity of their hosts. Eventually even the most naive reporter could not help but uncover the Northern Alliance's past record—resistance against the Taliban certainly, but also factional fighting, rapes, and massacres.

For the main player in the conflict, the United States, this was a difficult propaganda war, despite a great deal of patriotic self-censorship from much of the US media. (One network, for example, told its correspondents not to discuss Afghan civilian casualties without mentioning the victims of the September 11 attacks.) In other conflicts—the Falklands, the 1991 Gulf War, and the 2003 Iraq war—the military has been able to embed reporters with troops. Thus it largely controls what the reporters see and can impose news blackouts by interfering with satellite communications. A pool system often operates where the military gives selected correspondents privileged access on behalf of the entire press corps. This can act as a reward system for positive copy and trigger infighting among the journalists. Afghanistan was different. The United States had only media-shy Special Forces on the ground. The bulk of the US war effort on the ground was allotted to Washington's proxies, namely, the factions of the Northern Alliance, whom it had paid and armed. US attempts to set the news agenda, therefore, had to come from its home soil. The performances were often masterly. Secretary of Defense Donald Rumsfeld became an internationally recognized figure as he joked and dramatized his way through daily Pentagon briefings. For journalists on the ground in Afghanistan or Pakistan, it was often Rumsfeld's briefings (happening overnight in the South Asian time zone) that provoked questions on live broadcasts the next morning. Often we were asked to speak about newly announced types of weaponry or ammunition that had been deployed, but humanitarian and human rights issues were also part of the US public-relations effort.

George Bush encouraged US schoolchildren to donate money to help the Afghan people. Laura Bush spoke on television about the plight of Afghan women. Afghans were repeatedly promised that there would be large-scale reconstruction in any post-Taliban Afghanistan. Bush also decided that food rations should be dropped in addition to the bombs so that Afghans would know the intervention was not aimed at them. "I was sensitive to this [accusation] that this was a religious war, and that somehow the United States would be the conqueror," said the president, according to Bob Woodward's book *Bush at War*; "I wanted us to be viewed as the liberator."[2] Woodward reports that "the idea of feeding the poor Afghan people appealed" to Bush. Bush also wondered if food aid might persuade "starving" Pashtun tribes in the south to revolt (but later discovered that they were not that hungry). The food drops were purely a propaganda exercise; the rations could not feed anyone beyond a day and were not targeted to those who were hungry, a fact that aid agencies fiercely pointed out. The exercise also backfired when US PSYOPs (psychological operations) had to broadcast a radio warning to Afghans cautioning them against confusing food rations in their yellow bags with yellow-colored cluster bombs.

The demand for news—particularly since the advent of twenty-four-hour programming—puts pressure on the military as well as journalists. If reporters and editors have nothing new to report, they tend to start questioning the wisdom of the whole operation—or even cast around themselves for fresh material—which can be very dangerous from the military's point of view. In the 1991 Gulf War, Major General Patrick Cordingley, commander of the Seventh Armoured Brigade—the Desert Rats—described the impact of having two hundred and fifty journalists embedded on his patch. "Each one of them or their editors wanted a story from us every day. It became very intrusive and actually forced us to deploy into the desert before we were ready, just to give the media something worthwhile to report."[3] Cordingley almost lost his job in 1990 for being too honest with the media when he said the war would involve causalities.

In the Afghan campaign, the week or so before the fall of Mazar-e Sharif was a difficult time for US military spinners. Commentators began wondering whether the bombing campaign was actually having any effect. Part of the problem was the lack of targets for the US Airforce to hit in such a resource-poor, underdeveloped, war-ravaged country.

Front lines were stationary, and there had been few defections from the Taliban. Just before cities started falling like dominoes, it seemed that the war might be a long one.

Despite all these problems for the US public-relations machine, the American bombing of Afghan cities was a largely invisible war. We still do not know how many Afghan civilians were killed, although some attempts (for example, by the Agency for Rehabilitation and Energy Conservation in Afghanistan, an Afghan aid agency) have been made to collate information. The United States—and to a lesser extent the Northern Alliance—briefings were the main source of information on the fighting. Taliban claims were reported, but with strong caveats. It was extremely difficult to get independent confirmation of losses, strikes, civilian casualties, and indeed any information or views from Afghan civilians. Any Afghan caught using a satellite phone in Taliban-controlled areas could be hanged as a spy. UN and aid agency radio rooms were closed down, although many brave staff continued to get information out from public call centers or by traveling to Pakistan.

Until the very last few days of Taliban-controlled Afghanistan, when the Islamic Emirate allowed a few, mainly Muslim, journalists into Kabul, the world was reliant on reports from the three Afghan news agency correspondents, plus Al Jazeera. Sayed Mohammed Azam, the correspondent for AFP, Amir Shah of AP, and Sayed Sallahuddin of Reuters, who was given the 2001 Reuters Cameraman of the Year award, worked under extremely dangerous circumstances. Azam was arrested by Arab militants, held for nine days, and threatened with the death penalty when he unwittingly framed Arabs in a photograph of Kabulis struggling to survive economic hardship in the secondhand clothes bazaar.

Journalists who had contacts in Taliban areas could attempt to relay eyewitness accounts by people whose cities were being bombed. The BBC Persian and Pashtu services managed to interview Afghans, and these voices were some of the few to be broadcast to the world through the wider BBC network. Getting such voices was a difficult task. I spent three days setting up an interview with an English speaker in Dara Souf in the Central Highlands of Hazarajat. I wanted to record someone speaking about the famine deaths there, but the only possible interviewee was a teacher who had to travel in from another village. My main method of getting information from the northern city of Mazar-e Sharif was to telephone a call center there. The Taliban commander in charge of Mazar, Mullah Dadullah, could be contacted by operator, but it was also interesting to speak to whoever picked up the phone. This was how we got confirmation of the fall of Mazar and the first eyewitness accounts of life under the new regime.

It was important to get Afghan eyewitness accounts and some reactions out to the world. The people's opinions were mixed. Many described to me how frightened their children had been during the bombing raids on Kabul. However, for those who had experienced the random rocketing of the mujahedin in the battle for Kabul in the 1990s, the targeted bombing of the Americans actually came as something of a relief. There was often a certain pragmatism about suffering; one man told me, "We can take sacrifices, if it means the end of the civil war and getting rid of the foreign militants."

In the end it seemed that most of the media reported what they wanted or expected to happen. When Mazar fell on November 11, there were reports by journalists who had never set foot in the city that women were discarding their face-covering veils—the *burqa*. The reports were not true, but for journalists and editors who assumed that unveiling was the main preoccupation of Afghan women living under the Taliban, it must have seemed obvious that they would throw away their *burqa* at the first chance. For anyone who knew Afghanistan at all, it was impossible to imagine women rushing to uncover their faces when three different armed factions had taken their city—all with well-established records of abusing civilians and raping women—records which the factions continued to maintain in the aftermath of the fighting.

Similar reports of women discarding the *burqa* flooded the media when Kabul fell, even though journalists in the capital could see that this was not the case. There were also pictures of jubilant Afghans welcoming the "liberating" troops of the Northern Alliance. It was certainly a moving experience to walk into Kabul amid crowds of cheering Afghans, but apart from the northern suburb of Khair Khana, where many people shared ethnic or family ties with the Shura-i-Nazar faction of the Northern Alliance that captured Kabul, those joyful crowds soon petered out. In the rest of Kabul, there had been looting and some revenge attacks. There was a mix of emotions—widespread joy at the fall of the Taliban tempered by real anxiety as the same troops who had wasted the capital several years previously drove back in as the city's new masters. However, those pictures of jubilant Afghans—maybe 5 percent of the population—will go down in history as the true story of the fall of Kabul.

It was many months before even a significant minority of Afghan women felt secure enough to contemplate walking in public with their faces uncovered. A few men shaved their beards on day one, and many people played music openly. One of the high points of the day was "Radio Kabul" reclaiming its name from its Taliban "Radio Sharia" days and playing music with a female presenter.

Kabul was now the new focus of world media attention. Bureaus were opened and many agencies deployed reporters to Bagram airbase just to the north, where American forces were based. For a while reporters competed with one another to be taken on trips by the American forces (known as "facilities") as they went to hunt down remnants of Al Qaeda and the Taliban. Irish journalist Maggie O'Kane referred to such trips as "dog and pony shows." They have the effect, she says, of distracting journalists from the real news. However, when American air raids have gone wrong and killed civilians, some journalists have traveled through hostile terrain to get the full story out. The arrival of British Marines was greeted with a patriotic outburst of support from the British media, encouraged to do so by the ministry of defence public-relations machine. Later, in characteristic fashion, the British press turned on the soldiers after they failed to find any militants to kill or arrest.

Journalists were not the only people descending on Kabul. Hordes of NGO and UN agency staff swiftly arrived to form a mushrooming aid industry. Spokespeople had tales to tell of aid and reconstruction: the return to education for girls after years when going to school had been an illegal act (in areas of the country that had schools); the few Afghan women who had jobs outside the home returning to work; and the return of over a million Afghan refugees from camps in Pakistan and Iran. Human rights agencies opened offices, also wanting to get their views into the news. An Afghan interim administration took power in December 2001. After the Pashtu-speaking Taliban (no English, barely any Persian speakers), it was good to be able to interview ministers and officials in English and to have the media-friendly Hamid Karzai answer questions at press conferences.

Kabul has become much more like other capital cities to report from. It has a full complement of ambassadors and a mobile telephone network that sometimes works. The vast increase in road traffic means that it is now much easier to sit in the bureau finding out information by phone than struggling through traffic jams to investigate news firsthand.

The national media has flourished in the post-Taliban era with a whole spate of new Afghan publications, many independent, although most are very wary of criticizing the new powers that be. For the first time in six years the BBC Persian, Pashtu, and Uzbek language sections have been able to open a Kabul bureau safely and to employ a nationwide network of stringers. Afghanistan in 2002 became a much more secure place to do journalism. However, in 2003 a resurgent Taliban began launching attacks. The deliberate targeting of aid personnel, including the first murder of an international aid worker in Afghanistan in twelve years, has made everyone, including journalists, more cautious about traveling, especially in the south and west of the country. However, even in Kabul there are still stories that are dangerous or difficult to tell—stories to do with corruption, warlordism, and human rights abuses. Afghans are less nervous about expressing their views, but most are still too cautious to criticize openly members of the armed factions that now wield power in the central government and in the provinces. Delegates who tried to speak out against the armed factions at the Loya Jirga held in June 2002 received death threats.

The aid industry and the media have both done well out of the Afghan campaign. Awards have been won, donations made, and operations and audiences increased. Eventually, though, the media circus has moved on as the world's attention has turned to Iraq. The American public-relations machine and aid-agency spokespeople—and indeed many aid workers—have also refocused their attention. However, there are many stories still to be told: Will the United States really stand by its promise to help Afghans reconstruct their country? When will a genuinely broad-based government, as promised by the Bonn Accords, take office? When will the cities be demilitarized, as promised at Bonn? Will the 2004 elections actually allow Afghan voices to be heard after the 2002 Loya Jirga effectively silenced ordinary delegates?

Because America's campaign was portrayed as pure liberation, there has been no urgency to demilitarize, demobilize, deal with human rights abuses, or ensure proper representative government. The political map of Afghanistan has remained essentially the same as it was in the winter of 2001/2002, with warlords and factions allowed to consolidate their fiefdoms militarily, politically, and economically. The US-led campaign has been held up as an example of what military intervention can do for a benighted country. It is still far from clear, however, whether the war has generated the changes needed to build a future in which Afghan citizens will be able to enjoy peace and freedom from injustice.

NOTES

[1] Bridget Kendall, quoted in Jessica Hodgson, "Journalists Fight 'Hidden War' in Afghanistan," *The Guardian,* April 26, 2002.

[2] Bob Woodward, *Bush at War: Inside the Bush White House* (New York: Simon & Schuster, 2002), 131.

[3] Major General Patrick Cordingley, interviewed by the author, "The World Tonight," BBC Radio 4, March 2003.

6

Afghan Women
on the Margins
of the Twenty-first Century

SIPPI AZARBAIJANI-MOGHADDAM

The turn of the twenty-first century saw Afghan women reemerging from under the *burqa* to join the modern world. The relentless oscillation between women's emancipation and marginalization in Afghanistan has been linked to state actors' efforts at expanding or limiting centralized state control.[1] Women's status, comportment, and especially dress code have often been used as potent symbols to indicate a regime's success in exerting influence on the populace:

> The woman in Afghan society, and particularly . . . among the Pushtuns, is a figure loaded with symbolic significance, embodying the *nang* (disgrace) and *namus* (reputation/chastity) of the whole kin group.[2]

In relation to shifting state policies and the ensuing public response, gender relations have been in a constant state of flux on some socioeconomic levels while static on others.[3] This chapter will give a historical overview of major changes in the situation of Afghan women from the late nineteenth century to the present, looking at issues related to intermittent gains and losses for women since the early twentieth century, the role of male and female elites in transforming gender relations, and the impact of the international community. All these factors have contributed to the creation of a fragmented reality, a morass of opportunities and threats, upon which external assistance and pressure should be applied with extreme caution. The basis of this chapter is a set of interviews with Nancy Hatch Dupree, an internationally recognized expert on the history, art, and archeology of Afghanistan. Dupree has dedicated a lifetime to documenting and preserving Afghanistan's cultural heritage. She runs the Afghanistan Resource and Information Centre, the world's most comprehensive resource center on Afghanistan.

AFGHAN WOMEN—A HISTORICAL PERSPECTIVE

It is misguided to perceive female poets, heroines, and harem intriguers in the course of Afghanistan's history as evidence of a women's movement or of "feminism," as these characters were motivated more by inter- and intra-familial power struggles than by those between the sexes. Even though Afghan history has its fair share of strong, learned, and resourceful women manipulating events from the wings, changes have been initiated by men and the history of women's rights starts with the efforts of individual men, at times aided by women.[4] The first, Amir Abdur Rahman, undertook a series of reforms with a view to improving the lot of women in the 1880s. He forbade child and forced marriages and supported inheritance and divorce rights for women, a policy repeatedly emphasized by a succession of powerful men, from King Amanullah to Prime Minister Daoud and later by Communist Party leaders. Abdur Rahman also imposed the death penalty for adultery in an effort to safeguard against loss of national and family honor through the dishonorable conduct of women who, he believed, should be protected and kept in seclusion from corrupting influences beyond family confines.[5] This motif has resurfaced time and time again, for example, under the mujahedin and their successors, the Taliban, who were "opting for a position in a pre-existing discussion"[6] rather than initiating a hitherto unknown "gender-apartheid"[7] policy in Afghanistan.

In granting an amnesty to families exiled by his father, Abdur Rahman's son Habibullah (1901–19) allowed echoes of debates held in other parts of the Near East, on women's emancipation and participation in public affairs, to reach Kabul with returned exiles. Notable among these was Mohamad Beg Tarzi, who advocated education and employment for women while his daughters introduced Western dress to women at court. Tarzi's daughter, Soraya, married Prince Amanullah, who succeeded his assassinated father, Habibullah, in 1919. Soraya and Amanullah (1919–28) promoted their ideas on women's emancipation perhaps a little too zealously. In addition to female emancipation,

Amanullah's other political reforms, and Soraya's penchant for shock tactics using dress code, successfully alienated conservative elements, who found another leader for their foment.

The revolt of Bacha Saqqao overthrew Amanullah's reign in November 1928, but his own rule ended nine months later when Nadir Shah (1928–33) toppled him in return. Bacha's revolt foreshadowed a scenario that would be repeated again when women's emancipation, entrenched in modernization programs, would be perceived as a threat and result in the imposition of "rural" values on urban populations as a countermeasure. During this period the gains made for women were lost; as Dupree relates, there was a thirty-year gap before women could once again appear unveiled in public.

The reign of Nadir Shah's son, Zahir (1933–73) saw slow but steady gains for women and girls, in particular once Zahir's cousin, Daoud Khan, became prime minister. This time modernization plans were formulated by male elites backed by a powerful military. The celebration of the *jashn* (feast) in 1959 was a turning point for this process:

> Prime Minister Daoud, other members of the royal family, the cabinet and high-ranking officers appeared at the celebrations, without any prior announcement, with their wives and daughters unveiled. In response, a delegation of religious leaders had an audience with Daoud *Khan* in which they accused him of being un-Islamic. . . . The Prime Minister informed the delegation that veiling was going to be a voluntary matter and if they could find incontrovertible justification for *purdah* and the veil in Islamic Law, he would be the very first to reimpose *purdah* on his womenfolk.[8]

In urban areas girls' schools increased, as did medical services for women. Women had increasing employment opportunities as administrative staff within the government, in service industries and by 1978, on a smaller scale, in the police force, army, industry, and all government departments.[9] The changes for elite Kabul women began to filter out into the urban middle class and slowly into rural areas. In 1964 Afghanistan's new constitution simply handed women their rights, at least on paper. As Dupree relates, they did not "lift a finger," and most never even heard that they had been accorded rights:

> "Women were automatically enfranchised [Art. 43], accorded dignity and liberty [Art. 26:1], were to receive compulsory education [Art. 34] and have access to public health facilities [Art. 36]. They also had the freedom to choose work and benefited from equitable labor laws [Art. 37]."[10]

By the mid 1960s and the 1970s small numbers of urban, educated women were more prepared to raise their voices and organize protests for what they perceived to be their rights.[11] Daoud's (1973–78) reforms, even after the palace coup that exiled his cousin Zahir and made him president of the Democratic Republic of Afghanistan, never satisfied leftist detractors, who claimed that the government's efforts for women were "cosmetic gestures."[12] Daoud's reign succumbed to the Saur Revolution of April 1978, followed by the Soviet invasion of Afghanistan in 1979. Communism was ushered in under the People's Democratic Party of Afghanistan, which would eventually split into the Khalq and Parcham factions. Murderous divisions between party leaders made it an unstable period, and the socialist "state" ultimately lost control of conservative rural areas. Marital practices including levirate, the obligation of a dead man's brother to look after his brother's widow by marrying her, were once again challenged, but new practices, which even urban, educated families found distasteful, shocking, or intolerable, also appeared.

For the first time women were jailed or tortured for ties with political groups opposing the PDPA regime.[13] According to Dupree, the stigma attached to having a career and leaving the home had been removed for many urban women, but the policy of encouraging unrelated men and women to socialize in the work place remained anathema to many families. They perceived it as an attempt to weaken strong family ties, which have always formed a powerful obstacle to social engineering attempts by successive Afghan regimes. In rural areas women and girls were forced to attend literacy classes. Political indoctrination, coupled with several documented cases of sexual abuse in these classes, led to popular outcry and the bombing of some schools.[14]

Despite sporadic attempts to accommodate their ideology with Islam, the communists alienated the more conservative elements of Afghan society and, bolstered by the United States' geopolitical ambitions to dislodge the Soviets, the mujahedin factions formed and the jihad started. In this period foreign support mostly took the form of weapons and financial assistance to fighting factions. Women's needs were buried under military interests and the rhetoric of jihad, which produced many warlords whose minions would later make life hell for large numbers of Afghan females.

Many Afghan women became heavily involved in the jihad effort. Women were told that they had equal obligation with men to participate because it was sanctioned by the prophet Mohammed, as reported in *Hadith*.[15] Strong, vocal women took leadership roles, enjoining others to support the jihad in order to provide essential moral support for men, home from the front. These women also chased funding for education and health care while male counterparts attracted military support. Many Afghans perished as lives, limbs, families, homes, livelihoods, and ways of life were blown apart by war. This period was marked by double standards: Women were expected to be veiled and housebound but were often victims of the unbridled lust of commanders and their troops, who were responsible for violent rapes, multiple forced marriages, and pressure to provide sexual favors in return for humanitarian assistance. Displacement to urban areas and neighboring Muslim countries also exposed people from rural backgrounds to the benefits of health, family planning, education, and employment for women. This resulted in a transformation in attitudes and a demand for those services once back in Afghanistan.

In 1989 Soviet forces withdrew, leaving Najibullah's communist regime to struggle on. In 1992 Najibullah's government fell and the constitution, which guaranteed the fundamental rights of women, was suspended. Afghanistan descended into anarchy as mujahedin commanders fought among themselves with complete disregard for civilians. Many parts of Kabul were bombed to rubble, and flagrant human rights abuses became even more commonplace than they had been throughout the years of Soviet occupation. With the Soviet departure international interest in Afghanistan fell dramatically, and faced with an intractable civil war, many governments simply turned their backs on the country. The excesses of this period in part led to the rise of the Taliban, the religious students whose mission was to "purify" the Islamic state of Afghanistan.

UNDER THE TALIBAN

The Taliban movement emerged from remote rural communities to overthrow the mujahedin for absorbing what the Taliban perceived as profligate urban values. The Taliban took over where the mujahedin left off in terms of repressing women with edicts and threats. In fact, the Taliban achieved a high profile in succeeding to overcome the failures of their predecessors in this respect. Taliban decrees prohibiting a variety of activities for ordinary Afghans are well publicized and need no further elaboration here. In many cases changes were superficial, short lived, quietly abandoned, or circumvented. The Taliban's enforcement of decrees and bans was in no way homogeneous because of the nature of the movement as well as changes that had occurred within Afghan society.

Urban and rural communities in Afghanistan have always been linked through kinship ties. Urbanization in Afghanistan has been slow—it is estimated that less than 10 percent of the population live in urban centers. After the Communists took power, people became increasingly mobile, fleeing fighting and political repression or seeking improved economic opportunities. By the time the Taliban took Kabul in 1996, the geographical division between rural and urban had been blurred, but socio-cultural distinctions remained largely intact. As a consequence, many rural women in Kabul saw Taliban restrictions as an extension of those imposed by their own men.

Taliban justice, consisting of public hangings, stonings, and amputation of limbs, was unpalatable by modern standards. The dreaded "vice and virtue" religious police enforced draconian measures with brutality, although these never stretched as far as the apocryphal "she was beaten until her white shoes ran red with blood" stories that were widely circulated. Taliban success in imposing a "medieval" way of life on Afghan people brought to the attention of the international community what had gone unnoticed in parts of Afghanistan for centuries. And yet, as discussions on the radio filtered into remote villages, Taliban actions and subsequent international outcries resulted in many Afghan women hearing for the first time that they had "rights."

Some Taliban leaders were aware of the sensitivity of the Afghan "women's issue" and used it to their own advantage whenever possible. In common with their *mujahedin* predecessors, the Taliban occasionally used "women-and-children" as a front when they needed to divert food supplies to their troops.[16] Overall, a patchwork of Taliban attitudes to women's programs, along with an equally inconsistent and uncoordinated range of gender policies from international agencies, led to unpredictable patterns of clamp downs or frenzied bursts of activity with women and girls in some areas, while in others, projects progressed relatively undisturbed.

THE INTERNATIONAL RESPONSE

Complexity and nuances notwithstanding, unprecedented international interest, misinformation, and hysteria have surrounded the situation of women and girls since the Taliban set foot in Kabul. In recent years Afghan women have been used by countless media, political, and humanitarian entities, as well as publicity hungry women's rights' groups, to pursue their own objectives. Dupree is appalled at how images of Afghan women have been shamelessly exploited by "self-interested" groups, providing an unbalanced, inconsistent, and unfair view of Afghan women. Media manipulation has created two extremes: vocal, jet-setting, lipstick-wearing superwomen in the limelight and downtrodden, *burqa*-wearing, vulnerable widows in the shadows. With notable exceptions even Afghan women have joined this cynical game, taking advantage of their countrywomen to become famous through the pursuit of well-publicized and gimmicky charitable acts that fail to make the slightest dent in the structural bedrock of gender inequity in Afghanistan.

The darlings of the media circuit have undoubtedly been the Revolutionary Association of Afghan Women (RAWA). Founded by Meena Kishwar Kamal in 1977, RAWA, described as Maoists by Emadi, seeks "to mobilize and organize women and girls into the armed struggle for national liberation."[17] With its founder assassinated by Islamists, RAWA was exceptionally well placed to jump on the publicity band wagon. Wholeheartedly milking rumors about women under the Taliban, and cashing in on the naiveté of journalists and researchers content to be hoodwinked and manipulated, RAWA fuels Orientalist notions of veiled Afghan women living in seraglios, jealously guarded by bearded Musulmans wielding scimitars. RAWA has as yet to prove that its relentless self-promotion has contributed in any significant way to the betterment of Afghan women.[18]

The faddishness and painfully short attention span of the international community are nothing new. Throughout the jihad, women's rights activists, who in recent years have espoused the cause of Afghan women with great fervor, somehow failed to protest against abuses perpetrated by US-backed Islamic warriors. When the Soviets left and warring factions began to perpetrate the worst abuses, international attention had turned to the Balkans and Bosnian rape testimonies had become fashionable. Those who were working to draw international attention to the crisis of Afghan women lacked an attentive foreign audience.

Journalists, women's rights activists, academic researchers, and high-level staff from respectable international organizations have at times resorted to twisting respondents' words to validate their prejudices and to grab attention through sensationalizing stories.[19] The small outcropping of Afghan women who form the Westernized, urbanized middle class has our undivided attention, thanks to media bias against the rural and urban majority, who do not speak English and who adhere to Islam as true believers. The Taliban decision, for example, to limit female employment in foreign-run and funded organizations in 2000 led to an international outcry that ignored the situation of millions of women engaged in unpaid or low-paid work that contributed to the household income, the rural economy, and the handicraft sector.

Presently, it seems that all "useful" changes for Afghan women must take place while they hold media attention and the fickle goodwill of the international community. This is putting pressure on donors and aid agencies to push through "feel good," gimmicky programs with very little analysis. It was inevitable that such widespread self-delusion, goaded by an orgy of media misinformation, would lead to a post-Taliban transition period in which the international response to the situation of Afghan women would be tainted with sentimentality rather than decision-making informed by the views of Afghan women.

LESSONS LEARNED—
AFGHAN WOMEN POST–SEPTEMBER 11

Historically, the struggle to bring Afghanistan under the control of a Kabul-based centralized government has resulted in a very complex dynamic reflecting the ebb and flow of resistance from conservatives and the fluctuating socio-political status of Afghan women. As Dupree points out, making the transition between public and private has generated a great deal of confusion and disorientation for both women and men since, on the one hand, women are promised independence, and yet, on the other, they are still subject to the dictates of patriarchy:

> "In the last fifty years, Afghan women have been buffeted by confusing ideologies. From 1959 to 1978 they were encouraged to go to work and walk in the streets by themselves but still expected to socialize only within the family. Then, a heavily socialist period was followed by the mujahedin, the Taliban and now, 'instant democracy.'"[20]

By January 2002 the aid community had descended on Afghanistan en masse. A national Back to School campaign returned thousands of girls to education. A small number of women returned to work in ministries and aid agencies. Several months later Massouda Jallal, a relatively unknown Afghan woman, ran for president against Hamid Karzai at the Loya Jirga. Beauty salons reopened all over Kabul, and many diaspora women rushed back to help their beleaguered sisters. But this is the latest swing of the pendulum and effecting sustainable change requires accepting the lessons presented by Afghan history.

DEFINING THE LIMITS OF OUR IGNORANCE

Since the arrival of the Taliban, gender issues have been oversimplified for the consumption of secular, consumerist societies addicted to speed and happy endings. The *burqa* has become symbolic of Afghan women's struggle against a repressive, Islamic patriarchy embodied by the Taliban. With the Taliban gone, the outside world wishes to see only Kabul's liberal face, and many, including some whom one would credit with more subtle powers of analysis, are amazed at the *burqa*'s resilience. As Dupree explains, it is dangerous and even stupid to assume that the legacy, the centuries-old prejudices, and threats to personal security have disappeared overnight. The tendency of Afghan women not to conform to shallow stereotypical images is symptomatic of a widespread ignorance and superficiality in understanding gender relations in the Afghan context.

The Afghan government and the international community are faced with a perplexing multitude of beliefs, ideologies, and attitudes related to the situation of Afghan women. In addition, gender considerations are not mainstreamed into strategic planning and coordination processes at the highest levels because gender is a complicated, emotive, and conflict-producing issue that leaders can usually afford to ignore. The complexities of gender programming are a long list of do's and don'ts navigated by isolated gender advisers. Knowledge of gender relations in the broader Afghan context, among internationals and the urban elite, has always been a patchy affair presenting itself as a Gordian knot, presumed better left alone. Thanks to the efforts of a few social scientists and long-time aid workers, there has been a small degree of change in this situation in recent years. However, progress is slow, while the expectation of rapid results tends to be the norm.

The male-dominated diplomatic and assistance communities tend to choose interlocutors in their own image: predominantly male, elite, urban, English-speaking and, in most cases, gender blind. We are inclined to forget that those fitting our criteria are from a minority group, often with unrepresentative views. Feeling compelled to project our values, some accommodate a range of seemingly incompatible ultra-modern and ultra-conservative stances, utilizing all the correct gender vocabulary and concepts while still having to control the dress code and mobility of their female colleagues and womenfolk in order to convey the right impression of honorable manliness in their own extended family and socio-political networks.[21] We prefer dealing with people who share our values because, for most, Islam is unknown territory. We have a preference for written communication in a country where the vast majority are illiterate and rely on memory. Linguistic, cultural, and religious sensory deprivation leaves most over-reliant on a small group, from a narrow stratum of society, that has historically misinterpreted the myriad nuances of Afghanistan through its myopic social lens with unsuccessful results.

The danger of ignorance and weak analyses regarding gender relations in Afghanistan is that some interventions can be very disruptive. Badly conceived and facile analyses based on the assumption that Afghan women are vulnerable individuals living in a vacuum may eventually isolate rather than reintegrate women. For instance, women have learned to exert influence in family, community, and political life from behind the scenes, in private, while male involvement in politics is articulated through public language. Women find ways to lobby leaders, either through male relatives or by making direct appeals in audiences with provincial and other authorities.[22] With little knowledge or analysis of such processes, the newly established Ministry of Women's Affairs (MoWA), pushed by foreign donors and adopting the age-old method of justifying its existence through leaving a visible trail of infrastructure, is establishing women's centers, isolated from mainstream governance bodies at provincial level, with a nebulous plan to help women achieve their rights.

Within the Afghan government the number of people with gender expertise is still negligible in comparison to requirements. As in many international organizations, simply being female is regarded as ample qualification and experience for taking up gender posts. With exceptions, many people still misunderstand the concept of gender, equating it with "doing stuff for women." Policymakers and implementers persistently take the road of least resistance, engaging women through their traditional gender roles and leaving inequitable gender relations unchanged. It should be obvious from looking at the last twenty years in Afghanistan that six months' funding for a handicraft or chicken-rearing project purporting to transform gender relations is utterly useless. The question is whether we want to gloss over gender inequities and celebrate short-lived quantitative results or to facilitate far-reaching, sustainable changes, requiring more time, commitment, and money.

MALE ELITES—SAVIORS OR TRAITORS?

Analysis of any Afghan "women's movement" must depart from the realization that until recently women's rights agendas were predominantly formulated and driven by male elites. Although the history of male support for Afghan women's rights is littered with miscalculation and betrayal, some men have genuinely supported an improvement in women's status. According to Dupree, this crucial point, although clearly evidenced in the 1964 constitution, which gave women a head start, is often lost on outsiders. Dupree believes that the key is to identify male support from what she calls the "modernist period, before the Communists and extremists."[23]

As Dupree points out, however, previous Afghan regimes enjoyed varying degrees of support from a united military that regulated the former's success at implementation of reforms and policies, including those on women's status. US distribution of funds and arms to competing mujahedin factions created competing armies that still pose a threat to the fledgling Kabul government. Warlords mostly see their power in the failure of centralized state control. Although some are mobilizing rights rhetoric to support their claims that they have reformed, many others are still not under any pressure to adopt liberal, pro-woman agendas or policies enhancing human security for their "constituencies."

Even supportive male elites, however, could not sweep away conservative and patriarchal prejudice in one fell swoop. Loopholes for the exercise of patriarchy remain intact from the reign of Zahir Shah:

"The legal system interprets the constitution, and there is the ca-
veat that 'there shall be no law repugnant to the basic principles
of the sacred religion of Islam.' It is in writing specific laws that
the patriarchal and discriminatory beliefs and practices become
sparklingly clear. The penal code [1976] and civil law [1977] are
where contradictions are found. For instance, Penal Code, Article 398 [states]: 'A Person, defending his honor, who sees his
spouse, or another of his close relations, in the act of committing
adultery or being in the same bed with another and immediately
kills or injures one or both of them shall be exempted from both
punishment for laceration and murder, but shall be imprisoned
for a period not exceeding two years.' . . . Articles in the civil law
pertaining to marriage and divorce [60–216] and children's rights
[217–88] meld basic human rights principles with customary law.
. . . It is obvious from these that social customs favorable to male
dominance are entrenched in the legal statutes."[24]

Since the Great Game,[25] and increasingly in the past two decades,
the international community's primary engagement with Afghanistan
has been through military support based on geopolitical considerations.
Women have never been major players in this "militarization" scenario
and have been accommodated within its structure as victims, collateral
damage, and media icons.[26] Providers of military assistance to more
recent, insalubrious male leaders, simultaneously mobilizing "women-
and-children" rhetoric, have never balked at their own duplicity. From
time to time cooperative women who have unwittingly or knowingly
provided a feminine mask for more unpalatable ideologies have even
been allowed to share male power. Mujahedin faction leaders, who
pulverized Kabul's residential areas in the early 1990s, supported
women's active involvement in advocacy work on behalf of their factions. According to Dupree, they succumbed to pressure from determined women in order to improve the party image:

"Hekmatyar and Rabbani were being 'good' Muslims by allowing women to engage in education and medical work, as long as
these activities took place in separate facilities for men and
women."[27]

Such women must at some stage agree to repress other women or
suffer the consequences. Tajwar Kakar, an activist jailed during the
jihad, was approached about setting up a women's prison in the refugee context and felt compelled to distance herself from the mainstream
of the mujahedin movement since her agenda was swiftly diverging
from that of male leaders.[28] The slightest challenge to patriarchy brought

swift reprisal, even for women who knowingly took on extra burdens and risks during the jihad and contributed within and beyond their prescribed gender roles, including bearing arms. Kakar's efforts at educating young girls on their Islamic rights were violently nipped in the bud by the very men who had promoted her as a leader; she had to flee for her life. Disillusionment from this period has led many women activists to stay in exile rather than risk disappointment, or worse, repression once again.

Regardless of women's enormous contribution to the war against the Soviets, the Bonn Declaration only thanked the mujahedin while many women are still stigmatized for being imprisoned by the Communists. Assumptions about sexual assault in prison led to many women being disowned or ostracized by family members fearing disgrace. Kakar believes that the marginalization, neglect, denial, and betrayal that surround women jailed for supporting the jihad have deterred subsequent generations from making a stand for their political and ideological beliefs and trying to emerge as women leaders in their own right.

Foreign military donors, currently going to war on behalf of democracy and Muslim women's rights, did not argue with their protégés for "humanitarian space" at the beginning of the jihad, when aid workers struggled to provide health and education for women and girls. Their proxy troops and handpicked leaders had to safeguard their Islamic credentials by keeping women, the purveyors of honor in Afghan culture, unsullied by contact with the outside world. Similarly, when the Americans withdrew their assistance to Afghanistan shortly after the departure of Soviet troops, "women-and-children" were callously abandoned to their fate at the hands of leaders trained in guerrilla warfare by American instructors.

Despite the rhetoric utilized by the Bushes and the Blairs following the events of September 11, and despite United Nations Security Council Resolution 1325 on Women, Peace, and Security, at no stage were any Afghan women consulted on Operation Enduring Freedom. The same nefarious warlords were paid handsome sums and empowered to act as proxy agents once again, while analysts justified these actions by saying there was no other choice. For Kakar and other politically conscious Afghan women, the betrayal continued at the UN-led talks that led to the December 5 signing of the Bonn Agreement. International scrutiny necessitated the involvement of women but, according to Dupree, the international community simultaneously colluded in maintaining the gender status quo by allowing male Afghan leaders to exclude politicized Afghan women. After much deliberation and worldwide pressure to include women at the Bonn conference, the three female delegates, and later, the women who would take up posts within the interim authority were all chosen from among the ranks of those who were politically inexperienced and would therefore pose no real threat to the patriarchal status quo.

Today, Afghan women simply do not believe that political, military, and security structures, along with the international armed forces deployed in Afghanistan, are in any way accountable to them. They do not even have recourse to a reliable police or security force and suffer from the absence of the rule of law. The fact that ISAF has ignored repeated requests from women to have its mandate expanded to cover areas other than Kabul demonstrates that, for the time being, such structures are unresponsive to the attempts of women and others to address the security problems faced by Afghan females outside the capital.

ECONOMICS AS A VEHICLE OF CHANGE

Since the 1960s Afghanistan has been one of the most underdeveloped countries in the world, with a weak formal economy bolstered by international aid packages. Two decades of war exacerbated Afghanistan's poverty by hastening the disintegration of the skeletal economic infrastructure, leaving the economy increasingly reliant on opium production and a network of transport interests smuggling a variety of goods. Substantial international assistance in the form of military backing has also been a feature of Afghan economics. Women have become commodities in this system, but their active involvement in and ownership of the "national" economy have always been infinitesimal. The economy at the macro level is male-dominated, while women operate at the micro level. And yet small and disparate economic changes for women have been some of the most far-reaching and transformative in the past few decades:

> "Economics are forcing old prejudices to give way to new priorities. Economics have probably done more to modify male-female relations than all the human rights rhetoric of the past fifty years or more."[29]

One reason for the effectiveness and sustainability of economic change has been that it is primarily owned and promulgated by families themselves. Policy and program formulators must understand that it is futile to address women as individuals in a vacuum, without understanding their position in the family, a crucial source of opportunities and threats where women are repressed, sustained, or propelled forward as a result of gender relations built on gender roles. These relationships can evolve as a result of well-planned interventions and social policies designed to bring about changes that Afghan women and their families desire. Since Daoud's time some Afghan families have been moving away from the attitude enshrined in the Pashtun saying, "A woman's place is in the home or in the grave." Certain ideas have incubated in the home and emerged slowly, spending a lengthy period maturing, halfway between private and public domains:

"Hair dressing salons do not provide the most meaningful work for women. But in the sixties and seventies, women opened hair salons and boutiques with the permission of their families. They would have a room on the outer wall of the family compound, with a door onto the street for customers to use. It was half in and half out of the family home and represents very well the cautious emergence of some women into self-employment."[30]

Similar to hair-dressing salons, home schools were developed as an alternative to a brash and forceful strategy to compel communities to accept primary education for girls in more conservative rural communities even before the rise of the Taliban. With careful, culturally appropriate exposure, communities gradually took ownership of girls' education and even successfully lobbied Taliban authorities who tried to stop programs.

Since 1959 realistic economic opportunities and necessities have been changing dynamics in a number of urban households. Implicit in the family decision to allow women to work is the decision to give them increased mobility and to allow them to benefit from education and vocational training. But women's involvement in economic activities also brings other changes:

"In many educated families you will find girls in their thirties who are still unmarried. They are used to their income and their independence.[31] Those with skills are working in ever increasing numbers and, in many cases, are becoming primary wage earners. They will pave the way in an evolutionary manner, just as in 1959. This is an urban phenomenon with Kabul as the nerve center. These women have gotten training, but the men from the same age group were deprived of an education when they went off to fight. They cannot enter into meaningful, productive activities, and they are not intellectually or emotionally capable of functioning in 'normal' society. The traditional male role has been eroded as a direct result of the war, and women have replaced them. He cannot assume the 'patriarchic' voice and expect to be obeyed. Traditionally, in Islam, the wife's right to maintenance is in consideration of her submission to her husband's authority. When she becomes economically self-sufficient, this premise is challenged. Male expectations of total obedience are thus eroded, while women who once accepted diminishment in exchange for security no longer need to do so. She doesn't need to be accommodating anymore. Modernization, the socialist experiment, and refugee experiences have given women more strength. Men must bow to the economic leverage women can now use. This can have important consequences and deserves to be studied."[32]

Quantifying such changes is difficult, and not all women have been successful in achieving the results mentioned by Dupree.[33] Women from other families followed a different path to contribute to family income.

Economic vicissitudes have steadily transformed attitudes along with the feminization of poverty, due to loss or absence of male providers, which left many, especially urbanized families headed by females, with little choice but for women to contribute to the household's cash economy. Previously, it was considered shameful for males to shirk their responsibility to provide for the entire family and to allow women to come into contact with corrupting influences by working outside the home, but men from rural and provincial families, as well as different income groups, gradually came to realize the benefits of allowing women to earn money or to have contact with foreign organizations that might give them assistance.

Evidently, involvement in family economics can only follow the pattern of markets for products and services as well as employment possibilities. These were and are predominantly provided by the government in urban areas. Aid-agency efforts to provide services to women, including those in rural and provincial areas, led to an increasing number of educated provincial women finding employment as health providers, educators, and project staff. Not all women were so lucky however. As the fighting dragged on, economic changes left a number of women who were not part of the educated elite open to destitution and exploitation. Illiterate women with no formal work experience can sell assets, become part of agency "widow" programs, enter prostitution, beg, choose work as domestic labor, or force their children into similar work.

Women's economic activity is still mostly controlled by men. For instance, handicraft production, especially of carpets, is an area of home-based economic transformation rife with exploitative gender relations. The war displaced skilled women to crowded camps where their expertise could be passed to others and used to derive an income. This income usually means a small wage for women and children but large profits for carpet dealers.[34] Carpet weaving is an acceptable option for many families because it is home based and does not require mobility and literacy. Many organizations have adopted carpet weaving as *the* women's income-generation project par excellence. But the employment of women in such low-paid, labor-intensive work perpetuates the belief that women's time is worthless and spent idling away. Approaching economics as a vehicle for transformation evidently requires detailed analysis of gender relations among producers, service providers, their families, middlemen, and markets.

THE ROLE OF WOMEN LEADERS

Obstacles notwithstanding, a number of Afghan women are trying to carve leadership positions in their own right, without allegiance to any male party. They emulate the male model of leadership based on the accumulation of power by, among other things:

> Attracting many regular guests through lavish hospitality; . . .
> channelling resources from the outside world to one's followers;
> . . . [and] demonstrating superior rhetorical gifts and regular sound
> judgement.[35]

Like elite, urban men, women of the same standing are generally out of touch with the reality faced by the majority. In this case, efforts to represent majority views are replaced by relentless promotion of their own personality cult.

The MoWA was recently set up as a direct result of the Bonn Conference. Male leaders agreed, some probably because they thought it would be good publicity and others out of genuine support for the cause of women. The MoWA is politically and economically marginalized within the Afghan government, with the leadership chosen to avoid challenge to patriarchy and male dominance. Without international financial and moral support, it could easily be starved out of existence. Despite this, with the right approach from donors and ministry staff, Dupree sees the MoWA as occupying a unique position from which to become an effective advocate for the majority:

> "The ministry should advocate for women's voices to be included. It should form advocacy groups in a manner that is compatible with Afghan culture—persuasive but not strident or too confrontational. The status quo of women in Afghanistan must be challenged, but in a way that is educational, not just with aggression. If women want to raise voices, they need tools."[36]

Advocacy is currently being pursued by another group of women. Since the mass exodus of Afghans to Pakistan and Iran, increasing numbers of women have begun working for NGOs and UN agencies, both in the refugee camps and inside Afghanistan. They have taken the lead in advocating for the health and education needs of Afghan women and children, and some eventually have become the heads of Afghan women's NGOs. They have faced hostility from conservative elements but continue undeterred. The work of women's NGOs has evolved rapidly, and they have moved into new areas dealing with more sensitive issues such as women's rights, protection, and domestic violence. A number of Afghan women's NGOs have the grassroots contacts and professionalism to represent women's majority interests effectively, but compared to men's organizations they are still hugely under-funded and have very little contact with mainstream donor agencies. Since their work has received relatively small amounts of funding, they have not been able to scale up their operations sufficiently to occupy a strategic position in pursuing women's advancement.

CONCLUSION

Fast in some areas and painfully slow in others, the pace of change is unevenly spread for Afghan women. The daunting challenge for women is to be an indispensable part of processes such as the drafting of the new constitution and the review of the judicial system. Afghan society now speaks with many voices, from a range of political backgrounds, from royalists and mujahedin supporters, to socialists and Taliban supporters. Ethnicity, socio-economic backgrounds, and waves of emigration and return each adds its own nuances. Intra- and inter-family rivalries still set men and women against each other. The international community often contributes to the fragmentation of the bigger picture in Afghanistan by taking sides and fueling tensions rather than communicating with all Afghan counterparts, literate and illiterate, rural and urban, conservative and moderate.

It has been said quite rightly that in order to follow international commitment to the Afghan women's cause one should follow the money. In comparison to the verbal support and enormous international interest to date, women's effective involvement in male-dominated national and international forums and discussions on Afghanistan has been minimal. Fund allocations, foreign diplomacy, and the role of the military are determined with no input from women. The challenge is to engage male leaders, Afghan and international, and convince them that change for women will not occur in a gender vacuum. There is an urgent need to form an alliance of men who will stand together with women for their rights.[37]

Between gradual, externally driven, state-sponsored change, supported but not enforced by military power, and change internalized, owned, and pushed by individual families, one can find the most fertile ground for sustainable gain. Helping significant numbers of women successfully negotiate the change into the twenty-first century involves specially designed and intensive capacity building and vocational training programs in Afghanistan, rather than short, overly expensive, and utterly useless showcase trips abroad. With such assistance women will be able to control their own access to their rights.

Lack of substantial and sensible support for "home grown" women's groups and women-run NGOs will starve a potentially powerful driving force for transformation and for the development of a women's movement in Afghanistan. Female Afghan leadership cannot be developed on a weak knowledge base. There is a need to explore indigenous models for women's organizations and leadership in the Afghan context. Effective engagement with the reality of Afghan women requires deeper analyses, a readiness to deal with complexity, and avoidance of acting on superficial impressions.

The future of an Afghan women's movement lies in transferring more power and resource control to the new group of capable women leaders and to women's NGOs, who are increasingly outside the network of tainted political factions, who have increased access to women at the grass roots, and who have an understanding of women's needs in the broader Afghan context. The reverse face of such a move is disempowering male leaders, thus far supported by the international community, who abuse their military power and trample the rights of women and children. If they are not brought to justice, stripped of their power, and punished, women will always live in fear and never find an effective voice.

NOTES

[1] Maliha Zulfacar, "The Pendulum of Gender Politics in Afghanistan," paper (2000).

[2] Asta Olesen, *Islam and Politics in Afghanistan* (Surrey, UK: Curzon Press, 1995), 136–37.

[3] "Gender relations are concerned with how power is distributed between the sexes" (Candida March et al., *A Guide to Gender-Analysis Frameworks* [London: Oxfam, 1999], 18).

[4] Contemporary examples are Fatima Yassar and Aziza Azam, both consulted on matters pertaining to women as laid out in Islamic texts.

[5] Nancy Dupree, *The Women of Afghanistan* (Office of the UN Coordinator for Afghanistan, 1998), 1.

[6] Peter Marsden, *The Taliban: War, Religion, and the New Order in Afghanistan* (London: Zed Books, 1998), 97.

[7] A term coined by the Feminist Majority Foundation.

[8] Olesen, *Islam and Politics in Afghanistan*, 195.

[9] Dupree, *The Women of Afghanistan*, 4.

[10] Interview by author with Nancy Dupree, Peshawar, December 2002.

[11] Hafizullah Emadi, *Politics of Development and Women in Afghanistan* (New York: Paragon House Publishers, 1993), 66.

[12] Dupree, *The Women of Afghanistan*, 5.

[13] Gulalai Habib, "Afghan Women and Religious Fundamentalism" (Islamabad, May 1998), 3.

[14] Emadi, *Politics of Development and Women in Afghanistan*, 77.

[15] Dupree, interview, 2002.

[16] Cynthia Enloe, *The Morning After: Sexual Politics at the End of the Cold War* (Berkeley and Los Angeles: University of California Press, 1993), 166; and interviews with families in Northern Afghanistan and Ghorbandi displaced in 1998.

[17] Emadi, *Politics of Development and Women in Afghanistan*, 85.

[18] The author's recent guided tour of "secret" RAWA projects in Kabul provided ample evidence of the group's painstaking charades aimed at manipulating, misinforming, and giving anything but the right impressions regarding the reality of life for ordinary Afghan women.

[19] For example, BBC television reported that a young girl talking about changes in Afghanistan said in Pashtun, "Now there is television." This was translated into English as, "Now we are allowed to watch television," skewing the meaning considerably.

[20] Dupree, interview, 2002.

[21] Ibid.

[22] Communication with Matthew B. Fielden, January 2003. Fielden is completing his Ph.D. on governance in Afghanistan at the London School of Economics.

[23] Dupree, interview, 2002.

[24] Ibid.

[25] The colonial contest between the British and the Russian empires to control central Asia.

[26] See Cynthia Enloe, *Bananas, Beaches and Bases: Making Feminist Sense of International Politics* (Berkeley and Los Angeles: University of California Press, 2001).

[27] Dupree, interview, 2002.

[28] Interview with Tajwar Kakar, deputy minister of Women's Affairs, November 2002.

[29] Dupree, interview, 2002.

[30] Ibid.

[31] Reluctance to marry may also be due to lack of suitable life partners and migration of male siblings to find work and better life opportunities, making it a necessity for at least one daughter to stay unmarried in order to care for aging parents.

[32] Dupree, interview, 2002.

[33] Sippi Azarbaijani-Moghaddam, "Take Our Words Abroad" (Islamabad: UNOCHA, October 22, 2000), 13.

[34] According to the *Frontier Post* the export of Afghan-made carpets from Pakistan alone reached US$130 million in the fiscal year 2000–2001 (May 9, 2001).

[35] Bernard Glatzer, *Is Afghanistan on the Brink of Ethnic and Tribal Disintegration?* in *Fundamentalism Reborn?—Afghanistan and the Taliban*, ed. William Maley (London: Hurst & Company, 1998), 177.

[36] Dupree, interview, 2002.

[37] Interviews with Carol Le Duc, gender adviser at UNHCR, Kabul, 2002.

Part Two

POLITICS AND HUMANITARIANISM AFTER SEPTEMBER 11

7

Principles, Politics, and Pragmatism in the International Response to the Afghan Crisis

ANTONIO DONINI

The international community's response to the Afghanistan crisis spans a twenty-year period that saw the demise of the Cold War; the ensuing disorder and reshuffling of political, military, and economic agendas in Central and South Asia; and the tentative emergence of a new hegemonic order based on globalization and the anti-terrorism agenda.

Humanitarian action has remained a constant in Afghanistan. It has, of course, been affected both by the structural changes in the nature of the conflict and by the superstructural developments in the international community's approaches to conflict and crisis. These changes relate to policy shifts within the humanitarian arena itself (where, for example, working on "both sides" of an internal conflict has become the norm rather than the exception) as well as the changing status of humanitarian action in relation to the other variables affecting the Afghanistan crisis—political, economic, and human rights in particular.

This chapter examines the interactions among principles, politics, and pragmatism in the international response to the crisis. It takes a broad view of this relationship and concludes with some considerations on issues that, at the time of writing, remain unresolved and are likely to affect the Afghan transition. The perspective is primarily humanitarian, but it must be said at the outset that in Afghanistan, as elsewhere, it is particularly difficult to separate out humanitarian issues from the political context and its ramifications. The Afghan crisis was primarily political from day one. The military vicissitudes that went with it in turn gave rise to massive humanitarian need. The manner in which the international community responded to these needs and to the related human rights violations, as well as the fluctuations of the response over time, were heavily influenced by political agendas that were often at odds with humanitarian objectives. From the start, as in most complex emergencies, the space for humanitarian action was determined by politics. This intrusion of the political has ranged from relatively benign pressure to the overt manipulation of humanitarian and human rights action for partisan purposes.

As we shall see, there are two important lessons to reflect upon. They are quite obvious and commonsensical, but all too often disregarded. The first is that there seems to be a negative correlation between international politics, understood as direct superpower involvement, and the ability of the international system to engage with crises in a relatively principled manner. In Afghanistan the "highs" in politics (Cold War proxy interventions; post–September 11 peace-building) correspond to "lows" in principles. Conversely, superpower dis-attention to the Afghan crisis, as in the 1992–98 period of internecine conflict, allowed more space for issues of principle and for significant innovations in how the United Nations and other external actors could do business in a crisis country. The corollary to this law is that when great power interest is high, as a rule the political people in the donor and UN bureaucracies take over policy and decision-making, including humanitarian and human rights decision-making, displacing the humanitarian folk who often have a better understanding of realities on the ground.

The second lesson is that the "instrumentalization" of humanitarian assistance for political gain, in addition to constituting in itself a violation of humanitarian principles, does not pay. Subordination of principles to so-called higher imperatives of realpolitik may allow for short-term gains, but in the long term the chickens come home to roost. And in Afghanistan, the "blowback" of the politics and the manipulations of humanitarian assistance of the 1980s continue to this day.

It is useful, for analytical purposes, to separate the humanitarian response to the Afghan crisis into four distinct phases:

1. *From the Soviet invasion to the fall of Najibullah (1979–92), or the Cold War period and its aftermath.* In humanitarian terms, there were two distinct phases to this period: the cross-border

solidarity phase during which UN agencies operated, by necessity, in neighboring countries, and the second phase, which saw the arrival of the UN agencies on the scene and which was accompanied by the first attempt to set up a robust UN humanitarian coordination mechanism while simultaneous UN attempts to broker peace followed a formulaic Cold War script.

2. *The civil war and the triumph of warlordism (1992–96).* The volatility of the situation in Afghanistan, which included the devastation and complete breakdown of institutions, hampered the provision of assistance and provoked great soul-searching in the assistance community—What are we doing here? Are we fueling the war?—as well as growing disillusionment in a UN peace process that was increasingly reduced to "talks about talks."

3. *The Taliban period (1996–September 10, 2001).* The rise of the Taliban regime triggered a resurgence of interest in humanitarian principles and was coupled with a second attempt at robust and coherent coordination among, at least in theory, the assistance, human rights, and political dimensions of the international response.

4. *Post–September 11 or "nation-building lite"*[1] *in a fragmented state.* The heavy engagement of the international community (and great powers in particular) that has accompanied renewed interest in Afghanistan since the events of September 11, 2001, has, again, been characterized by politics trumping principles in the quest for a durable peace.

During each of these periods there is a corresponding shift: from weak unitary state to fragmenting state; from fragmenting to failed state; from failed to rogue state; and from rogue to recovering "protégé" state.

A note on sources is relevant here. In contrast to the vast literature, analytical and sentimental-journalistic, on the Soviet intervention and its bloody aftermath, there has been very little scholarly research on the evolution of humanitarian action in Afghanistan across the span of the last quarter century and even less on how humanitarian issues have intersected with the other dimensions of the crisis.[2] Few, if any, researchers probed the effects of Cold War political agendas on donor government aid policies or on UN and NGO activities in Afghanistan. Much of the academic research spawned by the latest spike in international interest has focused on the political economy of the crisis, on the dynamics of tradition and modernization,[3] and after September 11, on the challenges of nation-building.[4] Humanitarian and human rights issues (except as the latter related to the Taliban) have generally been dealt with as an afterthought. Recent studies and reports commissioned by aid agencies or donors have an obligatory opening overview of the historical context, but few scratch below the surface or draw linkages to the present. Studies dealing with assistance issues, with few exceptions, have focused on the trees rather than the forest and how it has grown over time.[5] Most recently, in 2002–2003, a wave of Afghan-specific or comparative studies have been commissioned or published, including some of the "chickens coming home to roost" variety, which focus on the institutional aspects of the post–September 11 integrated UN mission and its implications for broader peace-building approaches.[6] Thus, while there is a growing body of accessible documentation on the tail end of the Afghan crisis, the absence of solid research on humanitarian and human rights issues over the past quarter century is a finding in itself.[7] The dearth of documented research suggests the neglect with which the politicization of assistance in the earlier periods of the international response to the Afghan crisis has been treated. In this light, this chapter aims to discuss the high and low points in principled engagement in Afghanistan.

FROM THE SOVIET INVASION
TO THE FALL OF NAJIBULLAH (1979–92):
THE CROSS-BORDER YEARS

The Soviet intervention in December 1979, and the rapid escalation of what was until then a low-intensity guerrilla war between small and disparate Islamic resistance groups and the central government, triggered a massive outflow of Afghan refugees, primarily to Pakistan and secondarily to Iran. Until the mid 1980s the humanitarian effort was essentially confined to refugee camps in Pakistan and undertaken, in accordance with the precepts of the time, by UNHCR and its partner NGOs, albeit with strong Pakistani government involvement and control. The situation in Iran was different in that the refugee population was scattered around the country and access by the few aid agencies present was severely constrained by the authorities. UN agencies were present in Kabul, as were a couple of small medical NGOs and the ICRC but, in compliance with Cold War dictates, access to areas outside government control was out of the question. UN agencies based inside Afghanistan therefore worked in partnership with government authorities and focused on such residual development activities as the situation and the very limited funds available allowed.[8]

    Cold War parameters defined the limits of humanitarian action. Bona fide UN and NGO humanitarian agencies working in the refugee camps soon found themselves enmeshed in a much larger game in which the Afghan resistance groups, their Pakistani backers, and covert or overt support from Western governments and their partners in the Gulf were heavily involved. The relationships, conditionalities, and compromises that this proximity entailed had wide-ranging consequences at the time as well as in the years to come. The Carter and Reagan foreign-policy doctrines agreed on one point: avenging Vietnam and giving the Soviets a "bloody nose." In order to justify its support to the so-called Afghan freedom fighters, the US government deliberately magnified the threat posed by the Soviet intervention, stating that it threatened "vital interests,"[9] a euphemism for oil and sea lanes. This included the deliberate manipulation of information with claims—now clearly disproved—that the Soviet objective was to gain access to the warm waters of the Indian Ocean and the Gulf.[10] In fact, it is now clear that the US policy was aimed at deliberately provoking the Soviet Union into invading Afghanistan.[11]

This starting point was in many ways the lowest point of principled engagement. The refugee camps became hotbeds for militancy and recruitment, as well as safe havens for combatants.[12] Support went to the most fundamentalist groups. In an "anything goes" atmosphere, literally anything went to groups who later became "our" enemies: political support, cash, training, weaponry, and Stingers. The fundamentalist agenda of the resistance groups that were given preferential treatment—first and foremost Hekmatyar's Hezbi Islami—was well known to the CIA and US policymakers. Gulbuddin Hekmatyar, for example, had an established track record of being anti-women (responsible for acid attacks against unveiled female students at Kabul University in the 1970s), virulently anti-American, allegedly responsible for the killing of moderate pro-king intellectuals, using his weapons primarily against other mujahedin groups, and later doing everything in his power to scuttle international peace initiatives. Further, at least with tacit connivance of the CIA, US funds were utilized by the Pakistani ISI to recruit and equip thousands of foreign radical Muslim fighters in camps straddling the Pakistan-Afghan border. The short-sightedness of the US policy has now been well documented.[13] The Soviets, of course, never ceased to point out that the Reagan administration was supporting international terrorism, a claim which now seems self-evident, but which was then easily dismissed as Cold War rhetoric.

A parallel low point obtained in the humanitarian arena. The anti-Soviet "cause" attracted a motley crowd of young journalists, adventurers, and would-be humanitarians, many of whom had earlier visited Afghanistan as tourists on the hippy trail. They ranged from the innocent and inept to the conspiratorial, with a sprinkling of professionals. Afghan-specific international "solidarity" NGOs soon emerged and, building on the experience gained in the refugee camps, started to provide assistance (initially medical) to mujahedin groups inside Afghanistan. With the exception of a few medical NGOs, the traditional and reputable international NGOs kept their distance from these cross-border operations. In those days of miracle and thunder, mafia-style deals, which strike us as anathema today, were the norm. Crossings of the Pakistan-Afghan border were controlled by the ISI, which in turn was able to determine which areas and commanders could be reached. Many a naive expat aid worker was prepared to endure terrible hardship and danger and to place personal security and hard-collected cash in the hands of often unscrupulous military commanders. Bonds were created from which it proved difficult to disentangle. Many agencies were practically hostages to "their" commanders and found it extremely difficult to move, say, to the next valley, where the needs might have been greater. When assistance was not medical, it was often in the form of cash, a commodity easier to transport on donkeys than food or agricultural implements. Under such "cash for assistance" projects, commanders would purchase food locally and distribute it to their communities. Accountability was minimal if not impossible, given the difficulties of monitoring such activities. In the case of US-financed projects, monitoring could only be done by proxy through Afghan counterparts because, in order to maintain the fiction of "plausible deniability" of US support to the mujahedin, US citizens were banned from crossing into Afghanistan.

The manipulation of assistance was strategic. It allowed commanders at the end of the food and weapons chains to increase their standing in their communities, and it bolstered the legitimacy of the parties to which they bore allegiance. Much competition over the spoils of aid ensued, in which many NGOs were complicit.[14] Moreover, manipulation did not occur only inside Afghanistan. The fast-growing cottage industry of assistance agencies based in the towns of Peshawar and Quetta located near the Pakistan-Afghan border, was infiltrated by staff loyal to resistance parties and became highly politicized. Just as an affiliation to one of the parties was a prerequisite for refugees to receive their ration books, the employment of Afghans by aid agencies was controlled by these same parties. In the larger agencies there was a quota system largely controlled by Hezbi Islami and Jamiat-e-Islami (a more moderate Islamic party headed by Professor Rabbani).[15] Conflicts among resistance parties often spilled over into the assistance community, with threats, racketeering, abductions, bombings, and even killings of Afghan aid workers. In the main, NGOs accepted this reality as the price to pay in support of the Afghan "cause."

This legacy of complicity and collusion between assistance and political agendas that characterized the Cold War period proved very difficult to shake off. When the United Nations appeared on the cross-border scene after the April 1988 UN-brokered Geneva Accords, it had to grapple with the same unsavory reality. Although the first UN Coordinator, Sadruddin Aga Khan, came armed with well-tested humanitarian credentials and a formal agreement with the Kabul authorities and the mujahedin leaders ("humanitarian consensus") that UN agencies could work both in government and mujahedin-controlled areas ("humanitarian encirclement"), most NGOs were unimpressed. UN staff working in government areas—the "bad" United Nations—were seen with particular suspicion, and some NGOs refused to meet with them when they visited Peshawar. The arrival of international assistance through the Soviet Union into northern Afghanistan was also met with a hue and cry. When the USSR itself provided some wheat for delivery to mujahedin areas, the reaction in Peshawar was that "Afghans would prefer to die rather than eat Soviet food."[16] More important, the United Nations found it very difficult to free itself from the shackles of ISI control and from American political pressure. The United Nations as well as the NGOs needed permits to cross the tribal areas bordering Afghanistan. It was thus easy for the ISI to "filter" missions and deliveries.

As the vast majority of refugees in Pakistan were Sunni Pashtuns from the border areas who had tribal and ethnic bonds on the Pakistani side of the border, ISI political and military support went to Pashtun groups such as Hezbi Islami to the detriment of other ethnic or religious groups. Invariably, when the United Nations wanted to go to areas that were not a priority for the ISI, such as Hazarajat—a historically neglected, impoverished, Shia and Iran-friendly area—it would be told that it was "unsafe" to go there or that it was first necessary to provide assistance to all the (Pashtun) communities on the way in order to comply with a "no leapfrogging" principle. UN activities in Pakistan were not immune to such arm-twisting, especially since the ISI had tight control over the refugee camps. UNHCR and WFP were obliged to accept that food was distributed through party-affiliated "ration maliks" rather than to individual refugee families. Diversion to combatants was high and accountability low.[17] Even the fledgling UN mine action program was compromised by partisan agendas because it had to rely on the ISI for the identification of trainees—again on the basis of party quotas—for the procurement of explosives and the selection of the first areas to be cleared of mines in Afghanistan.

Heavy political pressure was often brought to bear on assistance actors. For example, at various times in 1989–91 the United Nations was asked by the ISI and the US Embassy in Islamabad to pre-position food around towns besieged by the mujahedin, such as Kandahar or Khost, to act as a magnet in order to "draw out" the civilian population and facilitate the capture of the towns. This writer recalls one such episode in the fall of 1989 when he was sent, with ISI "minders," to assess the situation of IDPs allegedly fleeing Khost. The UN team was chaperoned by Jalalauddin Haqqani, a senior mujahedin commander (and future Taliban minister) with the closest of links with the ISI, and taken to the hills overlooking Khost from which the town was being pounded. Nicely fingerprinted lists of "IDPs" were presented and caves to be used as wheat warehouses inspected. Attempts to interview IDPs failed as there were only a few nomad families in the vicinity. It became clear that we were being used. Had we pre-positioned the food, the message to the besieged civilians of Khost would have been: Come out! The United Nations is ready to help you. In this particular case the United Nations was able to resist, but faced with stronger pressure, or with implicit threats that access to certain areas would be curtailed, agencies often agreed to pay such "tickets" in order to safeguard their programs. Western donors, in particular the United States, were also initially critical of the "cross-line" programs that the United Nations began to establish from its bases in government-held towns, as these were seen as bolstering the flagging image of the Soviet-supported government. For example, it was occasionally alleged that UN food convoys from government-held cities to mujahedin-controlled areas were being used as cover for government military operations.

Infiltration and manipulation were not the sole prerogative of one side in the conflict. The government authorities in Kabul, and their extensive security apparatus, were adept at harassing local staff (or worse), at putting pressure on UN agencies to undertake high-visibility projects in the cities, and at denying access to certain areas or groups of vulnerable Afghans. However, given their embattled condition and the fact that, apart from the ICRC and small UN offices in Kabul and the major cities, the bulk of the aid bazaar was based in Pakistan, their leverage was minimal. Generally speaking, government authorities prided themselves in respecting the "humanitarian consensus" they had subscribed to at the UN's behest.

The instrumentalization of assistance during the cross-border period had a number of lasting negative effects: it contributed to the legitimization of the Peshawar-based Pashtun resistance parties and allowed them to increase and consolidate their patronage, including through Afghan "NGOs" they established; it resulted in the concentration of assistance in Pashtun areas and the neglect of equally or more deserving communities further afield in the center or north of the country; it corrupted the culture of the aid community for many years by encouraging "happy-go-lucky" approaches to accountability, if not outright identification with the "muj" cause and its objectives; it delayed the emergence of more professional and principled approaches such as those already being developed in other conflict situations (for example, the Ground Rules negotiated in the southern Sudan between the aid community and the belligerents); it fostered one-sided approaches and selective amnesia on the issue of human rights violations by the mujahedin; and finally, it thrived on the demonization of the enemy and preempted for several years the emergence of any substantive discourse on peace and reconciliation, subjects considered taboo at the time.

THE CIVIL WAR AND THE TRIUMPH OF WARLORDISM (1992–96)

It took the collapse of the Kabul government in April 1992 and the infighting among the mujahedin that ensued to clear the air somewhat. All of a sudden there was no longer a cause. The humanitarian imperative to alleviate human suffering took center stage. The glamour of the cross-border days rapidly evaporated. The stubborn fact that the conflict was a ruthless struggle for power with no real ideological stakes, coupled with donor and public disillusionment, triggered considerable soul-searching and a healthy debate on the need for professionalism in the humanitarian community. This was facilitated by staff turnover and the arrival on the Afghan scene of individuals and organizations that had experience in other crisis settings. This process had already started under the stewardship of the United Nations after the Geneva Accords, which, in addition to defining the timetable for the Soviet withdrawal, set the stage for a major assistance effort and a strong assistance coordination mechanism, the UN Office for the Coordination of Assistance to Afghanistan, also known as Operation Salam. Coordination was facilitated by strong leadership and, importantly, the availability of relatively high amounts of un-earmarked funds for which UN agencies and NGOs were vying. After the fall of Kabul, greater emphasis on transparency and accountability in the aid community accelerated the demise of many "truck-by-night" NGOs and put a premium on professionalism.

Nevertheless, it took years to weed out the infiltration of Hezbi Islami and other groups in the NGOs. As late as 1995 it was still difficult, if not impossible, to raise certain issues that were deemed too sensitive.[18] When an NGO organized a workshop on "reconciliation," the UN coordination body was loath to participate because the subject was still considered anathema by all mujahedin factions; the same applied to the issue of human rights where the ritualistic condemnation of the abuses of the Soviet invaders was not complemented by any desire to address those of the mujahedin.

1996–SEPTEMBER 10, 2001: PRINCIPLES SAVED BY THE TALIBAN?

Fast-forwarding to the "Taliban years," the situation was very different. A conjunction of factors made it a high point for principled intervention by aid agencies. Once the Soviets had been defeated, Afghanistan practically fell off the political map of the international community. The internecine fighting was of little strategic interest. The conflict had become an orphan of the Cold War; the factions had lost their "parents" and were left to their own, violent devices. UN peace initiatives went nowhere. Instead, humanitarian action was the only form of actual international engagement and was just sufficient, perhaps, to prevent the crisis from spinning out of control and engulfing the region. When the first stirrings of the Taliban movement gripped southern Afghanistan in late 1994, the aid community on the ground and at headquarters was busy asking itself hard questions: Are we unwittingly fueling the war? How can we be more effective and accountable in a volatile and warlord-ridden environment? New ideas, some imported from other crisis situations, influenced the debate, including the "do no harm" approach, which was predicated on the idea that capacities for peace could be built through carefully targeted assistance at the local level.[19] There was also growing recognition that in Afghanistan the humanitarian/development distinction did not make much sense because there were large swathes of the country where there was neither war nor peace, just grinding poverty and relative stability. In these areas more durable rehabilitation projects were deemed possible; the key constraint was not insecurity but lack of funds. Some, in Afghanistan and elsewhere,[20] started airing the notion that it was necessary to "do development" in conflict situations or at least to maximize the logic of peace wherever possible through assistance, including those interventions aimed at the promotion of sustainable livelihoods.[21]

Breaking new ground: The Strategic Framework for Afghanistan

The combination of soul-searching at the local level and the global quest for improved UN action in crisis countries resulted in a quantum leap in policy development. In 1997 the secretary-general of the United Nations proposed, and his UN agency counterparts agreed, to test an innovative and more unitary approach in Afghanistan: the Strategic Framework. Recognizing the failures of the recent past, the aim was to bridge the disconnects among the political, assistance, and human rights strategies relating to Afghanistan so that the combined synergies would contribute to the quest for peace.[22] The starting point was the realization—at a major workshop of donors, NGOs and UN agencies in late 1997—that no one knew if assistance was part of the problem or part of the solution. There were no tools to measure the impact of myriad small-scale projects. Hence the need for a more unitary and accountable approach based on clear principles and human rights objectives while at the same time nurturing a better dialogue with the "political UN."

Policy innovation in Afghanistan benefited from the fact that in Western capitals and at UN HQ political interest in the Afghan quagmire had fallen to an all-time low. The UN political mission had lost credibility, a view shared by Afghans and the aid community.[23] As a result, the only people paying attention to the crisis were the humanitarian players in the headquarters of the United Nations and donor capitals as well as in the field. They had a relatively free rein to test out new ideas. Also, the absence of high political stakes facilitated consensus-building among donors and assistance partners. Concern for the plight of Afghans, coupled with growing frustration with the Taliban and their perceived imperviousness to the basic tenets of international behavior in general, and humanitarianism in particular, resulted in a widespread realization that the most reasonable option for effective action had to be based on enhanced coherence among the various instruments at the disposal of the international community. An additional important factor was the emerging deviousness of the Taliban themselves, who were becoming masters at giving conflicting signals and playing one part of the aid community against the other. An agreed overall strategy and "speaking with one voice" became widely recognized objectives.

The SF was officially launched in September 1998. All UN agencies formally endorsed it, though some did so reluctantly. Its success was predicated on coordination arrangements that were more robust than in any other crisis situation (with the possible exception of the first UN-led coordination structure in Afghanistan, 1988–91). Disbelievers and naysayers abounded in the NGO community and within the United Nations. The former were concerned that their wings might be clipped if donor funding became conditional on subscription to the SF and that their independence of action would be curtailed by what they saw as a coordination straitjacket. The latter, UNHCR, WFP, and UNICEF in particular, were resistant to coordination by bureaucratic instinct and retreated behind their "mandates" in an effort to escape it. The strong support of donors saved the day: they saw in the SF the potential for a new approach in failed state environments as well as an opportunity to increase the accountability and effectiveness of the aid system. In the words of one senior donor representative, "We had to read the riot act to the UN agencies" to make it clear that their full compliance to the SF was expected.[24]

On the assistance side, a coherent and principled approach was facilitated by the strengthening of the UN Coordinator and his office. The humanitarian and (residual) development coordination functions had been merged into one office in 1997. Human rights and gender advisory functions were added in early 1999. Public information/spokesperson functions, information management, security and flight operations for the aid community, as well as the largest mine action program in the world, were put under the same roof. The UN field coordination office, based in Islamabad for security reasons, and its seven sub-offices within Afghanistan became the service centers for the assistance community, providing information, particularly on security matters, and space for meetings and coordination of programs. More important, UNCO became the hub of policymaking for humanitarian and human rights matters in the assistance community as well as a key player in interactions with the Taliban and the peace process.

Substantively, as a result of the SF, UN agencies, NGOs, and donors had for the first time subscribed to a set of common principles and strategic objectives aimed at maximizing the synergy among assistance, human rights, and political action, as well as the internal coherence of the assistance effort itself. Unusually, the principles and some of the modalities (for example, do's and don'ts with the Taliban, speaking with one voice on issues of principle, security arrangements for staff) were binding for the United Nations.[25] Some more radical ideas contained in the first drafts of the SF had to be abandoned because of the tooth-and-nail resistance of the UN operational agencies, notably the idea of a common fund for Afghanistan from which a single assistance program would be financed. Nevertheless, the SF provided a coherent strategy and instilled a sense of meaning to the disparate projects and activities of what had been until then a fractious assistance community. Principles took center stage, the key issue being how to engage with the Taliban (and the other presumptive authorities) while simultaneously maximizing the opportunities to alleviate suffering and protect sustainable livelihoods.

Technically, the normative aspects of the SF applied only to UN entities. It was therefore seen as a "UN thing." The principles, however, were translated into practice through principled common programming (PCP) mechanisms on the ground, which involved UN agencies, NGOs, and donors and which elicited wider subscription. In addition to a donor-coordination body, the Afghanistan Support Group, which met twice a year in a donor capital, and a tripartite (donor, United Nations, NGO) Afghanistan Programming Body, which met regularly in Islamabad, an array of thematic, sectoral, national, and sub-national programming bodies was established. The servicing of this architecture by UNCO was a complex and sometimes ungrateful task. The bodies worked more or less well, as did the UNCO sub-offices in the field. The transaction costs of coordination were high, and given the general scarcity of resources, some agencies felt that the elaborate architecture of the SF and PCP worked against effectiveness. PCP worked better the more it was focused. For example, compared to other countries in crisis, real progress was made in the preparation of the annual program and appeal for funds that included the combined requirements of UN agencies and NGOs. The coordination of efforts to combat the effects of massive drought and displacement in 1999–2001 was also relatively successful. Both processes—SF and PCP—generated continuous debate in the aid community that was matched by frequently diverging positions and acrimony on how to deal with abusive authorities. Overall, however, from mid 1998 to September 2001, there was more unity of purpose and support for principled engagement in the assistance community in Afghanistan than at any time previously.

On the political side, things were more difficult. The three pillars of the SF—political, assistance, and human rights—did not have the same height. Although formally on board with the SF, and in fact originally entrusted by the secretary-general with the overall development of the concept, the "political UN" was institutionally averse to working closely with its humanitarian and human rights counterparts.[26] The UN Department of Political Affairs was allergic to the notion that humanitarian and human rights objectives were of comparable value to those of a political nature. The problem related in part to authority and control: As in other crisis countries there were different views at UN headquarters and in the field as to who was in charge overall, a sensitive issue made more acute by the relative size of the UN humanitarian establishment—large and with roots all around the country—and the political mission—small and with a credibility problem, given its track record.[27] Moreover, the disagreements and misunderstandings among the political, assistance, and human rights pillars within the UN system were also cultural. The political pillar saw itself as the emanation of the secretary-general (if not the Security Council), while the human rights pillar claimed a legitimacy inherent in the UN Charter, and the humanitarians set their bearings on the basis of international humanitarian law. This led to tensions between the UN humanitarian and human rights staffs, on the one hand, and their political colleagues on issues related to abuses and how to deal with information on mass killings (see Chapter 4). Other problems arose over the sanctions against the Taliban and their humanitarian implications.

In the final analysis the "political UN" either did not understand or was not interested in the SF's main assumption; namely, that it made sense from a peace-making perspective to pursue systematically synergies among the three pillars of UN action in Afghanistan. No less important, perhaps, humanitarian and human rights action got caught up—again—in superpower politics. The UN humanitarian agencies on the ground, under the leadership of the UN Coordinator, took a strong position on the first UN-mandated sanctions against the Taliban (November 1999), and again when these were strengthened to include a one-sided arms embargo (December 2000) which most aid workers saw as a recipe for the continuation of the war. In an unusual step the UN Coordinator was invited to address the Security Council in early 2001, where he made a strong intervention highlighting the humanitarian implications of sanctions. This did not go down well with those council members bent on demonizing the Taliban (US, UK, and Russia) nor with the Northern Alliance in Afghanistan. While the UN country team remained united in its approach of principled engagement with the Taliban—which was seen as the only possible strategy for effective humanitarian action on the ground—UN headquarters, the United States, and Russia, and occasionally the media, were sometimes critical of the approach, which was seen as "accommodationist."[28] The counter-argument from the field was that painting the Taliban into a corner would not work; rather, it would strengthen their siege mentality and the hand of the hard-liners. Distance tended to reduce the situation to black-and-white terms, whereas the difficulties of engaging with the Taliban to alleviate the massive suffering of Afghans ranged from pitch black to various shades of gray.

In conclusion, while on the political side the SF had relatively little impact on how business was conducted, on the humanitarian front, after some initial confusion on how to interact with the Taliban,[29] the SF provided a template for principled engagement. The reasoning that prevailed was that principled engagement would provide a better environment in which humanitarian needs could be met, that the Taliban would come to understand and respect the principles and modus operandi of assistance agencies, and that interaction with the aid community would bear fruit in terms of an "opening up" of the regime. By and large in 1999–2000 the consensus within the donor community in Islamabad supported this approach. Donors and the UN Coordinator regularly worked together, including through joint démarches with the Taliban leadership and public statements to ensure that the Taliban received the same message. As we shall see, the results were mixed.

FROM FAILED TO ROGUE STATE

As the Taliban regime's hold on Afghanistan strengthened and its prospects for international recognition waned, the regime hardened. This not only made life more difficult for Afghans and for aid agencies trying to provide much-needed assistance, but it also resulted in more partisan politics and more attempts to instrumentalize humanitarian action. The United States was initially benevolent to the Taliban takeover.[30] Soon, however, hopes for stability and pipelines were replaced by concern for Taliban policies toward women, poppy production, and the safe haven provided to Osama bin Laden and various other groups of similar ilk.[31] Feminist rhetoric and demonization of the Taliban began to clog the airwaves and had direct negative consequences for the aid community, including various attempts by the United States and the UK to impose conditionalities on UN and NGO assistance. Citing security concerns, after the US missile strikes against Osama bin Laden's training camps in Afghanistan (August 1998), the US and UK governments asked the UN secretary-general to refrain from deploying nationals from these two countries to Afghanistan. Despite the objections of his field staff, who pointed out that such selective treatment was not in line with the UN Charter, the secretary-general complied.[32] Pressure on the NGOs was even stronger: While the United States strongly cautioned its nationals not to travel to Afghanistan, the UK made its funding to NGOs conditional on respecting the travel ban for UK nationals. Several NGOs refused to comply and lost their funding. The UK also tried to force the United Nations to stop flying UK-funded NGO staff on its planes. The UN Coordinator refused to do so, and the UK withdrew its pledge, equivalent to US$1.5 million, to subsidize NGO travel on the UN aircraft. This resulted in a doubling of fares, increased overhead costs, and greater difficulties in access to vulnerable communities.

Taliban-bashing became a sport in which feminist and human rights groups, international media personalities, a European Union commissioner, and a variety of self-appointed experts on things Afghan distinguished themselves for the sophistication of their analyses. Black-and-white reporting abounded, with little attention to the many nuances of the situation on the ground. Visitors and remote control experts on Afghanistan were quick to condemn the Taliban for their abuse of women and girls. They failed to note, however, that women's access to health was as much a function of derelict health structures as of Taliban restrictions, that, despite official policy, NGO-supported girls' schools were often tolerated by local leaders, and that there were probably more opportunities for girls to go to school in many rural areas than at any other time in Afghan history. The Taliban were by and large a mean and uneducated bunch, but their mujahedin predecessors were hardly paragons of enlightenment. Dispassionate analysis became more difficult with rhetoric and single-issue politics obfuscating a reality that was grim but not uniform. The one-sidedness of much of the analysis and reporting, including on human rights matters, may well have been a factor in the hardening of the regime and the increasing influence of Osama bin Laden and the other foreign "guests" on the Taliban leadership. There were other factors as well: the failure to gain international legitimacy, which the Taliban saw as a conspiracy against them; and the stalemate on the battlefield.

Engaging with the Taliban was an exhausting task made more difficult by the fact that Taliban interlocutors frequently changed and that positions on policy matters taken in one location or ministry were often different in another. More important, the language, principles, and objectives of the Taliban and external actors were often incompatible. Discussions shifted from "two steps forward, one step back" to "two steps back, half step forward." While such discussions led to important advances in some areas (access of women to health care, immunization, some improved humanitarian access), progress was elusive on the core issues of girls' education, women's rights, protection of civilians, and human rights in general.

A good example of the difficulties and frustrations of negotiating with the Taliban is provided by the ill-fated Memorandum of Understanding (MOU) signed by the United Nations and the Taliban in May 1998 to try to resolve a standoff between the Taliban and the aid community on the issue of girls' education and various other problems relating to the functioning of the aid community in Afghanistan. A team specially dispatched from UN headquarters held a series of high-level meetings with Taliban ministers to try to unblock a tense situation—made worse by posturing on both sides—with the aim of arriving at an agreed modus operandi. The two teams entered the negotiations with very different expectations: The New York team wanted the Taliban to subscribe to the precepts of the UN charter and human rights instruments as a prerequisite for an agreement; the Taliban wanted to tie any agreement to increased levels of assistance and to international recognition of their regime. Predictably, the result was a shaky compromise with the Taliban accepting that girls' education opportunities would increase over time and that the issue of women's rights would be settled on the basis of advice to be provided by reputable (but undefined) Islamic scholars, while the United Nations on its side agreed to a number of specific assistance projects (eleven schools for girls to be financed by Norway, various medical/hospital projects, and so on).

Problems with the MOU started even before the ink was dry. The pragmatic approach taken by the United Nations was heavily criticized in the media. Trade unions in Europe condemned it as a violation of UN International Labour Organization standards, and feminist groups demanded its revocation. Implementation of the agreement was supposed to be ironed out in technical committees that proved unworkable; Taliban delegations changed constantly or appeared not to be in the picture as to the specifics of the agreement and what it entailed. Differing interpretations emerged in Kabul, the formal capital, and Kandahar, Mullah Omar's capital. Attempts to set up a schedule of meetings on specific issues failed amid accusations by the Taliban that the United Nations was reneging on the agreement.

In the end, the technical committees achieved little. The schools to be rebuilt were never identified, and the opinion of the Islamic scholars that had been chosen from the Islamic University in Cairo (modestly favorable to female employment) was denounced by the Taliban. By early 2000 the MOU process had ground to a halt. Both sides, it seems, had learned that more could be achieved by lower-profile technical meetings. In noncontroversial sectors such as immunization, water and sanitation, and agriculture better understandings were reached. Progress was constrained more by constant lack of funds than by Taliban policies. Nevertheless, the Taliban kept on reminding the United Nations that it had not delivered on its part of the MOU deal. The wording on the "gradual" advancements for girls education continued to be seen by many as a blemish on the UN's conscience.

What had been a process of slow and painful incremental progress came to an abrupt halt in the summer of 2000 when the Taliban supreme leader, Mullah Omar, signed Edict 8 banning employment of Afghan women by aid agencies except in the health sector. The relationship further worsened when UN-mandated sanctions were strengthened in December 2000 to include a one-sided arms embargo and because of the increasing negative press on the Taliban human rights record. A last attempt to negotiate an agreement on "minimum operational requirements" for humanitarian action collapsed in the spring of 2001, when the Taliban insisted that international humanitarian law principles would be acceptable only if they did not contravene their interpretation of Islamic precepts and Taliban Emirate policies. Principles also came under stress from donor capitals and UN headquarters. There was a sense that the field was going too far in raising "sensitive" issues such as the UN *fatwa* banning US/UK nationals from UN postings in Afghanistan, the public position taken by UN staff in the field against the humanitarian implications of sanctions, and their criticism of the public discourse on rights issues where only the abuses committed by the Taliban were seen and condemned.

As engagement became more and more difficult and the authorities more abusive, it became evident to aid agencies on the ground that the Taliban were deliberately transitioning from failed to rogue state. Humanitarian action, including greater attention than before to the plight of civilians in need of protection, had helped to reduce suffering. But the crisis was deepening; the worst drought in living memory combined with the continuing conflict and increasing violations against civilians were taking a heavy toll. The Taliban were still bent on defeating their opponents on the battlefield. Their offensives north of Kabul (late 1999) and in Takhar (summer 2000) were particularly brutal, as were their repeated forays into Hazarajat. Hundreds of thousands of civilians were involuntarily displaced. Scorched-earth tactics included the burning of houses, crops, and agricultural assets. Several thousand civilians were deliberately killed.[33] In 2001 the numbers of people internally displaced by drought and conflict exceeded one million. The plight of families too poor to move, or prevented from moving—"internally stuck people"—was even worse. The capacity of the assistance agencies was stretched to breaking point, and resources were woefully inadequate. In retrospect, the underlying assumption of the SF—that aid could help advance human rights and contribute to the quest for a political solution by creating "spaces" for rehabilitation and even development as well as fostering the logic of peace—had reached its structural limits.

This does not necessarily mean that the theory was wrong; it could be that it did not have sufficient time to mature. The objective of the SF was to minimize the disconnects and maximize the synergy between political, humanitarian, and human rights actions. This was based on two assumptions: that synergy would in itself have a positive impact on conflict resolution; and that as the three pillars of UN action were meant to subscribe to the same clearly defined principles, this would provide better insurance against instrumentalization of the humanitarian or human rights agendas to achieve short-term political gain. That there could be friction or even opposing perspectives between political and humanitarian actors was to be expected, but it was assumed that day-to-day proximity, commitment to core UN values, and a clear understanding of each other's perspectives would result in a more unified and informed response than separation or insulation of the humanitarian and human rights component from the political endeavor.

POST–SEPTEMBER 11: PRINCIPLES UNDER STRESS

In mid 2003 it was already difficult to recall the misery and dereliction of Afghanistan prior to September 11. Profound underdevelopment had been compounded by twenty-two years of war, massive displacement, human rights abuses, grinding poverty, and the unending drought. Socio-economic indicators—health, education, access to food and water—were at rock bottom, practically the worst in the world. Afghans eked out a bare-bones existence, sometimes alleviated by international assistance. For the vast majority, life was dark, cold, and vulnerable to illness, to the vagaries of war, and to the abuses of a brutish regime.

Moreover, there was no state to speak of. There was barely a nation, in the sense that, while none of the parties in conflict openly advocated changes to its borders, Afghanistan had succumbed to massive external interference, cross-border criminalized economic pillaging, and some incorporation into the external economies of its neighbors (at least of Pakistan and Iran). The unitary state, which historically had been very weak, had failed and fractured. Temporary "statelets" had waxed and waned during the 1992–96 period, while large swathes of rural Afghanistan remained for all practical purposes stateless.[34] The Taliban appeared less as a state-building entity than as an inchoate movement driven by rigorous Islamic principles, jihad, and later, an anti-Western agenda. Semiliterate rural religious zealots, led by fundamentalist ideologues trained in Pakistani *madrassas*, had taken the reins of power. They had very little to offer in terms of a state project. Instead, they focused on security—successfully de-weaponizing the areas they controlled and coopting or eliminating local mujahedin commanders—

and on repression by imposing dress codes, compulsory prayers, and other restrictive measures of social control. In the vast Pashtun crescent, from south of Herat to north of Jalalabad, *Pax Talibana* was imposed and cautiously welcomed—it corresponded, after all, to traditional Pashtun mores. In the non-Pashtun provinces and front-line areas, where the Taliban were reviled, terror tactics were the key instrument of governance.

Over time, after the combined failures of rapprochement with the international community, the UN-supported peace initiatives, and attempts to win decisively on the battlefield, the Taliban regime fell prey to its hard-liner elements and, to an extent as yet unknown, to Osama bin Laden and his cohorts. Afghanistan thus spiraled deeper into a complex crisis with many ramifications: internal and external; political and military; social and economic; humanitarian and human rights.

In addition, and important for the future, the failure of the institutions of the state had become a central element of the crisis and had to be addressed as such. There were hardly any functioning institutions, and those that existed were not legitimate in the eyes of the international community. This meant that the United Nations and the NGOs, spurred by their Western donors, turned their back on the remnants of the state and worked in a kind of parallel universe. The assistance community created its own institutions (coordination bodies, SFs, common programs) that were functional to its needs. It committed itself to a more coherent and principled approach aimed at maximizing synergies among humanitarian action, the advancement of human rights, and the elusive quest for peace. Working under, and often in confrontation with the Taliban was not easy. Aid agencies faced a double challenge: to expand and safeguard humanitarian space in the face of blatant disregard for international humanitarian norms; and to convince donors that investing in Afghans was not a lost cause and that it was possible to work in a principled manner to save lives and rebuild livelihoods without supporting abusive authorities.

The UNCO, supported by the entities comprising the Afghanistan programming body (donors, UN agencies, and NGOs) de facto assumed the functions of a surrogate "Ministry of Planning." It provided a framework for the prioritization of the scarce resources for humanitarian and rehabilitation assistance and a forum where issues of principle and strategic concerns could be discussed. It did its best to coordinate and maximize complementarity between disparate programs and to ensure that the many agencies substituting for "governmental" functions—education, health care, mine clearance—did so as part of an agreed common program. This approach was not without problems, and the results were mixed; it was nonetheless a step ahead of other countries in crisis.

Then came September 11, and the Afghan crisis was blown into another dimension. At the time there were perhaps twenty UN international staff in Kabul, another forty around the country, and a couple of hundred expatriate NGO personnel. Humanitarian action—protection of civilians, food aid, drought relief, mine clearance, basic health services—was the only show in town. Less than two years later the scenery has changed utterly. The aid bazaar has set up shop with a vengeance; there are now several thousand internationals in Kabul alone (more than four hundred for the United Nations); and white Land Cruisers with strange, insect-like antennas speed around every corner.

And there is an internationally recognized government, brought in, as some Afghans say, "walking on American legs" or "singing an American tune." The calendar, if not the contents, of the Bonn Agreement has been formally respected and, after a somewhat fractious Loya Jirga, a transitional administration is now in place.[35] Pitfalls abound, but there remains room for some optimism that Afghanistan will successfully manage the transition from failed/rogue state to a "recovering" and hopefully "democratic" state based on the rule of law while at the same time avoiding the quicksand of a "beggar" state surviving on international handouts.

Optimism should be tempered, however, because the perils of nation-building are momentous. A number of key issues need to be resolved.

WHO SHOULD DO IT?

The "light footprint" approach adopted, at least in principle, by the SRSG and head of UNAMA Lakhdar Brahimi—which is by no means "light " in terms of staff—refers to the fact that, unlike Kosovo or East Timor, the international community has no stomach to run Afghanistan or to involve itself directly with troops, tanks, and administrators in patching the country together. Rather, the UN's role as outlined in the UNAMA mandate is to capacitate the interim and transitional administrations and thereby promote and defend Afghan ownership of the state recovery process. To many this is a dangerous gamble. The ATA has little influence outside Kabul. Security remains volatile around the country and in mid 2003 seemed to be deteriorating, with more remnants of the Taliban reemerging and reorganizing. Support from the regional warlords, who are militarily and financially entrenched, is tenuous, and the prospects for the deployment of peace-keepers around the country are dim. Moreover, the ATA derives its legitimacy from international processes (namely, the Bonn Agreement and Security Council resolutions) and from an emergency Loya Jirga that many Afghans see as orchestrated by outsiders (read: US envoys)[36] rather than from an endogenous political process. In the absence of "heavy" international commitment to ensure the security and protection of Afghan citizens or of a thorough reconciliation process percolating through the fabric of society, the approach has been characterized as "nation-building lite."[37] International support is hostage to fortune: The Coalition forces may tire of "imperial policing," declare victory and leave; or the donors may tire of lack of progress and move their chips elsewhere. Ordinary Afghans, who see little evidence of change, were showing growing impatience by mid 2003.

THE KABUL BUBBLE

The deployment of ISAF troops, the establishment of the ATA, the "aid rush," and the return of many expatriate Afghan technocrats (as well as more than half a million refugees) make Kabul the "Klondike of the new century."[38] While fledgling government institutions are slowly re-emerging, assorted teams of nation-builders are frenetically working on development frameworks, national plans, feasibility studies, aid-tracking systems, employment strategies, and the like. "Aidspeak" is all. The beehive feel of Kabul makes the contrast with the rest of the country even more stark. The writ of Kabul on the provinces is more theoretical than real, and not only because the regional leaders run their own show, often with resources and other support provided by external patrons. Capacity and institutions of governance are weak or nonexistent outside the capital. When they exist, they are disconnected from the center, sometimes by design but most often by default, since provincial departments have very little opportunity or means of communicating with their respective ministries in Kabul. Policies and decisions can take weeks to travel to the provinces or do not travel at all. The further from Kabul, the thinner the aid presence becomes. In many areas, remoteness, volatile security, attacks on civilians, attacks and threats against foreigners, the erosion of coping mechanisms, abject poverty, and the near absence of any functioning state institutions offer a very different perspective to the upbeat mood in Kabul.

AFGHAN OWNERSHIP

Under the Taliban, because of their abusive policies, capacity building of state institutions was taboo except in those areas—like health, agriculture, or mine clearance—where it could be assumed that the rights of Afghans would not be undermined by interacting with the authorities. This meant that the bulk of assistance was humanitarian in nature and that the limited development assistance that was possible basically short-circuited Taliban institutions. With the establishment of the first Karzai administration in December 2001, this policy was turned on its head. While enormous humanitarian needs remained, the emphasis of the discourse shifted to development, and with it national ownership became the mantra. The United Nations eschewed its earlier "surrogate government" role and placed itself behind the new administration. In theory, aid agencies fully supported this as well as the mental gymnastics required to adapt to the new situation. In practice, old habits die hard. Donors were not confident that the authorities could effectively handle money in large amounts. As late as the summer of 2002 joint UN-ATA missions to the regions demonstrated that aid agencies were still "doing their own thing" with little reference to the authorities, whether regional or central. This was partly due to the center-periphery disconnects mentioned above. But two additional reasons stand out. On the one hand, aid agencies are still very much in humanitarian mode. They are also suddenly fully resourced and under pressure to show results, and they have little time to nurture local capacity. On the other hand, the multiplication of actors, disparate donor policies, and the bilateralization of aid have made coordination on the ground and by the government that much more difficult. Proposals for a development trust fund, echoing the ideas of the original SF, which would have allowed for a more rational allocation of resources were—again—not supported by key donors. This resulted in bouts of animosity between President Karzai and the aid community made worse by the perceived reluctance of donors to fulfill their pledges amid accusations that funds were being spent on the high salaries of an army of expatriates rather than on Afghans.[39]

PEACE WITHOUT JUSTICE?

One of the paradoxical and unsavory results of the Coalition intervention to topple the Taliban is that the warlords that ruled Afghanistan in the 1992–96 mujahedin period are back in power, courtesy of the US military. For many Afghans who lived through that anarchic period this brings back sinister memories. Human rights abuses were rife then, and a well-documented pattern of abuse has continued post-Bonn.[40] The conventional wisdom among senior UN and donor officials in Kabul throughout 2002 was that "politics is the art of the possible" and that it was not opportune to tackle issues of impunity and accountability for war crimes in the immediate post-Bonn period. Karzai indicated that, for now, justice was a "luxury," and Brahimi said that the welfare of the living had to take precedence over accounting for the dead.[41] While in early 2003 there was wider recognition within and outside Afghanistan that the warlord issue had to be tackled, as has so often been the case in the Afghan crisis, politics still trump principles. This may well work in the short term. In the long term, it may turn out to be morally unsustainable, if not politically unwise. Experience elsewhere has shown the risks of not linking peace with justice.[42] Unless the issue of impunity is tackled—and the vicious circle of abuses, deteriorating security, and jeopardized development opportunities is broken—durable and sustainable peace will remain elusive.

A stable social compact in Afghanistan is unlikely as long as warlords with a disreputable past are able to wield political, military, and economic power and are able to threaten the formal legitimacy of the ATA as well as the rights and well-being of the populations they control. This is not only an issue of principle—and one that needs to be tracked in the months and years to come—but it is also an issue of survival for some twenty-five million Afghans who are concerned that their hopes for peace and stability may be dashed. As we have seen at the beginning of this chapter, short-term gain in Afghanistan is often a prelude to long-term pain. The failure of the international community to support the ATA on the issues of impunity and accountability, and to provide it with the means to rein in warlordism, carries the threat of yet another spiral of violence and abuses.

Notes

[1] Michael Ignatieff, "Nation-Building Lite," *The New York Times,* July 28, 2002.

[2] For example, I have been able to find only one real-time analysis of the role of NGOs in Afghanistan written during the Cold War period (Helga Baitenmann, "NGOs and the Afghan War: The Politicization of Humanitarian Aid," *Third World Quarterly* [January 1990]). Between 1990 and 2002 only two studies deal with the issue, albeit tangentially (Antonio Donini, *The Policies of Mercy: UN Coordination in Afghanistan, Mozambique and* Rwanda, Occasional Paper 22 [Providence, R.I.: Thomas J. Watson Institute for International Studies, 1996]; and Nigel Nicholds with John Borton, *The Changing Role of NGOs in the Provision of Relief and Rehabilitation Assistance: Case Study 1—Afghanistan/Pakistan,* Working Paper 74 [London: ODI, 1994]). Fiona Terry's recent book, *Condemned to Repeat: The Paradox of Humanitarian Action* (Ithaca, N.Y.: Cornell University Press, 2002), includes a chapter on the Afghan refugee issue and its implications for humanitarianism; it analyzes in part the cross-border solidarity days.

[3] See, in particular, works by Barnett R. Rubin, William Maley, Gilles Dorronsoro, Ahmed Rashid, and Michael Barry. All are strong on analysis of political-military developments but short on the political economy of humanitarian action in the Afghan context.

[4] See, for example, Ignatieff, "Nation-Building Lite."

[5] For exceptions, see in particular Mark Duffield, Patricia Gossman, and Nicholas Leader, *A Review of the Strategic Framework for Afghanistan* (Kabul: Strategic Monitoring Unit, now AREU, 2002); and Antonio Donini, Eric Dudley, Ron Ockwell, *Afghanistan: Coordination in a Fragmented State,* a Lessons Learned Report (New York: UN/DHA, 1996).

[6] Nicholas Stockton, *Strategic Coordination in Afghanistan* (Kabul: AREU, 2002); Centre for Humanitarian Dialogue, *Politics and Humanitarianism:*

Coherence in Crisis? (Geneva, February 2003); and the "Beyond Brahimi" report, *A Review of Peace Operations: A Case for Change. Afghanistan (A Snapshot Study)* (London: Kings College, 2003); as well as other reports commissioned by AREU, OCHA, ODI, and ICG (available from their respective websites).

[7] A vast gray literature exists in the archives of aid agencies (and in the memories of aid workers), which remains largely untapped.

[8] After the Soviet invasion most internationally supported aid projects were frozen. Post-1989 some UN funds were unfrozen with the concurrence of the Kabul regime for emergency rehabilitation activities in mujahedin-controlled areas.

[9] Jimmy Carter, State of the Union address, January 1980: "The Soviet invasion poses an incredible threat . . . to vital resources and to vital sea lanes."

[10] See Andrew Hartman, "'The Red Template': US Policy in Soviet-occupied Afghanistan," *Third World Quarterly* 23/3 (2002).

[11] In an interview with *Le nouvel observateur,* January 15, 1998, Z. Brezezinski, President Carter's national security adviser, boasted that the United States through its support to fledgling Islamist and anti-communist guerrillas, had deliberately "drawn" the Soviets into Afghanistan (quoted in Hartman, "The Red Template"). The Soviets were worried by the explosion of Islamic fundamentalism on their southern flank and by the prospects of its expansion into the "stans" of Central Asia. One is left wondering what might have happened had the United States seen this "axis of evil" coming a bit earlier.

[12] See Terry, *Condemned to Repeat,* chap. 2.

[13] See Hartman, "The Red Template"; see also works by William Maley cited later in this chapter. As Fiona Terry, puts it, "The greatest irony is reserved for the United States, which ended up at war with the very forces it had been instrumental in creating" (*Condemned to Repeat,* 78).

[14] "Some rebels have given the right to work in their areas to the highest-bidding NGO" (Baitenmann, "NGOs and the Afghan War," 73).

[15] It was not uncommon for aspiring employees to change party affiliation if a particular quota was full with a particular aid agency.

[16] Internal UN memo (October 1989).

[17] See Baitenmann, "NGOs and the Afghan War"; Terry, *Condemned to Repeat.*

[18] Author's interviews with NGO and UN staff in Peshawar and Kabul in April 1995.

[19] The influence of the "building communities for peace approach," developed by Mary B. Anderson, is discussed in Chapter 2 in this volume.

[20] See, for example, Jan Pronk, minister for Development Cooperation of the Netherlands, in his speech at the International Forum on Afghanistan, Ashkabad, Turkmenistan, January 1997.

[21] See Michael Keating, "Dilemmas of Humanitarian Assistance in Afghanistan," in *Fundamentalism Reborn? Afghanistan and the Taliban,* ed. William Maley (New York: New York University Press, 1998); and Donini et al. *Afghanistan.*

[22] On the origins of the SF, see Duffield, Gossman, and Leader, *A Review of the Strategic Framework for Afghanistan;* and Antonio Donini, *The Strategic Framework for Afghanistan: A Preliminary Assessment* (Islamabad: UNOCHA,

1999). The Donini article and related documents, including the text of the SF, are available online.

[23] William Maley, "The UN in Afghanistan: 'Doing Its Best' or 'Failure of a Mission,'" in Maley, *Fundamentalism Reborn?*

[24] At a donor meeting in London in June 1998 donor displeasure was evident. When some UN agency representatives questioned the usefulness of the SF (which had not yet been formally adopted), the chair instructed them to call their executive heads on the phone to explain that they were expected to go along with donor support to the SF. The executive heads reluctantly complied.

[25] This was the case for the so-called Next Steps Papers, which defined the conditions for return and reengagement with the Taliban after the missile strikes of August 1998 and the killings of one international and two national UN staff.

[26] This was a situation by no means unique to Afghanistan (see Larry Minear, *The Humanitarian Enterprise, Dilemmas, and Discoveries* (Bloomfield, Conn.: Kumarian Press, 2002), 34.

[27] Afghanistan was a "graveyard for UN mediation" (Maley, *Fundamentalism Reborn?*, 183). Skepticism about the "talks about talks" approach of UN political representatives was high in 2000–2001. At the donor meeting in Ottawa in December 2000, the UN Coordinator called for an "audit" of the effectiveness of UN peace-making efforts in Afghanistan.

[28] William Maley is unfairly critical of the coordinator for "detecting specks of light at the end of a tunnel which other observers found completely black" (William Maley, *The Afghanistan Wars* [New York: Palgrave Macmillan, 2002], 246).

[29] In 1997 and early 1998 major controversy developed in the UN system when WHO took a "collaborationist" line, while others, UNICEF and WFP in particular, took a much "harder" line to the extent that WFP shut down food for work projects where it was not possible to certify that men and women were benefiting equally.

[30] See Maley, *The Afghanistan Wars*, 226-28; see also Ahmed Rashid, *Taliban: Militant Islam, Oil and Fundamentalism in Central Asia* (New Haven, Conn.: Yale University Press, 2000).

[31] "Sex, Drugs, and Rock 'n Roll" (or gender, poppy, and terrorism) was how some field staff described US policy toward Afghanistan.

[32] The "US/UK ban" remained in force until the summer of 2001.

[33] The largest single massacre of civilians occurred in the wake of the Taliban takeover of Mazar-i-Sharif in August 1998 (at least two thousand civilian deaths and possibly many more according to a HRW November 1998 report). Repeated incursions by the Taliban into Hazarajat in 1999–2001 resulted in a string of massacres involving hundreds of Hazaras.

[34] In the pre-Taliban years, Kabul had varying but generally decreasing degrees of control over the provinces. Herat, Kandahar, Jalalabad, Mazar-i-Sharif, Bamiyan, and Taloqan became the capitals of independent fiefdoms. There were up to three different currencies in use and several "national" mini-airlines.

[35] See ICG, "The Afghan Transitional Administration: Prospects and Perils" (Kabul/Brussels: ICG, July 30, 2002).

[36] Ibid.

[37] Ignatieff, "Nation-Building Lite."

[38] Ibid.

[39] As of the time of writing, in mid 2003, only approximately half of the US$1.8 billion pledged at the Tokyo conference in January 2002 had been disbursed. Much of this was indeed being spent on salaries (with seven hundred international staff costing each approximately US$0.3 million per year, the United Nations's share alone would have been in excess of US$210 million pledged for Afghanistan).

[40] For example, SRSG Brahimi handed over to the three northern warlords during the Loya Jirga a catalogue of over seventy incidents of abuse of civilians that had occurred in the areas under their control since November 2001. This had been prepared in the wake of the rape of an expatriate aid worker and threats of aid agencies to withdraw from northern Afghanistan because of growing insecurity.

[41] Hamid Karzai, "Hard Talk," BBC World interview, June 2002; Lakhdar Brahimi, press conference, August 27, 2002.

[42] "The failure to grasp that democracy works only when it goes hand in hand with the rule of law has been the costliest mistake in the Balkans" (Ignatieff, "Nation-Building Lite").

8

The Dilemma
of Humanitarianism
in the Post-Taliban Transition

ALEXANDER COSTY

The international intervention in post-Taliban Afghanistan comes in the wake of a decade-long sea change in the international aid environment, marked by an ever closer interface between the provision of aid and the political imperatives of long-term security and social stabilization in conflict-affected countries. This interface has developed under the banner of peace-building, a conceptual framework through which humanitarian assistance has been recast, no longer as a justifiable end in itself or as a "fig leaf" of half-hearted engagement, but as an integral component of a larger agenda of global ordering.[1]

Under the logic of peace-building, aid has been employed as a device to achieve deep behavioral changes and institutional reforms in recipient countries. In Angola it has been calibrated to encourage greater social investments by a historically disconnected elite.[2] In postwar Mozambique, humanitarian and recovery assistance was consciously programmed to encourage a "de-Sovietization" of the state and society. In Afghanistan itself during the latter 1990s humanitarian assistance became the centerpiece of international efforts to obtain changes in the Taliban's position on human rights, and specifically on the treatment of women.[3]

Most recently, and most significantly perhaps, peace-building interventions have appeared increasingly not to recognize the need to engage with existing political or social institutions in recipient countries. Rather, an emerging doctrine of *regime change*, supported by multinational war efforts and financial aid to armed opposition movements, has underpinned efforts to fundamentally transform the balance of political forces inside war-torn states. Full-scale armed force has entered the peace-building "tool box" of the 2000s, testifying to a new realism about the use of external power to resolve distant civil wars. In this context international assistance has increasingly taken on a role of *regime consolidation*: feeding and servicing war-affected communities; regulating population movements; shoring up internal security systems; stimulating social and economic recovery; and rebuilding state institutions of new, more accommodating elites. With these developments traditional distinctions between different types of foreign intervention have further blurred, and the neutrality and integrity of the humanitarian agenda itself have come under renewed strain.[4]

Afghanistan after the fall of the Taliban has provided a fertile testing ground for the evolving peace-building model, one that promises to generate new lessons in the ongoing search for global order. The experience of 2002 also highlights a number of fundamental tensions that exist between the perceived requirements of peace and regime consolidation and what many see as an ongoing need for the neutral and impartial delivery of humanitarian aid to populations in acute distress. This chapter briefly outlines the main patterns of "integration" between external political and assistance efforts under the Afghan peace-building effort in 2002 and highlights two issues that have caused significant debate over "humanitarian space" in the post-Taliban transition. The first involves the leadership role claimed by an internationally legitimized but as yet unconsolidated central government in controlling and managing international assistance entering the country. The second, more widely publicized issue is the growing involvement of military combat forces, operating under the aegis of the international coalition against terrorism, in relief and recovery activities.

These discussions have prompted a resurgence of humanitarian discourse in defense of an independent space for action. Yet in Afghanistan's transitional context the proper role of the humanitarian enterprise is unclear. There are fundamental differences among state and assistance actors over the way the humanitarian problem should be posed and over who retains custody over its resolution. Interpretations of what constitutes humanitarian action, and views on how core principles should apply in the transition toward statehood, vary widely. Critically, the ambiguity is compounded by a persistent lack of precision about the socio-economic situation in the country; by contradictory signals from the donor community; and by hesitation from the United

Nations, governed by a mixed mandate, in providing clear guidance and leadership on the humanitarian front.

In the midst of this uncertainty there is a concrete risk that the humanitarian agenda may be used in order to preserve operational independence and funding guarantees for aid actors accustomed to collapsed-state environments. The Afghanistan debates of 2002 and 2003 are likely to affect future practices and interactions elsewhere. For the integrity of humanitarian action to be preserved in future peace-building interventions, it is critical that the definition of humanitarian space in the current Afghan experiment be based on an accurate knowledge of needs, a careful and balanced reading of core principles, and their focused application in the local context.

POLITICS AND AID:
PATTERNS OF INTEGRATION IN 2002

Throughout the twenty-three-year Afghan conflict, different patterns of linkage between international political and humanitarian responses have taken place, including the SF initiative in the late 1990s, which sought to bring together donors, NGOs, and UN political and assistance agencies within a common framework of principled intervention in support of peace.[5] Yet for many years Afghanistan remained marginal to the global security agenda and faded from view as one of several forgotten emergencies. Humanitarian assistance stood as the preferred strategy for minimal engagement in the country, enabling the international community to respond to basic social needs of Afghans without supporting a regime universally perceived as illegitimate and repressive.

The events of September 2001 once again placed Afghanistan at the center of global attention. They generated a new "unity of purpose" among key Western states to reengage robustly against terrorism by supporting peace and national social, economic, and institutional renewal.[6] In this new climate a strategic consensus emerged among Afghanistan's key donors, the United Nations, and leading development banks on three central choices: First, that all international assistance efforts should coalesce into a unified effort to support the provisions of the December 2001 Bonn Agreement;[7] second, that the authority and capacity of Afghanistan's newly formed interim administration should be fully supported; and third, that a rapid transition should be made from short-term emergency relief to longer-term investments in poverty alleviation and national reconstruction.[8] These were the fundamentally *political* choices, which in early 2002 provided the conceptual basis for peace-building in post-Taliban Afghanistan. Critically, they generated a set of powerful working assumptions about the integrity of the peace process, about the legitimacy of the state, and about the expected utility of economic assistance as an instrument of transition that has set the tone of subsequent policy debates within the assistance community and shaped the policy dialogue between the international community and the ATA. By creating an impression of linear, forward movement toward peace and recovery, these working assumptions radically challenged the logic of humanitarian assistance after the Taliban. Yet for many observers, they have remained untested, more closely associated with the Kabul policy circuit than with the troubled, fragmented, and actively contested political and economic realities prevailing around the country.

INTEGRATION OF ASSISTANCE FUNCTIONS WITHIN THE UNITED NATIONS

Admittedly, and as discussed further below, the strategic consensus around these choices has been qualified.[9] Nonetheless, it was strong enough in early 2002 to prompt the UN system in Afghanistan to pursue an integration agenda that would impact visibly on the way in which the humanitarian problem was posed, and as such redefine the parameters of UN policy, programming, and action on the humanitarian front. Despite serious uncertainties and ongoing debate about the situation on the ground in several parts of the country, the overall approach of the United Nations was, from the outset, to move away from an expanded humanitarian mandate as a means of articulating confidence and support for the Bonn process. This choice was reflected both in the institutional design and in the programmatic options adopted by the United Nations as the international community prepared to return to Afghanistan in the wake of the Taliban defeat.

Institutionally, early steps were taken (by late 2001) to begin building a new, unified UN presence that would "integrate all the existing United Nations elements in Afghanistan into a single integrated mission" that would ensure that "all UN efforts are harnessed to fully support the implementation of the Bonn Agreement."[10] The formal mandate of the new mission, endorsed in Security Council Resolution 1401, made it abundantly clear that its primary function would be one of peace-building,[11] notably through the stabilization of the structures of a new state by political efforts and by using economic assistance to build legitimacy for the post-Taliban administration, what one observer has called "aid-induced pacification."[12]

Neither the design nor the mandate of the integrated mission provided a strong basis for the United Nations to articulate a clear position or to exercise leadership on behalf of the international community in the area of humanitarian affairs. The design of the mission was itself closely linked to the recommendations of what became known as the

"Brahimi report," a review by the UN Department of Peacekeeping Operations that recognized the need for the United Nations to engage more actively in peace-building and that discussed key organizational measures that would be required to do this more effectively.[13] The report focused primarily on political aspects of UN support, such as elections, political reconciliation, and the rule of law. Yet, although it advocated a system-wide integration of the entire range of UN activities (including humanitarian efforts) undertaken in conflict and post-conflict situations, the report provided virtually no analysis of the mandates and operational priorities of UN humanitarian agencies typically working in such contexts or of how these might blend with political functions without compromising the integrity of core humanitarian principles. The report's definition of neutrality, linked to the UN Charter and to Security Council resolutions, was clearly problematic for the majority of humanitarian agencies and NGOs. The core of the institutional analysis that stood behind planning and design of the UN mission was therefore decidedly not of the kind to favor leadership on humanitarian issues.[14]

For its part, the mission's Security Council mandate gave a mixed signal on the way in which assistance generally should be provided in Afghanistan. On humanitarian assistance in particular, it specified the principle of needs-based response and proscribed assistance to local authorities that did not demonstrate their intention to improve national security and respect for human rights. At the same time, however, the text of the resolution was couched in language and a tone that overwhelmingly emphasized the need to promote, above all, the political provisions of the Bonn Agreement and to meet the requirements of institutional recovery. It is important to note that the text provided no specific guidance on the role or scope of the United Nations in coordinating or facilitating appropriate humanitarian responses in the country.[15] Given this mixed message, the humanitarian component of the mission's mandate in Afghanistan (in comparison to other components) was left open to interpretation in a context where, as noted above, core working assumptions about linear movement toward peace and development were rapidly becoming embedded among international planners and the new national leadership.

In addition to the design and mandate of the mission itself, the unfolding of developments on the ground directly affected the humanitarian profile of the mission. Early planning for the mission had envisaged an organization set up on the basis of two preexisting UN offices for Afghanistan and their eventual integration into a unified structure.[16] These were the UNSMA, a field support office of the Department of Political Affairs, which for several years had worked to find a political solution to the Afghan conflict; and UNOCHA, which had worked to support Afghan populations throughout various phases of the civil war.

With UNOCHA presumed to be incorporated as a core pillar of the new structure, there prevailed a reasonable assumption that a strong humanitarian identity would be maintained within the mission. In reality, however, two critical factors combined to weaken its humanitarian profile. First, the buildup of the new mission's political component rapidly outpaced the consolidation of its assistance arm. This was partially a result of the overwhelming priority accorded, in early 2002, to the political timetable of the emergency Loya Jirga.[17] But it was also partly a result of organizational linkages with the Department of Political Affairs, which ensured the early appointment of a deputy SRSG for political affairs (in December 2001) and a swift and smooth recycling of former UNSMA staff into the new structure. UNOCHA, by contrast, enjoyed no such natural organizational linkages to the mission, and the absorption of humanitarian staff into the new structure became subject to lengthy and painstaking interdepartmental negotiation, which resulted also in professional and contractual uncertainty. The appointment of a deputy SRSG in charge of assistance activities was announced almost two months after that of his political-affairs counterpart, and his assumption of the humanitarian coordinator function did not occur until March 2002, in spite of the pronounced humanitarian nature of the assistance intervention during the preceding period.[18]

Second, a solid humanitarian planning and response division did *not* emerge from within the new mission. The old humanitarian office was not absorbed as a unit within the new structure. Instead, capacities and expertise focused on thematic issues of reconstruction and development, in particular on issues of government capacity building and transitional planning. The human rights and humanitarian protection functions of the original humanitarian office were curtailed and transferred to the political wing of the mission. A number of key humanitarian staff, including seasoned practitioners in the central and field offices, chose not to continue under the new mission structure, while others were not encouraged to stay. Relations with UN headquarters (and in particular the Geneva-based OCHA) became increasingly complex, and the support and backstopping role of OCHA was reduced.[19] The small-scale emergency projects locally managed by the UN Coordinator's office originally meant to meet outstanding needs and fill humanitarian gaps identified in the field, were redesigned as longer-term reconstruction programs.[20]

As noted, these organizational developments took place in a broader assistance policy environment that openly emphasized rapid transition from short-term aid to longer-term reconstruction efforts as a necessary ingredient for building and consolidating peace in Afghanistan. Management decisions taken during early 2002 were consistent with that environment and "made sense" in light of perceived needs that it generated. In so doing, however, they greatly reduced the humanitarian profile of the United Nations, notably its capacity to exercise leadership among the community of aid actors in core humanitarian analysis, planning, and response. And as the integration of the political and assistance functions of the mission proceeded apace throughout 2002 and early 2003, increasing concerns began to be raised by key humanitarian NGOs about the ability of the mission to engage on humanitarian issues in a principled manner.

Alongside the institutional restructuring of the UN's presence in Afghanistan, there were likewise strong moves away from traditional humanitarianism at the level of substantive programming and coordination. The UN Consolidated Appeal, pioneered in Afghanistan and for years the central mechanism for annually raising and planning the humanitarian contributions of the international community, was transformed in two significant ways. First, the 2002 appeal document was recast, by the United Nations itself, as a "transitional assistance" program that incorporated important programming elements not normally associated with humanitarian aid, such as the reinforcement of internal security structures, support for the recovery of the legal and justice sectors, and direct support to ministries and local administrative authorities.[21] At the same time, traditional elements of the UN appeal, such as in-depth humanitarian analysis and the formulation of scenarios and contingencies that could challenge prevailing "working assumptions," were omitted.[22] Second, unlike appeals in other contexts, and in a radical departure from the past in Afghanistan itself, the United Nations submitted to a detailed review of individual programs by national authorities. The United Nations subsequently supported the incorporation of humanitarian and recovery programs into the national development framework and budget process, and facilitated the transfer of financial tracking data from Geneva headquarters to the national assistance-coordination authority.

INTEGRATION WITH THE STATE: THE FUTURE OVERTAKES THE HERE AND NOW

According to international law, states are responsible for providing humanitarian assistance to populations affected by conflict. In practice, however, humanitarian assistance over the past decade has been provided in situations where states have collapsed, or where they were considered internationally to be in breach of their obligations to satisfy basic needs and uphold the essential rights of citizens. Humanitarian interventions have thus developed into primarily independent, external actions that weaken state sovereignty on the basis of international legal instruments. In Afghanistan, the "primacy of the humanitarian" was established during the 1990s precisely because of the chronic collapse of state functions and institutions or, in the case of the Taliban, international nonrecognition of the government and its perceived unwillingness to address humanitarian needs. There, in the absence of sustained political attention to engage the Taliban regime in a "peace process," humanitarian assistance became the primary form of external engagement, and NGOs and UN agencies performed many if not most basic governance functions relating to the provision of services.[23]

When the Taliban fell in late 2001, Afghanistan's formal economy was left almost entirely dependent on external resources. Decaying institutions and the absence of working systems for taxation and revenue collection meant that the ability of the public administration to finance and perform even the most basic functions of statehood (fiscal management, internal security, social-service provision) was virtually nonexistent. Afghan sovereignty, in this sense, was more a concept of the Bonn Agreement than a reality. It comes as no surprise, then, that among the first actions of the new post-Taliban authorities was an attempt to steer international funding away from externally determined, largely self-regulated and parallel forms of humanitarian aid and to orient it instead through a nationally "owned" programming mechanism that would involve, ideally, greater direct support to the state. The new administration in Kabul moved quickly on this front, first by establishing by executive decree a national authority to coordinate assistance entering Afghanistan, and second by subjecting a significant proportion of internationally funded projects to government clearance and prioritization.[24] Third, in April 2002, on the occasion of the first donor conference to take place on Afghan soil, the government released a National Development Framework (NDF), a comprehensive expression of national recovery and development strategies, priorities, and commitments, and a key instrument of persuasion to attract funds away from the traditional humanitarian programming styles of foreign agencies toward an "integrated," developmental approach.[25]

Although it was never finalized and never submitted to any serious form of national consultation, the 2002 NDF was widely accepted by the international community as a strong statement of vision and government commitment, providing a central reference point for policy and an overall structure for assistance programming and coordination in the country. The NDF imposed a reformist vision on both the organization and substantive work of a largely paralyzed and dysfunctional government system. Not unjustifiably, it also directly challenged the structure and logic of externalized UN programming by requiring the UN agencies to rearticulate their sector strategies and priorities in a radically new manner. Critically, however, it also served to further entrench existing working assumptions within the aid community about linear, forward-moving recovery.

The NDF recognized in passing the need for continued humanitarian efforts to meet basic needs and alleviate the suffering of millions of Afghans. Yet its treatment of the humanitarian situation was decisively couched in a complex analysis of short-term and long-term objectives, with an emphasis on livelihoods recovery, poverty alleviation, and capacity building that had much to do with the requirements of state formation, regime consolidation and social "buy-in" to a fragile political process but little to do with an objective analysis of needs on the ground, in a situation marked by ongoing conflict, the purposeful displacement or abuse of populations, the limited scope of state legitimacy and authority, and potentially destructive internal divisions within the government itself. Indeed, the opening paragraphs of the NDF's "humanitarian" chapter immediately set the tone of analysis by recasting humanitarianism in terms of "social capital formation," institutional support, and in relation to the peace process itself:

> Humanitarian action must be provided in a manner that supports the capacity for local communities and populations to emerge from a state of severe destitutions and impoverishment. . . . A central function of the government will be to put in place a social policy that supports the creation of human capital. . . . Developing the social sectors means putting in place the medium-term policies, strategies and implementation mechanisms in the areas of health, nutrition, education, and specific actions to protect the vulnerable from risks. . . . They will be viable if they involve representatives from communities and are owned by the line ministries. This opportunity will arrive with the formation of the Emergency Loya Jirga.[26]

The NDF was a clear and genuine statement of government commitment toward the people of Afghanistan. It expressed a legitimate desire to nationalize the country's economic development agenda after decades of external intervention. Viewed from Kabul, its motives and rationale were compelling. Yet just how relevant it was to the immediate situation of most Afghans, and how realistic about national capacities to deliver urgently needed assistance rapidly and effectively, remained unclear.[27] This uncertainty was clearly reflected within the donor community; many donors, privately and in their management of funds, remained doubtful that direct budgetary support could be spent efficiently and be properly accounted for through an ailing and possibly corrupt central administration with virtually no functional ties outside the capital and with only uncertain chances of political survival. Thus, despite the donors' public commitment to the government and its well-intentioned NDF, the overwhelming share of their assistance to Afghanistan during 2002 continued to be programmed through external mechanisms, in particular through the UN agencies, which accounted for over US$1 billion dollars, or about two-thirds of all aid funds for 2002. The lion's share of this was spent through donors' "humanitarian" instruments, such as the US Office of Foreign Disaster Assistance and the European Commission's Humanitarian Aid office.[28]

The United Nations found itself caught in the middle of this underlying divergence of interpretations, between donors and recipient authorities, about how incoming funds should be spent. The sheer size of funding channeled through the UN generated significant tensions with the government's NDF architects, which saw UN agencies as a parallel funding channel and as possibly subverting plans to nationalize, integrate, and unify the recovery effort. As donors demurred, pressures multiplied on the United Nations to demonstrate its support for government plans under the NDF. In an increasingly contested and pressurized environment, the UN mission responded in mid 2002 by establishing an integrated coordination structure that would bring UN agency programs closer into line with government priorities of capacity building and nationally led recovery programming. For several months agencies were assigned as "secretariats" to work within "lead-ministries" under different chapters of the NDF, providing technical assistance and personnel to support the production of national plans, recovery strategies, and program budgets.[29]

Under this integrated arrangement, UN programs became progressively enmeshed with those of the state, with implications for the coordination of assistance in general and for humanitarian programs in particular. For several UN agencies with a strong profile in traditional developmental areas such as education, agriculture, and health, working closely with counterpart ministries was a familiar institutional practice, even if perhaps somewhat forgotten during the Taliban period. For the UN's humanitarian agencies, joint coordination and support to ministries for long-term recovery planning in Afghanistan represented a new and unknown challenge, compounded in some instances by cultural limitations and the absence of clear counterpart entities within the government structure.[30] This latter group experienced particular institutional difficulties in "fitting" into the NDF and reorienting its programming priorities toward longer-term objectives. Core issues of humanitarian mandate—overly bureaucratic, perhaps, but nonetheless traditionally perceived as intractable—became increasingly subject to negotiation with government counterparts and were soon caught in the quagmire of inter-ministerial politics. Major humanitarian programs, seen as internally coherent from the perspective of individual agencies, were broken down and submitted as separate projects across various program areas of the NDF, "shoe-horned," as it were, into its longer-term reconstruction perspective.

For the UN mission the integrated coordination structure was a mixed blessing. On the one hand, it provided an immediate response to government demands for stronger control over resources entering the country. Arguably, it also provided a means to "buy time" for hesitant donors still awaiting positive signs of political consolidation and administrative streamlining within government before committing large investments directly to the national budget. In this sense integrated coordination helped edge the Bonn process forward and served to mediate international engagement with the new Afghan authorities in the early months of transition from Taliban rule. Arguably, also, it forced independent-minded UN agencies to address the government, and its vision of recovery, more soberly.

On the other hand, the integrated coordination structure placed UN agencies in a strategic position to influence the policies of their counterpart ministries, some of which questioned the logic of the NDF. In some instances unforeseen alliances were forged between agencies and ministries, and as a whole, the United Nations was drawn into fierce internal political debates over who within the administration had what authority to allocate assistance resources in the different program areas of the NDF. Coordination among the UN agencies, and relations between the UN mission and the government, came under renewed strain as a result. Focused as it was on the politics of joint coordination with government, the UN mission's ability to direct serious substantive attention to real or potential humanitarian concerns on the ground was circumscribed. Because integrated coordination signified a concrete positional shift toward government, it simultaneously caused an increased distancing of the UN mission from the NGO community, the international community's only real front-line presence on the ground and a vital source of understanding of the humanitarian situation in the country.

SPACE, THE STATES, AND THE MILITARY:
DILEMMAS OF TRANSITION

The above discussion has highlighted some key elements of organizational, policy, and program integration, undertaken within an overall logic of post-Taliban peace-building, which shaped the way in which the issue of humanitarian assistance was approached by senior planners within the ATA, the UN mission, and the donor community during 2002. Throughout the year the concrete case for providing humanitarian assistance *strictly defined* remained unclear due to a lack of common (and commonly available) baseline data, a fragmented multiplicity of information sources, and contested interpretations of humanitarianism. What was clear, however, was that the era of expanded, perhaps overarching definitions of humanitarian assistance, prevalent during the Taliban period, had come to an end as a result of the creation of a recognized, sovereign central authority and of its energetic drive to move Afghanistan toward longer-term peace and recovery. It was also clear that the traditional monopoly over humanitarian discourse by NGOs and UN aid agencies was fundamentally challenged, and perhaps definitively ruptured, under the pressure of new working assumptions of the type expressed through the NDF. "Integration," within the context of the Bonn Agreement, and the strategic consensus of counter-terrorism meant that the United Nations had necessarily to be an active participant in this paradigmatic shift.

Yet although the humanitarian policy agenda was significantly cut down in Kabul during 2002, it was not altogether eliminated. Throughout the early months of post-Taliban transition, and at the height of national and international enthusiasms for moving quickly toward reconstruction, dramatic reminders of the acute distress suffered by several hundreds of thousands of Afghans were received in Kabul in the form of high-profile reports and surveys, which served to make the case for continuing to direct significant resources to support humanitarian responses.[31] These reports caused significant, yet temporary, ripples across the assistance policy community in Kabul and were ultimately absorbed into mainstream development planning processes.[32]

Toward the end of 2002, however, two particular developments caused a wave of heated reaction among assistance organizations that commonly understood themselves as humanitarian actors. The first involved a government-led restructuring of the national assistance coordination mechanism in a manner that moved assistance yet further along the road toward developmental assistance patterns. The second, much more widely debated and with broad implications for future peacebuilding practices, was the deployment of provincial reconstruction teams by international Coalition forces engaging in active combat in and around Afghanistan. Both developments reflected a denser mixing of assistance and political priorities and could be taken to represent the next logical steps on the path toward integrated peace-building. Both were seen to have important implications for humanitarian action and for its future, both in Afghanistan and further afield. The remainder of this chapter explores key points raised through these debates and attempts to provide some clarity about their implications for humanitarianism in current and future peace-building interventions.

THE CONSULTATIVE GROUP STRUCTURE

In late 2002 the Afghan government announced its intention to establish a new coordination mechanism of consultative groups (CGs) to support the longer-term recovery process. Much about the new system was familiar: assistance coordination would be structured around the NDF, would be led by selected government ministries in each sector, and would involve a credible range of stakeholders. However, important new elements stood out. For one, the new system was decisively donor-oriented, designed primarily to ensure stronger direct links between individual government ministries and external donor states and, as such, to bring donors more closely into the national policy and planning processes. Critically, this implied that UN agencies would in many cases cease to enjoy the privileged position that they had occupied under the previous joint-coordination mechanism. Second, the CG coordination system was decidedly developmental, reflecting Afghanistan's urgent desire to "normalize" relations with donors by adopting a national programming model used by the majority of developing countries around the world. The primary purpose of the new system was to provide a permanent structure for preparing Afghanistan's annual recurring and investment budgets for presentation to international donors and creditors.[33] In general, the new coordination system was embraced by key members of the donor community in Kabul, a number of which provided vital technical assistance to government in order to ensure its successful launch.[34] And while many within the UN felt, with some justification, that relevant agencies had not been sufficiently consulted in the creation of the CG mechanism, the United Nations nonetheless mobilized quickly to support what was seen as a nationally led process consistent with the spirit of the Bonn Agreement.[35]

A number of assistance actors, however, showed strong concern about the possible implications of the new system on future humanitarian action in the country. Chief among these concerns were, first, that increased donor involvement in the planning and programming of specific recovery sectors could lead to a "bilateralerization" of assistance to the country, whereby individual donors would gain increasing leverage to pursue their own interests within their preferred sector with selected national actors and, through this, greater scope to mix assistance efforts with their respective foreign policy priorities. From the humanitarian perspective this would potentially jeopardize the neutrality and impartiality of assistance programs, in particular those involving efforts to address conflict-related humanitarian needs.[36] Second, several humanitarian actors expressed discomfort at the government's insistence that all international aid should be programmed through the CG process and integrated into the national budget.[37] For NGOs in particular, this implied a serious loss of independence of action. For some donors and UN agencies, the requirement to pre-program assistance within an Afghan annual budgeting cycle potentially challenged the logic of flexible, short-term disbursements normally afforded by "humanitarian" or "emergency" budget lines. Finally, the question arose as to whether humanitarian assistance could be impartially planned and programmed within a highly politicized context of inter-ministerial competition over limited resources, and whether the perceived priorities of central ministries were in fact consistent with real needs outside of Kabul.

Apprehensions further intensified in December 2002 when an Afghan ministry sought to clarify the government's position by issuing a public statement that in essence argued the case for a stronger leadership role for the state in managing and coordinating humanitarian assistance to Afghanistan. The government's argument was premised on its legal obligation and ethical commitment to serve and assist all Afghan citizens in need.[38] While these points were not questioned, doubts were raised about the government's capacity to manage humanitarian responses effectively, particularly in areas of the country where central authorities were engaged in active conflict with opposing factions. Citing its own institutional definition of "humanitarian" assistance, the European Community's Humanitarian Aid office stated that government attempts to coordinate its aid activities could unacceptably compromise its neutrality and could lead it to reconsider its program in Afghanistan.

As a compromise measure, it was decided that a special, semi-autonomous advisory group on humanitarian affairs would be instituted under the broader CG structure, to be chaired by a collectively agreed-upon donor rather than by a government ministry, and consisting of government, UN, donor, ICRC, and NGO members. At the suggestion of the United Nations, it was further agreed within the group that, to the extent possible, discussions would focus on the practicalities of delivery in emergency situations. Issues of principle, such as the neutrality and impartiality of assistance, would be left to appropriate case-by-case consideration. These measures testified to a general desire for pragmatism in a politically charged aid environment but did not immediately resolve the inherent tensions that continued to affect the relationship between Afghanistan's new government and its traditional humanitarian actors. Core concerns about humanitarian roles, responsibilities, principles, and space were somewhat "papered over" rather than decisively clarified.

What did become clear from the CG debate of late 2002, however, was that greater national control over the management of external resources in a highly aid-dependent environment was a central issue that needed to be addressed as part of the peace-building agenda. As noted earlier, sovereignty is reinforced where there is domestic authority to control who gets what in the national economy on the basis of internal political decision-making. The tension between this logic of peace-building and regime consolidation, on one hand, and independent humanitarian action, on the other, goes to the heart of the humanitarian dilemma in post-Taliban Afghanistan and, arguably, in similar transitional situations elsewhere.

Critically, much of the international community's high-level strategic planning in support of the Afghan transition looked ahead confidently toward a future, more or less apparent, in which the social and economic momentum of national recovery would overtake external relief as the primary instrument for providing basic goods and services to a troubled Afghan population. Policy dialogue among the main actors moved quickly to focus on issues of capacity building and public institutional support. Yet in fast-forwarding toward an unspecified future point on the path of recovery, insufficient attention was given to the "residuals" of humanitarian action. An agreed strategic plan of phased transition from humanitarian to recovery modes of assistance delivery, based on a common understanding of changing principles, roles and responsibilities, or on an accurate knowledge of the situation on the ground, was not developed among key national and international partners. The inherent tension between humanitarianism and peace-building was thus not resolved from the outset of 2002 and remained hostage for much of the year to competitive political and bureaucratic positioning and to generally unhelpful exchanges of rhetoric.

The Coalition provincial reconstruction teams: A bridge too far?

Recent years have seen a growing interaction between humanitarian and military personnel in conflict and post-conflict situations, a pattern that has inspired discussion and a sizable body of analysis.[39] The civil-military interface has normally occurred between assistance agencies and internationally mandated peace-keeping forces within a common peace-building framework and has been supported to varying degrees by institutional guidelines. In Afghanistan, however, the assistance community was faced with the new challenge of engaging with non-UN-mandated multinational forces that, from late 2001 onward, assumed a variety of roles, including active combat operations, intelligence gathering, psychological operations, and the conduct of "hearts and minds" campaigns through the provision of what is termed humanitarian assistance, primarily in the form of basic medical services, food distributions, and small infrastructure projects.

Historically, assistance agencies, in particular NGOs, have addressed the civil-military dimension of peace operations with caution, if not trepidation. Profound differences in professional and organizational culture have led to uneasy relationships and frequent misunderstandings on the ground. A common criticism leveled against military personnel is that they are insufficiently trained in the different aspects of assistance delivery, unaware of principles and operational best practices. More important, the co-deployment of military and assistance actors has been seen as a potential obstacle to humanitarian neutrality and, as such, a constraint on humanitarian space. In Afghanistan during 2002 concerns of this sort were significantly amplified by the primary role and mission of international coalition forces, which were to engage in counter-terrorist war and not in peace-building.

Throughout 2002 the NGO community and some international agencies raised specific concerns about the practices adopted by military units as part of the military campaign. The coalition's hearts-and-minds projects were particularly criticized for supporting military objectives rather than following a strictly humanitarian or recovery logic based on technical criteria. Strong objections were raised that military assistance projects were frequently carried out by armed personnel operating in civilian clothing, a practice that could potentially confuse local populations and thus expose genuine assistance workers to the threat of misguided attacks. Increasing interaction with military field personnel for the purposes of local consultation and coordination, often perceived as a necessary evil by civilian aid workers, likewise raised concerns about the confusion of identities. Such anxieties intensified toward the end of 2002 as US forces began to implement an expanded plan for nationwide military support to the reconstruction effort. According to the plan, provincial reconstruction teams (PRTs) of up to one hundred combat forces and military assistance experts, supported by advisers of the US State Department and Agency for International Development, would be deployed to selected locations around the country. The stated objectives were, first, to provide more secure conditions, which would facilitate the recovery work of international agencies; second, to engage alongside other assistance partners in the recovery of national infrastructure; and third, to support the extension of central government authority in the provinces. In a concrete sense, this meshing of political, economic, and security objectives, and the fielding of integrated teams, was a reflection of the US military's own attempt to achieve "coherence" in support of a particular brand of regime consolidation and counter-terrorist "peace."

The large-scale and high-profile movement by foreign combat forces into the aid arena was supported by the central government as an additional platform for reconstruction and domestic stabilization in volatile areas of the country.[40] The PRT initiative was also acknowledged by the government for its potential role in supporting disarmament and demobilization, and the formation of a new national army. However, initial deployment of the integrated teams in early 2003 led to immediate unease among a large number of assistance partners and to renewed tension in the overall civil-military relationship. Three main factors contributed to this: first, a lack of clarity within the Coalition itself about the role and rationale of the expanded aid teams, and its initial inability to communicate these consistently and in a language that was intelligible to civilian aid agencies. Contradictory mission statements by different parts of the Coalition led to strong frustrations that the civil-military dialogue was ineffective and to suspicions that, despite stated goals, underlying geo-strategic agendas were being played out through the PRT structure. Second, many assistance actors became increasingly concerned that the PRT framework reflected the beginnings of a new doctrine of militarized aid that could have serious future implications for their operational space and ability to attract aid resources. This was compounded by suggestions, in early 2003, that donors might consider channeling bilateral assistance through the military teams. Finally, the PRTs were not able immediately to demonstrate the superior technical professionalism or cost effectiveness of their assistance activities, a point that was not lost on the aid community.

Critically, the core strategy of the broader assistance community in responding to the challenge of aid militarization was to invoke humanitarian principles and contrast them with the purposes and objectives of the Coalition's military intervention in Afghanistan. One widely circulated NGO advocacy paper, issued at the time of the first deployments of the PRTs in late 2002, boldly stated:

> Most NGOs are committed to the principles of humanity, impartiality, independence and neutrality. In practice, this means our decisions regarding the recipients, the type and the quantity of aid are based solely on our assessment of needs, without discrimination and without aiming to promote a particular political agenda or outcome. We are obliged, therefore, to maintain our independence from the agendas of both the donors that fund us and the governments and local authorities that allow us to operate in their territory. . . . Military forces engaged in assistance activities are driven by political and security objectives.[41]

Seen from a purely humanitarian perspective, the increasing involvement in assistance activities by military forces actively engaged in conflict raises legitimate concerns. However, given the mixed policy and programming context, it was not immediately clear in early 2003 how humanitarian principles might apply to an analysis of civil-military developments. As noted, making the case for humanitarian intervention would require an accurate knowledge of the social and economic situation in the country, or in specific parts of it. While the NGO community continued throughout 2002 to operate on the front line of international assistance programs, a comprehensive analysis of basic survival needs or of patterns of localized conflict did not emerge. The need for a neutral and impartial humanitarian space for the delivery of assistance was assumed but could not be verified in a manner convincing enough to argue for a retreat away from the PRT concept.

A major weakness in the strategy of invoking humanitarian principles was that by the end of 2002 the majority of assistance agencies working in the country were in fact no longer engaging in humanitarian operations strictly defined, despite the use of bureaucratically defined "humanitarian" funding instruments by donors. Nor were the majority of assistance efforts being directed at areas affected by open conflict. Nor, finally, did official PRT mission statements clearly entail a violation of core humanitarian space by the military, as traditionally understood. On the contrary, senior planners of the PRT deployment were quick to indicate their primary focus as agents of reconstruction, security, and support for government authority, in other words, a focus on distinctly non-humanitarian activities. In this ambiguous context the question emerged as to what kind of space reticent aid actors were in reality seeking to defend: humanitarian? organizational? nongovernmental? or simply financial? Quite possibly, genuine humanitarianism was no longer at issue but was increasingly running the risk of politicization, or at the very least of instrumentalization, by the assistance community itself, as it was swept up by the national and international politics of the post-Taliban transition. Importantly, throughout the civil-military dialogue of late 2002 and early 2003, military counterparts appeared consistently open to incorporating ideas about assistance programming not included in their initial planning models. Whether these would be concretely adopted, or whether they would be effectively put into practice in the field, remained to be seen. Traditional assistance actors, by contrast, were visibly less willing to adjust policies or practice.

The intensity and profile of the civil-military debate prompted the United Nations to seek a formula of accommodation between highly contested positions, and served also as an important opportunity for the integrated mission to clarify its position vis-à-vis a delicate combination of political and assistance issues. In a concrete sense the mission's mixed mandate positioned it well to mediate between the military and assistance spheres. And to its credit, it was able to engage successfully with the architects of the PRT to articulate the concerns of the assistance community and to influence, at the level of policy, military thinking about assistance implementation options and managing relations with traditional aid actors. At the same time, different perspectives emerged within the mission's own structure, between its assistance and political components, on how the United Nations itself would engage with the PRTs. Resolving these differences was not a straightforward exercise, but the effort generated a genuine internal dialogue that, to some degree, forced the mission in the direction of a more integrated approach.

CONCLUSION

Attempts by a broad cross-section of traditional assistance partners to use the moral high ground of humanitarianism as a safeguard against the emergence of important new actors on the Afghan aid scene—the state and the multinational military force—reflected a number of contrasts and tensions inherent to the transitional process that followed the fall of the Taliban. On the surface they represented an obvious defensive reaction by a professional community long accustomed to self-regulation and, over the last decade at least, to a virtual monopoly in determining who gets what in Afghanistan's troubled and long neglected society. Deeper down they may have also reflected the beginnings of an emerging crisis within an overstretched global humanitarian agenda, fed over the past decade by uncritical budget flows and creeping institutional mandates, and now beginning to see its limits. Perhaps most fundamentally, they highlighted the basic institutional and policy uncertainties surrounding the meshing of humanitarian and developmental politics under the rubric of peace-building.

By raising the humanitarian banner, traditional aid actors demonstrated an instinctive discomfort with, but also perhaps an insufficient understanding of, the requirements of state formation in an environment marked by ongoing crisis, where the state itself stands as the principal mechanism of transition toward social and political stability. There persisted a strong reluctance to recognize the state as a key instrument of the peace-building tool box. Traditional aid actors also ran the risk of jeopardizing the integrity and intent of the humanitarian idea, setting a dangerous precedent for future international engagements.

From the perspective of peace-building, the humanitarian debates of 2002 highlighted important issues that will need serious consideration if the model itself is to retain any utility. The first and most obvious is that basic tensions will continue to exist among the different instruments within the peace-building kit. Fundamental contrasts in the respective purposes of humanitarian, development, and military support, and in the powerful organizational cultures and interests of the institutions that represent and promote them, are unlikely to be reconciled. This suggests a need to rethink current models of functional and organizational integration, perhaps in the direction of a lighter form of integration in which coherence is recognized more as a matter of common purpose than of forced institutional realignment. Serious thinking will need to be done also to create a better match between the instruments and objectives of peace-building in the new era of realism that appears to be emerging in the post–September 11 context. In particular, externally controlled economic instruments, such as humanitarian budget lines, agency country programs and consolidated appeals, will likely need to be recalibrated to meet the requirements of sovereignty and state formation in many, though not all, other areas of engagement.

Second, despite the increasing doubts of aid analysts and practitioners in recent years, the Afghanistan experience during 2002 showed a persistent dependence on *linear transitional thinking* within assistance institutions seeking to engage in peace-building efforts. Transitional planning in Afghanistan, as expressed in the NDF, was dominated by precisely this type of thinking. Inescapably, the linear logic imposes a distinction between historical "moments" along a single time continuum, and different, often mutually exclusive, modes of assistance programming considered appropriate to each moment. Yet Afghanistan's highly complex socio-political environment made it clear that transitional support needs to become more sophisticated. Transitional peace-building strategies must recognize multiple and overlapping social realities within or across different geographical areas. For humanitarian intervention in particular, this may mean returning to a more specific reading, but more robust application, of humanitarian principles in those areas in which they are most relevant. For peace-building more broadly, a coherent approach may require a more selective, and not necessarily more integrated, use of humanitarian, development, and political instruments.

NOTES

[1] Definitions of humanitarian assistance have been hotly contested over the past decade. For the purposes of this discussion, humanitarian assistance is defined as "aid provided to an affected population that seeks, as its primary purpose, to save lives and alleviate suffering in a crisis-affected environment. Humanitarian assistance must be provided in accordance with the basic humanitarian principles of humanity, impartiality and neutrality" (this definition was proposed as part of the draft terms of reference of the Humanitarian Affairs Advisory Group by a cross-section of donor, government, NGO, and UN partners in Kabul in early 2003).

[2] Tony Hodges, *Angola from Afro-Stalinism to Petro-Diamond Capitalism* (Oxford: James Currey, 2001); see also Alexander Costy, "The Peace Dividend in Mozambique," in *Peacebuilding in Africa*, ed. R. Matthews and T. Ali (Toronto: University of Toronto Press, 2003).

[3] International engagement through humanitarian assistance was also perceived by observers and practitioners as a means to achieve a longer-term political objective; namely, to moderate the Taliban's extremist national and international policy positions.

[4] See Joanna Macrae, ed., *The New Humanitarianisms: A Review of Trends in Global Humanitarian Action,* HPG Report 11 (London: ODI, April 2002), 5–16.

[5] See "Strategic Framework for Afghanistan: Towards a Principled Approach to Peace and Reconstruction," UN internal document (September 15, 1998). For assessments of how the SF fared in practice in Afghanistan, see Chapter 7

in this volume; Antonio Donini, *The Strategic Framework for Afghanistan: A Preliminary Assessment* (Islamabad: UNOCHA, 1999), available online; and Mark Duffield, Patricia Gossman, and Nicholas Leader, *Review of the Strategic Framework for Afghanistan* (Kabul: Afghanistan Research and Evaluation Unit, October 2001).

[6] See the "Beyond Brahimi" report, *A Review of Peace Operations: A Case for Change. Afghanistan (A Snapshot Study)* (London: Kings College, December 2003).

[7] See the Agreement on Provisional Arrangements in Afghanistan Pending the Re-Establishment of Permanent Government Institutions, otherwise known as the Bonn Agreement, S/2001/1154.

[8] See *Afghanistan: Preliminary Needs Assessment for Recovery and Reconstruction* (Asian Development Bank, UNDP, World Bank, January 2002).

[9] Leader points out, for example, that consensus in support of the Bonn process has not translated into consistent international budgetary support for the ATA, nor has it generated a strong security commitment on the part of the international community (as evidenced by repeated calls for the expansion of the ISAF by the UN secretary-general and others that have consistently fallen on deaf ears). Short-term funding commitments continued through 2002 to figure prominently in overall assistance provisions (see Chapter 9 in this volume).

[10] UN General Assembly/Security Council, "Report of the Secretary-General on the Situation in Afghanistan and Its Implications for International Peace and Security," UN doc. A/56/875–S/2002/278 (March 18, 2002). The rationale for the integrated structure of the mission is laid out in the first paragraph outlining the mandate of the mission: "Given that all of these activities [critical humanitarian and immediate recovery efforts] in one way or another affect the peace process, it is essential that they be conducted in an integrated fashion."

[11] UN Security Council Resolution 1401 (March 28, 2002).

[12] Nicholas Stockton, *Strategic Coordination in Afghanistan* (Kabul: AREU, 2002), 21–25.

[13] See United Nations, "Report of the Panel on UN Peacekeeping Operations," UN doc. A/55/305–S/2000/809 (August 21, 2000).

[14] Tellingly, a specific type of aid intervention identified in the "Brahimi report" is the "quick impact project," which is "aimed at real improvements in quality of life, to *help establish the credibility of the new mission*" (7, emphasis added).

[15] See UN General Assembly/Security Council, "Report of the Secretary-General on the Situation in Afghanistan and Its Implications for International Peace and Security"; and UN Security Council Resolution 1401.

[16] UNAMA Mission Support Plan (April 11, 2002).

[17] The first meeting of the SRSG with the heads of agencies was held in Kabul on June 24, 2002, only after the emergency Loya Jirga and nearly three months after the formal creation of the mission on April 1, 2002.

[18] See *OCHA and UNOCHA: Response and Coordination Services Provided to the Escalating Emergency in Afghanistan, July 2001–July 2002*, an external evaluation carried out for OCHA by Carrol Faubert, Laurie Clifford, Humayun Hamidzada, and Colin Reynolds (November 2002), para 100. In fairness, as the report points out, the delay in the confirmation of the deputy

SRSG as humanitarian coordinator reflected primarily procedural delays on behalf of the Inter-Agency Standing Committee.

[19] Arguably, initial complications in the relationship between the new mission and OCHA can be explained by difficulties in institutional adaptation to a radically new operational and organizational environment on the ground. By the end of 2002 new arrangements for headquarters support for relief, recovery, and coordination activities were being formally discussed between the two bodies. Nonetheless, the initial difficulties raise a strong case for better advance planning of anticipated institutional changes, including issues of transitional programming, staffing, and appropriate support roles.

[20] See Faubert et al., OCHA and UNOCHA.

[21] See the Immediate and Transitional Assistance Programme for Afghanistan (ITAP) 2002, which was presented at the Tokyo Donors Conference in January 2002.

[22] See OCHA, "Technical Guidelines for the Preparation of Consolidated Appeal Documents" (September 1998).

[23] See Chapter 7 in this volume; see also Mohammed Haneef Atmar, "Politicization of Humanitarian Aid and Its Consequences for Afghans," paper presented at a conference on Politics and Humanitarian Aid: Debates, Dilemmas, and Dissension Conference (London, February 1, 2001); and Duffield, Gossman, and Leader, Review of the Strategic Framework for Afghanistan.

[24] The ITAP was submitted to two rounds of government review between March and June 2002.

[25] See "The National Development Framework" (Kabul, April 2002). Available online.

[26] Ibid., 14.

[27] For several months after the NDF was published in English in April 2002, authorities outside of Kabul remained unaware of its existence, testifying to the central government's incapacity to communicate policy decisions to the periphery.

[28] By conservative estimates, over US$600 million in aid that entered Afghanistan during 2002 was spent through short-term humanitarian budgets, channeled through the United Nations (see CARE International in Afghanistan, "Rebuilding Afghanistan: A Little Less Talk, A Lot More Action," policy brief (September 2002).

[29] "Program secretariats" were constituted in eight of the twelve NDF program areas on the basis of a formal letter of agreement jointly signed by the minister and head of the agency in question, as well as by the director of the Afghanistan Assistance Coordination Authority and the deputy SRSG for relief, recovery, and reconstruction.

[30] Several months passed after the launching of the NDF before the WFP, the UN's food aid program, could identify a clear government counterpart in the Ministry of Rural Rehabilitation and Development. The UNHCR, responsible for refugees, was required to engage with three separate line ministries and to broker agreements among them on programs relating to repatriation and initial reintegration.

[31] See, in particular, Sue Lautze et al., Qaht-e-Pool 'A Cash Famine': Food Insecurity in Afghanistan, 1999–2002 (ODI, May 2002). Available online.

[32] For example, the government's response to the Lautze et al. study (ibid.), which suggested that significant humanitarian assistance would be needed until well into 2004, was primarily institutional; it intensified consultations on "livelihoods" and established a livelihoods and vulnerability analysis unit in a key government department.

[33] The CG process, sponsored by the World Bank, is the primary instrument for developing countries to solicit international grants and loans on the basis of annual budget requirements. For details of its constitution in Afghanistan, see the Afghanistan Assistance Coordination Authority, *The Establishment of Consultative Groups for Furtherance of the National Development Programme* (Kabul, December 2002).

[34] For example, the United States deployed a senior State Department official to build political support within different government ministries for the new CG system. The European Commission provided technical expertise to assist in the preparation of a two-year national budget. Several other donors engaged actively to ensure early progress in the substantive work of the different sectoral CGs.

[35] In late 2002, as preparations for launching the CG process were being made, there was some sense that the role of the United Nations in assistance coordination was being deliberately reduced in comparison to earlier months. For several weeks UN agencies were not clearly informed by the government on what their role within the CG process would be.

[36] The "bilateralization" of assistance has been identified by analysts as a form of politicization of aid; it has been the focus of aid policy debates since the late 1990s. For an in-depth discussion of this and other recent trends in assistance, see Joanna Macrae, *The Bilateralization of Humanitarian Response: Trends in the Financial, Contractual and Managerial Environment of Official Humanitarian Aid* (London: ODI, 2002).

[37] Not unreasonably, the government argued that a wide range of activities normally defined as humanitarian, such as support for refugee returns, food distributions, de-mining, and the clearance or roads and pre-positioning of stocks for winter, could in fact be preprogrammed and, as such, integrated into Afghanistan's annual budget.

[38] Ministry of Rural Rehabilitation and Development, "Humanitarian Assistance and Social Policy in Afghanistan" (Oslo: December 2002).

[39] For a detailed analysis of the evolution of civil-military relations in complex political emergencies, see Jane Barry, with Anna Jeffreys, *A Bridge Too Far: Aid Agencies and the Military in Humanitarian Response,* HPN Paper 37 (January 2002).

[40] PRTs were initially made up of US forces and deployed to the politically volatile areas of Gardez, Bamyan, and Kunduz.

[41] Agency Coordinating Body for Afghan Relief, "Concerns and Recommendations on Civil-Military Relations" (Kabul, December 2002).

9

Political Projects

Reform, Aid, and the State in Afghanistan

Nicholas Leader and Mohammed Haneef Atmar

> *The lessons of the past two decades in Afghanistan and elsewhere are that only accountable and legitimate national institutions, though open to the outside world and subject to international standards, can protect human security.*
> —Barnett R. Rubin

The broad goals in Afghanistan since the fall of the Taliban in late 2001 are easy enough to state: Afghan men and women leading longer, healthier, richer lives; security, justice, and the rule of law; broad-based economic growth; an end to terrorism and drug trafficking; a prosperous, moderate Islamic democracy. But getting there is a dauntingly complex problem. It means nothing less than changing the political economy of the country from one based on unaccountable and arbitrary military rule, oppression, predation, and illicit economic activity to one based on democratic, civilian governance, rule-based authority, a thriving, licit, private sector, and political freedom. *Transformation* would be a better way of describing this process than the rather prosaic and pedestrian term *reconstruction*; here we have chosen to use the deliberately political term *reform* to capture the objectives of the triple transition from war to peace, from repressive to more open government, and from a controlled to a market economy.

Rebuilding the institutions of legitimate governance, in particular the state, is a necessary condition for this process; "the collapse of even

166

the weak state that Afghanistan once had is the source of most of the catastrophes that have befallen the Afghan people" and also has made it possible for Afghanistan to become a base from which to launch an international war.[1] Rebuilding the state is necessary but not sufficient. We will need to rebuild many other institutions—markets, a free media, political organizations—but the key to the reform process will be the twin tasks of rebuilding the state and ensuring that it is controlled by legitimate and accountable political actors. Without this, the rest of the reconstruction program will be in vain.

Our aims in this chapter are, first, to sketch out the elements of this reform process, in particular the rebuilding of the state, and, second, to assess the role and impact of aid and aid agencies in the process of reform. We will concentrate mainly on the "traditional" focus of aid—the humanitarian and recovery activities of donors, the United Nations, and NGOs—and not so much on aid to the rule of law and security sectors. This is not because these sectors are not important but because most of the aid money spent so far in Afghanistan has been on these traditional activities and because this area has been the main focus of other authors in this volume and elsewhere.

It could be argued that the primary aim of much recent aid work in Afghanistan is saving lives and livelihoods, not the "political project" of state-building. This is certainly not the case for UNAMA and the UN agencies, whose primary task is to support the implementation of the Bonn Agreement of December 2001,[2] or for the international financial institutions. But, more important than legal mandate, the context of a legitimate and representative government radically changes the nature of both UN and NGO operations and objectives; the political significance and impact of an aid project in the context of the reform process is very different from one under the Taliban. There is, we argue, both an obligation and an opportunity for aid to play an important role in supporting reform. We agree that humanitarian assistance, properly understood, should be exempted from this obligation. But defining humanitarian assistance in a substantive rather than bureaucratic way is difficult in this context, not least because of the activities of a number of humanitarian actors who have successively blurred and expanded the concept.

We examine how donors and agencies have contributed to reform in three related areas: the way in which the "problem" is defined by various actors, and so the solution implied; the planning, funding, and implementation of service delivery; and the vexed issue of humanitarian principles and the relationship between aid and the political process.

Our conclusion is that the contribution of both donors and agencies to the reform process to date is ambivalent and in some instances unsatisfactory. A number of actors have been reluctant to understand fully, engage with, and support the reform process, in particular the state-building project, as the key to long-term peace and development. And many institutional aspects of the aid system have also been unhelpful. This has meant that opportunities that could have benefited the reform process have been missed or delayed, and thus the process has been slower and more difficult than it need have been.

This is significant not only for Afghanistan but for the aid system globally. The end of the Cold War led to the eruption of a number of conflicts in what became strategically unimportant countries, and a decade in which "humanitarianism" was the defining concept for much intervention in collapsed or failed states precisely because there was little political will to intervene in any other way. The new strategic context of the twenty-first century, with the intimately linked emergence of a "hyper-power" and the "war on terrorism," may see a closing down of many conflicts, such as Afghanistan, Sri Lanka, Sudan, and a new emphasis on state-building and nation-building as one way of ensuring there are no more havens for terrorists. As it has done in the past, the aid system will need to redefine its goals, methods, and organization if it is to maintain its focus on poverty and exclusion in a new geopolitical context. The experience of Afghanistan should provide much useful material in thinking through these challenges and changes.

However, at the outset, we should emphasize the uniqueness of the Afghan context. The strong arguments for support of the reform process and state-building below relate very specifically to this context. Much of what follows depends on a political judgment by the authors about the current situation, in particular what we see as the significant potential for an effective reform process given the particular political circumstances that have developed since the Bonn Agreement was signed. We are not arguing that the type of reform process we outline below is essential or possible in all contexts, but rather that it is possible and necessary in *this* context, given Afghanistan's particular history and the current political situation. We also stress that much in this debate relies on a prior political judgment as to the current and likely future legitimacy of the current government; how the authors have made that judgment will be obvious. But while opinions among reasonable people vary on these questions, and we accept that reasonable people may disagree with our judgment, we cannot accept that, as the aid system often seems to pretend, such a political judgment can be avoided.

THE OBJECTIVE: REFORM AND THE STATE

The war in Afghanistan in late 2001 ended decisively. Thus we are not faced with the usual peace-building scenario where a number of previously conflicting parties collectively implement a peace agreement. Although it would be foolish to deny that there are tensions within the government, this political context means we can move faster than in situations where erstwhile enemies stymie each other at every turn during the reconstruction process. In this context it makes sense to talk of a reform process, as opposed to just a peace process. The goal of the reform process is nothing less that the transformation of the country from one dominated by warlords to a moderate Islamic democracy, and the goals and strategies for this process are outlined in the NDF.[3]

The reform process is obviously, and crucially, a political process. We believe that there is a significant consensus for the vision outlined in the NDF among Afghans and that the emergency Loya Jirga demonstrated this.[4] As with every political process, there will be winners and losers, and compromises will need to be made between actual power and ideal futures. There are a number of actors, both inside and outside Afghanistan, for whom adaptation will be painful, some to the extent that they will resist. Most obviously, warlords and their supporters, Taliban and Al Qaeda remnants, drugs traders, and smugglers all stand to lose from the reform program and can be expected to resist. For others, though they may support reform in theory, adaptation will be difficult and painful, for example, civil servants, poppy farmers and workers, individual members of militias, and even some aid agencies.

This makes reform a conflictual process and is one of the reasons why control of an effective state is necessary. "Unless the state in Afghanistan acquires a monopoly of power with respect to basic state functions, the country will not be able to break out of the vicious circle of political disintegration, endemic conflict, poverty and economic collapse."[5] Not only is a state monopoly of violence crucial, but state authority is necessary for macro-economic policy, dispensing justice, providing an enabling environment for the private sector, providing equitable service delivery, and managing Afghanistan's interactions with the rest of the world, including, of course, the aid system itself. As the Taliban demonstrated, there is simply no substitute for the state in this process.

However, despite the overwhelming need, the process of rebuilding the state and ensuring its control by accountable political groups is challenging, to say the least:

- The process of state formation in Afghanistan, as in many other countries, has involved a degree of conflict. Even during the comparatively successful period of the 1960s-70s, the state relied on external support as well as internal legitimacy. Politics was often clientelistic, and private enterprise was stunted by state interference. The state had little impact in remote villages. The state was not strong, but it was centralized.

- State institutions that existed virtually collapsed during the years of war. The state lost its monopoly of violence to warlords (raising important questions about the relationship between peace and justice), the national economy collapsed and was replaced with a number of local economies dependent on neighboring states, there was no macro-economic policy, the currency collapsed, service delivery was almost nonexistent, and many qualified staff left. Naturally, to survive, Afghans fell back on family networks. Some were even forced to develop illicit survival strategies such as corruption, smuggling, and poppy growing. Afghans' faith in and indeed experience of the impartial delivery of services by a rule-governed bureaucracy are limited.
- Whether the state is decentralized or centralized, it will not be rich. Reconstruction aid will decrease after three to five years or so, and therefore we must avoid creating expectations of the state that it will not be able to meet. We do not want to make the mistakes of the past and develop a state dependent on foreign aid and aid agencies. The state must focus on a few vital jobs and do them well.
- And, lastly, the state is necessary but not sufficient. Again, we want to avoid the problem that led to war in the 1970s: state-led development imposed by a small minority with no political legitimacy. The reform process will require other institutions for economic growth and legitimate government, active but regulated markets, a free media, political movements, and so on. Some have argued that a World Bank/IMF-imposed model state is a practical necessity in Afghanistan.

Afghanistan also needs to maintain good relations with its neighbors to avoid the competitive backing of rival factions by neighboring states that has caused so much conflict in the past. And, just to make things a real challenge, all this has to be achieved, initially at least, by persuasion, because the international community has not seen fit to support the rule of the center in the rest of the country through the expansion of ISAF. The problems are indeed daunting, almost to the point of paralysis.

However, on the other hand, almost because the problems are so great, the ending of the war and the Bonn process have given us a historic opportunity for radical and far-reaching reform, indeed for transformation; we have an opportunity now that we will not see again for many years. This opportunity for radical change will inevitably decrease as time goes on, so we need to seize this moment to carry through reforms, the impact of which will be felt for generations. The reform program outlined in the NDF provides a framework with which we can seize this opportunity.

The vision, in brief, comprises:

- A light but effective state with a monopoly of legitimate force and taxation through the national army and police and control of border posts, one which provides effective, affordable, and fair public services, a social protection policy for the most vulnerable, and coordination of foreign aid to ensure it is effective.
- Promoting economic activity by legitimate actors in the private sector, the state to provide an enabling role, with privatization of many previously state-run enterprises.
- An active civil society and political competition organized around stable political groupings, promotion of the rights of women, in particular their engagement in public and economic life.

The political process toward this vision is complex and uncertain. What has evolved is an inclusive political process led by a president (Hamid Karzai) elected by the emergency Loya Jirga in June 2002 and enjoying very widespread popular support, in fact the most legitimate president in Afghanistan's history. The emergency Loya Jirga was the most democratic and representative in Afghan history. An inclusive political process is necessary to prevent a return to war, and thus will need to include warlords, intellectuals, and religious and tribal leaders. This inevitably puts serious strains on the process, in particular the problems of past crimes and current control of elements of the state by forces many Afghans have little confidence in. But an inclusive process should not mean impunity. The government welcomes human rights scrutiny, in particular the establishment of the human rights commission, and the president has recently dismissed a number of officials around the country for various abuses. The formation of a national army is also crucial. In the medium term it will be necessary to encourage the political mobilization of stable interest groups around which political competition can be organized.

In terms of the economic and social counterparts to this political process, an approach has been developed that recognizes both the weakness of existing state capacity and the fragility of the political process. In terms of the economy, the state will concentrate on providing an enabling environment for the private sector, thus the successful currency reform and the new investment law. For service delivery, government will set policy, decide on the main priorities, programs, and overall strategic objectives, but will not implement; implementation will be by the communities themselves, the United Nations, NGOs, and the private sector, the choice being based on comparative advantage. This will use existing capacity, build up the private sector wherever possible, and avoid building an expensive, patronage-rich state apparatus. As far as possible, to ensure a national and programmatic approach, funding should be pooled through trust funds that can be jointly managed by government and donors. Government has already put in place oversight and control of funds by contracting internationally respected companies. A key principle is, as far as is possible, to remove decision-making from government and agencies and put it in the hands of communities. In much relief work, for example, this means shifting to labor-intensive, cash-for-work programs and away from in-kind distributions. And in much reconstruction work it means providing community cash grants, not NGO- or government-designed projects. As much as possible, service delivery contracts should be competed for by open tender to ensure value for money and to avoid corruption. This approach should also avoid creating parallel agency structures. This process has been enhanced by the post–Loya Jirga appointment of "technocratic" ministers to the main spending ministries. There is also a solid commitment to raising revenue and avoiding unsustainable levels of service delivery.

Reform is an integrated political, social, and economic process. The different strands come together in, for example, the National Solidarity Programme, where community grants will put decision-making in the hands of communities, enable the state to bypass warlord structures to provide resources to communities directly, and promote the development of community-level democracy and decision-making as the basis for a more democratic polity. Similarly, social protection and the provision of cash-for-work is as much about creating mutual obligations between the state and individuals as improving levels of well-being and income. By making the state more responsive to people's demands, Afghans will develop a stake in its future; in turn, this means they are more likely to demand accountability and so engage in the political process rather than look to non-state sources of protection and patronage. It is also important that state servants behave in systematic and ordered ways, providing service on the basis of rules not relationships. Civil service reform will be a key element of the process.

In order to pursue this program, we need the active support of many actors, not just Afghans, but aid workers, aid agencies, donors, and investors. We believe there is a broad consensus around this reform program, not only among Afghans but among much of the aid system and most international actors. However, despite this agreement in principle, our experience is that support for the reform process has been ambivalent at best.

THE ROLE OF AID

What, then, has been the role of donors and agencies in the reform process, especially state-building? We will focus here on that part of the system through which the bulk of aid has come so far, that is, the United Nations and NGOs, much of it labeled "humanitarian."

First, is it legitimate to ask this question at all? Is not the primary task of most of the money that has been spent to save lives and livelihoods? Should aid be judged against its contribution to reform? We argue that, with the limited exception of properly defined humanitarian aid, it should be, and that contributing to the broader reform process is an essential element for most aid interventions. Unlike during conflict, when it is now well established that the potential peace-building impact of aid ranges from limited to nonexistent, aid in the context of a legitimate government is very different.[6] Aid, particularly when it has gone from around an annual level of US$250 million during the Taliban period to the approximately US$2 billion that has been committed since the large donor conference in Tokyo in January 2002, has a significant political impact, and this must be in the direction of positive political progress.[7] Indeed, the potential for aid to influence the political process positively and to build the legitimacy of the state may be greater in post-conflict situations than during conflict or in normal development situations, when government revenues and private capital flows are that much more important. Donors and agencies have options—putting money in trust funds or directly into projects, putting money into agency-run in-kind distribution or government-run cash-for-work projects, for example—and one of the criteria in decisions on these options must be their impact on political change.

On the question of "humanitarian exceptionalism" we agree that humanitarian aid, strictly defined, should not be subject to such political considerations. However, much of what is called humanitarian aid now being conducted in Afghanistan is humanitarian only in the bureaucratic sense that it comes from humanitarian budget lines or is programmed by agencies that call themselves humanitarian. In the absence of active conflict, and in the context of a legitimate government committed to poverty reduction, it is hard to make any sense of a distinctly "humanitarian" vulnerability as opposed to poverty, and the best way to tackle poverty in the long term is to have an accountable and capable state. We will touch on this question again below.

So, given that it is legitimate to ask how aid has affected the reform process, we will do so by examining three features of current aid practice in Afghanistan:

- The way in which the problem is defined;
- the planning, coordination, funding, and implementation of service delivery; and
- the notion of humanitarian principles and the relationship of humanitarian action to the political process.

DEFINING THE PROBLEM

Definitions and perspectives are rarely neutral. Rather, the way in which a problem is defined, and thus a solution implied, is a reflection of institutional and political power. Often, definitions both serve and reflect the interests of the different actors engaged in a problem. Thus the "humanitarian" definition of many small wars during the 1990s reflected the lack of international political will to engage in dealing with them.

There are many competing definitions of the problem in Afghanistan, reflecting the nature of the reconstruction process as an arena of competing interests. A small example would be the use of the terms *regional leader* versus *warlord*. This range of competing definitions reflects the lack of agreement about strategic objectives in Afghanistan; not only do different actors disagree, but different parts of the same government often disagree.

Our definition of the problem is sketched out above, but, as we argued, it is by no means the only one. There are competing definitions, not only from other Afghan political actors but also from aid actors. We, of course, argue that the definition provided by a legitimate government should have priority.

We will look at these definitions at two levels: what might be called the strategic level, and the level relating more specifically to aid.

THE STRATEGIC LEVEL

At the strategic level there is a lack of consensus about the primary goal in Afghanistan. Candidates in this regard include an undefined "reconstruction" process, the more explicitly political reform process we outlined above, rebuilding the institutions of governance, containment of the problem, and destroying the remnants of Al Qaeda and the Taliban. The traditional donor policy goal of straightforward national interest, of course, is always present as well.

Within the political and military sphere there are two "parallel worlds" with different views of Afghanistan. The first, widely held by many in the military and intelligence community, sees Afghanistan as a country of warlords and drug barons with little chance of a political future. Policy goals are achieved by bribery, violence, and support of regional leaders. In this model there is little point in expanding ISAF or, more broadly, in nation-building. This approach is inconsistent with reconstruction because it has retarded the expansion of the center's authority and strengthened the hand of anti-reform forces—those who stand to lose from a rule-based state and want to see the perpetuation of arbitrary, personal, and clientelistic rule. The second view, more widely held by politicians and diplomats, believes the political process has some possibility and has led to support for the use of Loya Jirga mechanisms and an inclusive political process as the best way to prevent a return to war.

The events of September 11, 2001, undoubtedly played a significant role in terms of bringing much of the international community together over Afghanistan, as reflected in support for the Bonn process and the Tokyo meeting in particular. However, it would appear to be difficult for the international community to have an overall common definition of the problem and a common "strategy" in anything but the broadest terms; there are simply too many conflicting interests and differing goals.

THE AID LEVEL

This inconsistency in broader objectives feeds through to the narrower programming of aid, where similar processes operate; definitions of vulnerability tend to reflect agency mandates rather than poverty as experienced by Afghans or reform as defined by the government. The aid bureaucracy tends to define the problem in depoliticized terms such as *humanitarian* or *reconstruction,* not being comfortable with the more overtly political idea of *reform.*

Within the aid bureaucracy there has been some competition between those defining the problem in Afghanistan as humanitarian and those preferring to see it in terms of reconstruction and development. Many of the initial actors, both donors and agencies, were humanitarian in focus. They tended to react quicker and could access rapid funding, and this gave them an initial definitional advantage. Most of the funding that was received during 2002 went to humanitarian projects. This tended to sideline government calls for early attention to activities that would provide both short-term income and long-term benefits, such as roads, in favor of in-kind distributions. Defining the problem as humanitarian has also obscured state-building possibilities in favor of building the capacity of humanitarian agencies, many of whom had little or no presence in the country before September 11. Defining the problem as humanitarian has also tended to focus response on distribution of in-kind commodities by humanitarian agencies at the expense of the government's favored approach of focusing resources on labor-intensive, cash-for-work programs. Similarly, defining the nature of vulnerability in, for example, terms of food implies a certain response. The initial needs-assessment process also was done without any significant Afghan involvement.

A related problem has been the control of information by agencies, often related to their own mandates rather than common problems on the ground; UN agencies, for example, are still using their own definitions and maps of district boundaries and have not agreed on province groupings. In preparation for the winter of 2002, there were significant problems getting information from agencies about deliveries of commodities in a usable form.

Any society, through the political process, must decide for itself the balance between welfare and investment, short term and long term, and reconstruction priorities; the very weight of the aid system makes it difficult for this to happen. But in the long term, only a politically representative government has the right and the capacity to do so; indeed, the "strategic coordination" of the aid system will not be possible unless it is led by the Afghan government.

SERVICE DELIVERY: PLANNING, COORDINATION, FUNDING, AND IMPLEMENTATION

The NDF sees one of the state's primary roles as investing in Afghanistan's human capital, thus one of the key elements of the reform program is improving and expanding public service delivery. Better public service delivery also has a political significance and is one element of the new compact between state and citizen that is at the heart of the reform process; if the state is a reliable service deliverer, the position of local patrons and warlords will weaken.

During the war, services were delivered in a multitude of different projects by the United Nations and NGOs across the country, each funded by individual contracts between donor and agency, and each designed and planned by individual agencies with more or less coordination. There was little in the way of national policy, despite many attempts. The primary relationship remained between agency and donors, and the primary mode of intervention was the project.

But this approach is not workable for state-building and supporting a reform process with a government in place committed to poverty reduction and social protection:

- Coordination as exercised by OCHA in country is unable to deliver national strategy or policy because it is a matter of "good will" in a competitive environment. This means it is impossible to prioritize scarce resources, and actual allocation is the result of a series of disconnected negotiations between agencies and donors. This leads to unsustainable commitments in, for example, the form of schools and clinics that cannot be afforded.
- The project approach tends to be supply driven and typically focuses on outputs rather than impact.
- The project funding system tends to maintain a division between government and implementing agency by prioritizing donor/agency relationship and accountability.

- The project approach makes it very difficult to collect national level comparable data and so build up a national and comprehensive picture of vulnerability and impact.
- The project approach is anti-competitive and excludes the private sector; it gives agencies an effective monopoly of public money for projects they, not government or communities, have identified.
- The project approach tends to reinforce regional power structures at the expense of central policy and allocation, precisely when the need is to strengthen the center.
- There is a danger that the need for project implementation will create multiple and parallel delivery structures; project administration costs are a large part of agency budgets.

It was, in part, to remedy these problems that the government produced the NDF. The NDF was intended to ensure that the primary coordination mechanism is a plan, not a structure. The NDF is a comprehensive plan covering almost all aspects of the reform process but focusing on the role of government. It is divided into three pillars and twelve programs and forms the foundation for the coordination structure and the national budget.[8]

One of the government's most important objectives, in line with international best practice, is to make the national budget the centerpiece of planning and policymaking. Also in line with international orthodoxy, we argue strongly for funds to be put through the central budget rather than through a series of donor-supported project implementation units or agencies. We recognize that the government has weak implementation capacity, and much service delivery will be contracted out, strengthening the private sector, another of our key goals. Financial oversight mechanisms managed by internationally respected companies are being established to ensure transparency.

This approach has the following benefits:

- It allows government to set overall policy and objectives, which can be done with relatively few skilled people, but leaves implementation, where government capacity is weak, to the private sector, NGOs, and communities. These polices are then expressed through a limited series of national programs rather than a jumble of ad hoc projects.
- It ensures national-level policy and standards, ensuring that entitlements to services are the same everywhere, which is both just and essential if confidence in the state is to be rebuilt.
- It means the population will see the state, rather than the UN system or NGOs, as the primary service provider, a key factor in demonstrating the state's legitimacy and building reciprocity.

- It allows the allocation of scarce resources to be done at the national level on the basis of a national understanding of vulnerability and of priorities. This should avoid the problem of creating unsustainable demands the state will not be able to fulfill, and so avoid money being wasted on, for example, building schools where we cannot afford teachers.
- It makes the political process of resource allocation by ministers real. This is an essential part of normal politics, and thus should encourage responsible decision-making. If ministers are sidelined and the real allocation decisions made by donors, the government is unlikely to develop as an arena for peaceful conflict management and responsible decision-making.
- The way in which services are delivered—which should be client and community focused, not "Kabul knows best"—is as important as the objectives of improving livelihoods, reducing mortality, increasing literacy, and so on. In the context of degraded, understaffed, and poorly equipped state structures with a tradition of central control, contracted NGOs should be able to make service delivery more responsive to local needs than the state. Contracting out thus has a political as much as an efficiency rationale.
- It will contribute to the rebuilding of the private sector, key to the economic future of the country.

In other words, our approach to planning and budgeting is not just about a competition for control but is a key element of the state-building agenda. So, to what extent has it been supported by the aid system?

In terms of structure, we have moved rapidly from the confusion of early 2002 to the current CG structure. Donors have been asked to focus their funding on a maximum of three of the twelve NDF programs. The AACA has initiated a government aid-tracking system. We are grateful for cooperation in this from our partners, but it would not have happened without government taking the lead; that is, if donors and agencies had been left to themselves, it would not have happened.

However, the picture is much less encouraging in terms of funding and implementation. Funding and implementation are still primarily through agencies and projects rather than through government and programs.[9] In the early days there was a donor obsession with quick impact projects at the expense of capacity building. More recently the focus has been on individual donor-agency contracts rather than national, government-led programs. While there are limited amounts of money in the trust funds, and donors negotiate directly with agencies, this will remain the case. Of the US$1.84 billion in grant money disbursed since the Tokyo conference, only US$296 million, or 16 percent, has been provided directly to and received by the government.[10]

The reasons for this seem to be a mix of the political and technical. On the political side, as argued above, the reform process is still not seen as the primary objective by a number of aid actors, both donors and agencies. Many donors are also equivocal about both the political legitimacy and the administrative capacity of the government, making them reluctant to invest too much, though there is disagreement among donors on both these issues. Planning and coordination are as much political as technical issues; they are about who has the right to decide and allocate resources. This political role has been obscured by the practice of humanitarian coordination in Afghanistan prior to the Taliban, which operated to the exclusion of that regime. But with a new government in place, what seems to be happening is that donors are allowing the government to move ahead on the structural side—that is, the rapid move to the CG—while maintaining control of resources, where the real influence lies. This leaves government as a "coordinator" rather than a real government. This very qualified view of sovereignty is in line with the qualified legitimacy awarded to the government by donors.

On the technical side, there are the usual problems of high transaction costs for coordination, lack of commitment, desire to pursue individual agendas, competition among donors, and so on. Perhaps more fundamental is the extent to which "the project" is embedded and institutionalized in the system, which itself is the mediator of the symbiotic donor-agency relationship that often excludes government. It serves the interests of both donors looking for ever-tighter accountability needs and allows modular expansion by agencies. By working though agencies, it serves the interests of foreign policy bureaucracies that are wary of strengthening a government many donors are not sure of, and the interests of donor bureaucracies who need to justify their existence and maintain patronage rights over agencies, something that would be lost if money was pooled into programs run by the government. The reform process is not the only political project around.

The irony is that when the government tries to improve coordination and reduce dysfunctional competitive behavior between agencies and donors in line with best international practice, some donors and agencies complain. Much of the progress that has been made has been a result of government initiatives. The aid system needs the government to take charge to make it work properly, yet when it tries to do this it meets with resistance. It would seem that the structure of the aid system has as much to do with the slow progress as the government's lack of capacity.

POLITICS AND PRINCIPLES:
AGENCIES AND THE REFORM PROCESS

Much of the tension between government and aid agencies in terms of the state-building project has been expressed in the language of humanitarian principles; typically, agencies express their rejection or qualified acceptance of government-led planning, coordination, and resource-mobilization processes in terms of "humanitarian independence," and their continued provision of services on the grounds of the need for an "impartial" response to ongoing humanitarian need. What is implied, but only occasionally stated, by this position is that the state is unwilling or unable to provide service delivery impartially. It is the local expression of the broader issue of the relationship between aid agencies and the political process, the old chestnut of aid and politics.

There are several misconceptions in this position. First is the lack of an adequate understanding of the role of government and the state. In many encounters with NGOs in particular, but also with the United Nations, the impression has been given that the state is seen by agencies as a body of dubious legitimacy and uncertain capacity that is trying to impose tiresome and inappropriate structures on busy NGOs, who are doing all the real work, and that will direct resources according to "political" (i.e., bad) criteria. In fact, of course, not least because of the inherent patchiness and unsustainability of assistance, it is *only* a legitimate and effective state that could possibly deliver reasonably impartial services to the whole population, which purpose is indeed part of the justification of the state in the first place. Given the global inequities in humanitarian funding, agencies themselves are far from impartial and face, at a global level, the same constraints of which they accuse the government: the provision of funds for service provision according to criteria other than need.[11]

When the state is, grudgingly, accorded a special role, it is usually assumed to be a negative force and compared, inevitably and unfavorably, with civil society. The potential role of the state as a progressive force that promotes social justice and development is overlooked. It is galling to receive lectures on the importance of civil society from NGOs that receive most of their funds from other states. It is even more galling, for an Afghan government official who has worked here for his professional life, to be told by a Western NGO official who has been in the country a few months, and will leave in a few more, how much closer to the grass roots NGOs are. Perhaps the experience of too many complex emergencies in failed states and working with "non-state actors" has left the humanitarian system unsure of the unique role of the state in ordering public space and service provision, and of the meaning and purpose of sovereignty. If the state is not seen as inherently oppressive, it is just one more competitor in an already crowded space competing for contracts with Western donors.

Along with this perception is the common dualistic humanitarian attitude that "good" humanitarian action is somehow separate from "bad" politics. Rather than see themselves as political actors pursuing a distinct form of "humanitarian politics" with its own objectives and rules of behavior, most agencies still see themselves as somehow disengaged from the political process.[12] From a government perspective, agencies are most definitely political actors whose actions have political impacts whether they like it or not. The question is not whether they are engaged in political action, but how. It is merely incoherent for agencies to demand "political solutions for political problems" and then protest against the inherent workings of a political process in which policy determination and resource allocation are conducted by political actors, a process in which political actors will be held accountable for their decision to an Afghan electorate. But it beggars belief that unaccountable agencies can actively prevent the political process from working (through refusing to acknowledge domestic political guidance in directing the large resources provided to them by foreign states) and still maintain that they are "nonpolitical." Perhaps the sheer majesty of the self-deception is necessary to allow agencies to work at all.

A further confusion is the continued applicability and usefulness of the term *humanitarian* to describe vulnerability in the context of relative peace and a legitimate government committed to social protection and poverty reduction. As many studies have shown, analyzing and characterizing vulnerability in Afghanistan is highly complex. We do not pretend to have the answers here, and we readily admit that the notion of humanitarian action has continuing relevance in this context. However, currently the term *humanitarian* is used cavalierly; not only does it cover vulnerability and response, but it has substantial institutional and bureaucratic uses as well. This overlapping and elasticity leads to confusion. Is an activity humanitarian, and therefore subject to the full panoply of humanitarian principles, just because it is funded from a humanitarian budget line? Should a clinic funded from a humanitarian budget line, for example, consider itself outside the government-led health policy and structure because to be part of it would compromise its independence? Is an agency that has been doing humanitarian work but has now expanded into development a humanitarian agency? Should it retain its autonomy, or should it regard itself as part of the mainstream? Is the type of long-term service delivery in health and education that many humanitarian agencies have been doing for years humanitarian, or, as service delivery, the role of government? How can agencies both work with this government and yet maintain sufficient neutrality so that if there is a return to conflict they can work on all sides?

Such confusion has been harmful to the reform process in a number of ways:

- There has been little sophisticated analysis of the political situation by aid agencies, in particular about the reform process itself; agencies tend to lump all actors in "the government" together rather then seek to understand tensions and opportunities. This is unhelpful in itself, but it has also meant that there has been little thinking from agencies, in particular the United Nations, about opportunities for integrating political and assistance goals.[13] This is not to argue for crude "threats and bribery" models of the contribution of aid to the peace process, rather for initiatives such as the National Solidarity Programme mentioned before. It has also made many agencies parochial; with the proving-the-rule exception of CARE, the focus of much NGO advocacy work has not been on, for example, expanding security for Afghans through expanding ISAF, or the future of the reform process, or the different roles the state and NGOs in affordable service delivery, but rather on the narrower issue of civil-military relations, in particular the issue of soldiers doing humanitarian work.[14]
- Most NGOs have refused to get involved in so-called political activities such as helping the emergency Loya Jirga process or promoting debate among Afghans on the NDF, or on the reform process generally. The postwar political settlement in Afghanistan will depend on developing a consensus and a broad alliance for reform. NGOs could have a significant contribution in promoting and encouraging that debate among Afghans.
- Mistaken notions of agency independence and "politics bad, aid good" attitudes have tended to promote crude "they are trying to manipulate us" interpretations of legitimate government initiatives for greater coordination and to interpret government policy choices as political interference. Thus, policy discussion between government and agencies about certain types of interventions have led to accusations that the government is anti-humanitarian. It should be possible for the government to disagree with a humanitarian agency about its mode of intervention without being accused of being anti-humanitarian.
- There is a tendency for donors and agencies to misuse the notion of humanitarian space; at worst, it is not a vehicle for ensuring impartial humanitarian action but rather allows agencies and donors to pursue their own polices and justifies spending little time coordinating or negotiating with government. Coordination with government, after all, requires lengthy and tiresome translations into Dari from English, the internationally accepted language of humanitarian coordination.

The halfway house of post-conflict is particularly difficult for agencies. They are happier dealing with absolutes, that is, either with a situation in which need can be easily characterized as "humanitarian" and the authorities have no legitimacy, such as under the Taliban, or in which need is characterized as "poverty" and the authorities are accepted as fully legitimate, as in most development contexts. Agencies find it difficult to cope with the ambiguity of post-conflict, when the legitimacy awarded by the international community is usually partial and conditional. Post-conflict situations force agencies to make political judgments, something agencies seem unwilling and often incapable of doing.

But, as we argued above, the potential political return on aid is greatest in precisely this context. This means that, at a minimum, agencies must understand the reform process, what their role in it may be, and the impact they are having. The reform process demands of agencies a degree of political understanding and astuteness; agencies must make politically informed judgments about whether the reform process is likely to succeed or not and what the impact of their actions will be. It seems easier for agencies to resist or to ignore the state than to work with it. Working with a legitimate state is much more politically complex, judgments are less black and white, and it is harder to sell to the media or constituencies back home. The image of NGOs as providers of social services by contract to government is not one that sits well with the buccaneering NGO self-image as protector of the weak.

Because the notion of humanitarianism has become so elastic, in great measure because of the actions of humanitarian agencies, its use is undisciplined and often self-serving. Because the notion of humanitarianism comes with independence, it is tempting for agencies who want to assert their perceived right to do as they please to describe whatever they do as humanitarian. It smacks of "wanting to have your cake and eat it" for an agency to expand into development activities through accessing development funding that is only available because the government is internationally legitimate, but yet arguing that it cannot get close to that government for fear of losing its humanitarian neutrality. It is ironic that the concept of humanitarianism is now being used to defend agency isolation from "politics" precisely when a real reform process is possible in which aid can have a very positive role. There is a distinct danger that the idea of humanitarian principles is being misused to legitimate what are in effect unaccountable power structures rather than to ensure the best interests of the poorest.

We suggest that it is time for a return to a more well-defined notion of humanitarian action as an activity that is undertaken during active conflict, that focuses on the short-term, impartial relief of suffering, and that is carried out by specialist, neutral agencies that do not also get involved in development. This would provide a clear distinction.

On the one hand, the government would recognize the need for such action to be independent, on the other it would allow much of what is currently classed as "humanitarian" to be properly classified and programmed as part of normal, ongoing service delivery and so coordinated by the government. If agencies are concerned about whether or not they are perceived as neutral, then their proper course is to stick to humanitarian activities and refrain from undertaking development projects; engaging in development necessarily implies an acceptance of government *legitimacy*, if not of all government *policies*. Accepting money for development projects from donor governments who do recognize the legitimacy of the Afghan government, but refusing to engage with the government for fear of compromising neutrality, is simply incoherent.

CONCLUSIONS

Of all the "national institutions" referred to by Barnett Rubin in the quotation at the head of this chapter, the state itself is the most important, and reconstructing an accountable, legitimate, and effective state is the primary task facing Afghanistan. The outline of an Afghan-led reform process is in place; whether it will succeed or not is very hard to say, because the risks are almost too numerous to enumerate. However, no reform process can be successful without vision and risk. Afghanistan will be no different. Aid and the aid system will play an important, if not a defining role in whether or not it is successful. However, as we have argued, there has been a number of problems in getting the aid system to engage with the reform process, including two overriding problems.

First, despite a consensus on the need to rebuild the state at a theoretical level, donors have failed to agree on the detailed strategies necessary for reform as the overriding policy objective in Afghanistan. Instead, a number of often competing policy objectives have been pursued by different actors—destroying Al Qaeda, straightforward national interest, reconstruction, emergency response, and containment of population movement. Thus mechanisms fundamental to the process, such as pooled funding either through the trust funds or the government budget, have not been fully established.

And second, the structure, resourcing, principles, and ideology of large parts of the aid system have made it very difficult for it to even recognize, let alone adapt to the new realities of Afghanistan. Many of the features of the aid system operating in Afghanistan—some of which evolved in the context of the Taliban, and some of which are universal—have proved less than functional in the context of a legitimate government with a credible poverty-reduction program. Many of the issues we have raised here are far from new; they have been raised in similar reconstruction contexts, which raises serious questions about learning in the system.[15]

It is too early to tell how the outline of the settlement between aid and politics will work out in this new era. However, we suspect that the role of the state will return to center stage, after a decade or so when many have predicted its virtual demise. This may well be the case in arenas where humanitarian agencies have for years been virtually alone. There are risks here. In the Cold War, state violations of human rights were often overlooked in return for support, and the same could happen again. But the progress of the last decade in terms of asserting human rights over sovereignty is unlikely to be completely overturned. And there is probably greater consensus than for many years now among a broad range of development actors about the relative role of markets and the state in the development process and reducing poverty.

Afghanistan and the Afghans have been seen by the international community in many lights: resistance heroes against Soviet aggression, drug-dealing warlords and bandits, the arena for proxy wars, victims of Taliban oppression, and unwilling hosts to international terrorism. We hope that in this current phase of international engagement in Afghanistan the international community can unite behind a reform process that is led by Afghans themselves, one through which Afghans can determine their own future.

NOTES

[1] Barnett R. Rubin, "Statement to Implementation Group" (Kabul, October 12, 2002). Available online.

[2] "The next step, to ensure that all United Nations efforts are harnessed to fully support the implementation of the Bonn Agreement, would be to integrate all the existing United Nations elements in Afghanistan into a single mission, the United Nations Assistance Mission in Afghanistan (UNAMA)" (UN General Assembly/Security Council. "Report of the Secretary-General on the Situation in Afghanistan and Its Implications for International Peace and Security," UN doc. A/56/875–S/2002/278 [March 18, 2002], para. 95).

[3] "National Development Framework" (Kabul: AACA, 2002).

[4] For research into Afghan opinions about democracy and state-citizen relationships, see also T. O'Melia, "Afghan Perspectives on Democracy: A Report on Focus Groups in the Kabul Area on the Eve of the Emergency *Loya Jirga*," a report prepared for the National Democratic Institute for International Affairs, Washington D.C., 2002.

[5] Andreas Wimmer and Conrad Schetter, "State Formation First: Recommendations for Reconstruction and Peacemaking in Afghanistan," ZEF Discussion Paper 45 (Bonn: Bonn University, April 2002).

[6] Joanna Macrae, *Aiding Recovery?: The Crisis of Aid in Chronic Political Emergencies* (London: Zed Books, 2001).

[7] See AACA, "Preliminary Analysis of Aid Flows to Afghanistan" (Kabul: AACA, 2003).

[8] Pillar 1, humanitarian and social capital, comprises programs on refugees, education, health, livelihoods and social protection, and culture and sport. Pillar 2, physical reconstruction and natural resources, contains programs on energy, mines, telecommunications, transport, natural resource management, and urban management. Pillar 3 is private sector development.

[9] AACA, "Preliminary Analysis of Aid Flows to Afghanistan."

[10] Ibid.

[11] On humanitarian funding trends, see Joanna Macrae, ed., *The New Humanitarianisms: A Review of Trends in Global Humanitarian Action*, HPG Report 11 (London: ODI, April 2002).

[12] Joanna Macrae and Nicholas Leader, eds., *Shifting Sands: The Search for 'coherence' Between Political and Humanitarian Responses to Complex Emergencies*, HPG Report 8 (London: ODI. August 2000).

[13] *A Review of Peace Operations: A Case for Change. Afghanistan (A Snapshot Study)* (London: Kings College, 2003).

[14] See, for example, ACBAR, "NGOs Concerns and Recommendations on Civil-Military Relations," ACBAR Policy Brief (Kabul: ACBAR, December 2002). In this document with six recommendations, one is on the issue of expanding security for Afghans, but five focus on the role of the military in assistance activities, the thrust being against anything but a limited role for the military. See also, "French NGOs Say *'Stop the Confusion'* Between Military and Humanitarian Personnel," press release by Action Contre la Faim, ACTED, AFRANE, AMI, Architecture & Dévelopement, Enfants du Monde/Droits de l'Homme, Handicap International, Madera, MDM, MRCA, Solidarités, and Groupe URD (Paris, February 3, 2003). On CARE, see CARE International in Afghanistan, "Rebuilding Afghanistan: A Little Less Talk, a Lot More Action," Policy Brief (September 2002).

[15] For reviews of post-conflict assistance in a number of countries that raise many of the issues raised here, see, for example, Shepard Forman, Stewart Patrick, and Dirk Solomons, *Recovering from Conflict: Strategy for an International Response* (New York: Center on International Cooperation, 2000) and Macrae, *Aiding Recovery?*

10

Old Woods, New Paths, and Diverging Choices for NGOs

PAUL O'BRIEN

When I visited Kabul in 1999 for the United Nations, NGOs had become a de facto shadow government running many of the social services that the Taliban and their predecessors were unable or unwilling to provide. The Swedish Committee for Afghanistan was educating more than 160,000 children, employed more than 8,000 people, more than 1,500 of them women (mostly as teachers). CARE International, for whom I now work, provided clean water to more than 400,000 people in Kabul. NGOs were the social safety net for the Afghan people, and times were grim. The Taliban remained a hard sell to media and donors that had grown weary of complex crises. NGOs were left to scramble for emergency funds while Afghanistan floundered at the bottom of the world's poverty indices.

Little did they know that three years later they would be responding to a twelve-month media frenzy, their rents in Kabul would multiply tenfold, and many of their qualified Afghan staff would leave for more lucrative positions in the United Nations and embassies. They had no idea that they would be stretching their capacities to the limit as donors spent more than US$1.5 billion dollars in 2002 to fulfill pledges made in the political afterglow of the Taliban overthrow. Most of all, they were ill-prepared for a new reality in which *humanitarian space* became an oxymoron, and *aid politicization* a tautology. "You're with us or against us" was the mantra of post-Taliban Afghanistan, trumpeted by donors, the Afghan authorities, the international military coalition, and even our erstwhile humanitarian bedfellows, the United Nations.

This chapter evaluates how NGOs responded to that call and suggests a future choice for NGOs to consider. It first looks back at how NGOs saw themselves during the Taliban years, and then reflects on how post-Taliban Afghanistan has altered NGO perspectives and their reality. It goes on to consider how aid politicization has affected NGOs and suggests two ways that NGOs may respond to the new environment. Finally, it examines the benefits and costs of those choices.

THE GOOD, BAD, AND RIDICULOUS OF LIFE IN THE TALIBAN BORDERLANDS

At time of writing, a number of international NGO offices established pre–September 11 still have one or two foreign staff who have been here since the Taliban years. Many such "veterans," after years in the hinterland of assistance work, wanted the chance to make real progress with real resources. Finally, relative peace, a reform-oriented government, and serious international attention gave NGOs the opportunity to move from band-aids to rebuilding, to take on the kinds of interventions that require long-term significant resource commitments and a permissive operating environment. Yet, some NGO veterans cannot help but bring serious skepticism to the grand experiment of post-Taliban Afghanistan. To understand their concerns and some of the dilemmas now facing NGOs in Afghanistan, it is useful to reflect on NGO life under the Taliban.

Back then, as one NGO staffer told me, "there was a wall between us and them. Donors drummed it into us. The Taliban were on the other side, and we were not to give them so much as a pencil. Funding was to be used to serve the Afghan people, not their illegitimate government." The culture of separation was more prevalent in some sectors (such as education), than in others (such as health), but it was certainly different from today's reality. In keeping the Taliban at a distance, many NGOs relied upon humanitarian principles. As organizations committed to independence, neutrality, and impartiality, NGOs were comfortable maintaining an arm's length from the Taliban. They were there for communities, not for government. What little support donors provided, they gave from a distance. Political agendas were more subtly displayed. Humanitarian space seemed important and real.

NGOs were important in those days. The Taliban were too busy fighting wars and the world to provide services to ordinary Afghans.

Donors, beyond mandating NGO disengagement from the Taliban, were too far away to tell NGOs how to work with communities. The media were just not interested. Few came to Afghanistan if they didn't have to. Over time, NGOs became the eyes of the world and therefore its conscience.

Of course, NGOs were frustrated that, once again, ordinary people were paying for the sins of politics and religious extremism. Funding was short term and emergency driven. There were no reconstruction funds. Women-centered social change work was challenged at every turn. Nevertheless, NGOs found innovative ways to get important work done. When the Taliban partially lifted the ban on female employment to allow women health educators, NGOs changed the job descriptions of many female staff to include health education; some hired the husbands of female doctors so that they could "work" and travel together; NGOs who sponsored rural girls' schools kept a low profile, while local community leaders took ownership and simply ignored Taliban edicts. It was hardly a merry dance, but it lasted nonetheless, and as a result millions of Afghans fed themselves, educated their girls and boys, and found treatment for their sick.

It wasn't always possible to get around the more harmful and ridiculous sides of Taliban extremism. The Taliban specialized in cruel and often bizarre methods of punishing those who questioned their authoritarian madness. For five years the ability of NGOs to fight poverty and relieve suffering was undermined by the gender discriminatory Taliban edicts. Many talented Afghan women working for NGOs lost years of professional experience, forced to play backroom roles and hide their skills, when they could get work at all. Typical of the more ridiculous side of NGO life under the Taliban is the following tale related to me by a CARE colleague:

"We had some external visitors come in 2001, both men and women. Driving out to Nawal, the seating arrangements were no problem because there were few Taliban checkpoints. Coming back, however, it took us twenty minutes of discussion to work out how to seat the genders and the seniority in a way that would pass Taliban scrutiny. This was beyond respect for culture. It was daft."

Yet, it would be wrong to characterize the Taliban years as worse in every sense for NGOs. For one thing, there was far less bureaucracy at practically every level than there is today. The Taliban, ill-trained and largely uninterested in the art of governance, had little time for paperwork. They were frustrated that NGOs would not submit to their control, but they came to tolerate the constraints of funding and principle that NGOs faced. There was less infighting among government departments anxious to garner strategic control over resources, and far less opportunity to use NGOs as puppets in power games. Donor agencies faced nothing of the political or public-relations pressures that exist today in Afghanistan. Rather than designing initiatives at head-quarters to achieve maximum political impact, donors looked to NGOs to tell them what communities required and mostly listened to the feed-back they received. Their general disengagement meant fewer reports, fewer meetings, fewer site visits, and a lot more influence for NGOs.

Moreover, the Taliban were not the homogenous horde of back-ward-thinking ideologues that some imagine. Among their ranks were more moderate elements, who understood that survival demanded some accommodation with the international community. While letting NGOs know of their distaste for Western ways, they also saw the poverty of their communities and wanted help. One NGO tells this indicative story:

> While visiting Ghazni in 2000, the Taliban's minister for justice saw young girls in uniform going home. He went to the governor to demand the school's closure and the identity of the NGO spon-soring the school. The NGO representative was called to the governor's office, where, by coincidence, the minister for educa-tion had also turned up. After an initial inquisition, the NGO representative was asked to step outside while the two ministers engaged in a roaring argument over the need for girls' education.

Through the Taliban's time in power, NGOs and the United Nations found many ways to exploit their internal divisions on behalf of the Afghan people.

POST TALIBAN: A SITUATION CHANGED UTTERLY?

The post-Taliban era has been a roller-coaster ride for NGOs. From protagonists, NGOs faded to a pale reflection at many policymaking meetings. From safety net of last resort for millions, their service role was challenged both by a government anxious to prove its legitimacy and by for-profit contractors looking for aid dollars and willing to promise concrete deliverables quickly.

The so-called NGO community cannot entirely point the finger of blame elsewhere. The frenzy for donor funds in early 2002 saw hun-dreds of new NGOs setting up shop with little to offer beyond a sign-board and a proposal. Some were entrepreneurial Afghans who under-stood donor need to spend money quickly. By January 2003 the Ministry of Planning had more than one thousand NGOs registered—more than three times the number from a year previously. An Afghan colleague told me this story. Down in Gardez for a visit, he bumped into an old friend who had previously gone to Kuwait and set up lucrative work as a building contractor for international companies and the military. He asked the friend why he had left Kuwait. The friend responded, "Why stay there, when Kuwait has come here?" When asked to clarify, he said, "I learned in Kuwait how to talk to the US military. Now, when they need something built in Gardez, I'm here. I tell them what they need to hear and get the contract. It's good money and they need to spend it fast."

Other new arrivals included established international NGOs. Like Rwanda in 1994, the DRC (1996), and the Balkans throughout the 1990s, the influx of organizations with questionable Afghan experience and capacity may have damaged NGO reputations in 2002. NGO bashing once again became a (sometimes justified) sport played by donors ("NGOs are slow to respond, overstretched, and under performing"), the government ("NGOs are taking Afghanistan's dollars, refusing to submit to our authority, inefficient and unmanageable"), the United Nations ("coordinating NGOs is like herding cats"), and the media ("the military are out there building schools where NGOs fear to tread").

The roller-coaster ride was not all downhill, however. Most media, policymakers, and assistance functionaries understood that, flaws notwithstanding, NGOs were still essential. They had been on the ground through the lean years and were still doing the vast majority of the social work in rural areas. Those that had been here in the 1990s had trained or hired sometimes sizable staffs of Afghan professionals with precious health, education, engineering, construction, logistical, management, and emergency-response capacity, and not all those staff were willing to go to high-paying, low-responsibility jobs with the United Nations or embassies or to critical but critically under-funded positions in the new government. Amid the cacophony of short-term political mindsets and six-week contracts, NGOs provided a historical, grounded reality check. They had been here before and during the Taliban and would remain after the circus had moved on, as it now has. For all the anti-NGO rhetoric, they were called upon time and again when implementation was called for. Many a grand proposal emerging from the Afghan authorities, donors, the United Nations, or the World Bank closed with the acknowledgment that "much of this work will in the short to medium term be undertaken by NGOs."

While it is important to understand how things have changed, it is also worth noting that many things are not so different. Many NGOs that were in Afghanistan before 2002 found themselves doing essentially the same projects in 2002 as they did in years previously. Nor has the domestic political machinery with whom NGOs related transformed radically. If one goes to get a visa at the passport office in Kabul, one can see files everywhere dating back to the 1980s and early 1990s. And it is not just the files that are the same; below deputy minister level NGOs often find themselves dealing with the same faces in the government. Outside of Kabul, where most NGO work takes place, much of the political administration of the Taliban years remains intact. Often the governor and his deputy are the only new faces. More than once I've heard someone note that "one can switch from the turban [worn by the Taliban] to the pakool [sometimes known as the 'Massoud hat'], but the face is still the same."

That is not to imply that NGOs are ambivalent about the new Afghanistan. Whatever memories there may be of the critical role they played in the Taliban years, genuine nostalgia is rare, if it exists at all. Even if Afghanistan has been something of a circus since September 11, and even if NGOs have too often been painted as clowns, they recognize the critical importance of this moment in Afghanistan's history. It is a precious opportunity, perhaps a last chance, for Afghans living today to bring themselves out of abject poverty. There is no real debate that NGOs want this new great game to succeed. The challenge for NGOs is to determine which player they want to be and the rules for which they should fight.

The rest of this chapter addresses this challenge. If NGOs are to emerge from the post-Taliban experience stronger and more relevant in today's world (not just in Afghanistan), they will have to answer two critical questions (both discussed below): First, how do we respond to the drastic politicization of aid that has taken place in Afghanistan? Second, what ground do we stake out to ensure our practical relevance and comparative advantage under the "new rules" of relief and development?

AID POLITICIZATION FOR NGOS:
TAUTOLOGY OR TOTALITARIANISM?

I returned to Washington in December 2002 to do advocacy for CARE. Our concern at the time was that US military plans to engage in assistance work to further political and military goals would jeopardize humanitarian space. At the meeting, officials from USAID and the Office of Transition Initiatives presented their plans to co-locate with the US military to strengthen the overall coordination of aid. The officials had been frank that the primary objective of all US efforts in Afghanistan was to win the "war on terrorism" and had conceded that aid coordination would be used as one weapon in this fight. I raised the obvious dilemma: If NGOs participated in this effort, we would be taking United States funding in order to help achieve a military objective, not a humanitarian one, and asked what advice the US government had for us on resolving this dilemma. One official replied, "I feel like I'm in that Casablanca scene when the guy whispers, 'Do you know that there is gambling going on in the casino?'" The official went on to remind us that that aid is *always* used as an instrument of foreign policy, and in this regard, Afghanistan is no different.

I came away from that meeting wondering whether it was true. Was this just another example of NGO naiveté? Had aid always been used so politically? Have NGOs always been unwitting pawns in the global chess game?

My conclusion was that Afghanistan *was* different. It wasn't just the rhetoric of these policymakers—refreshing in its frankness, but worrying in its implications. It wasn't just that the assistance community, both donor agencies and implementers, had finally woken up to their role in the world. There was something profoundly new and troubling about what was going on in Afghanistan. Perhaps it really was, as David Rieff writes, the swan song of autonomous humanitarianism.[1]

Maybe after Somalia, Bosnia, Rwanda, and Kosovo, all of which further encroached on humanitarian space, NGOs should have been more prepared. Perhaps what was surprising in Afghanistan was how many sides it came from. Donors, the government, the military, and even the media seemed to have abandoned any pretense of respecting humanitarian neutrality. Instead, policymakers wanted to know whose side NGOs were on. The mission was clear—the new Afghanistan versus the Taliban legacy, state-building versus treating the symptoms of suffering, "real progress" versus incremental development. Either we got on board or lived with the consequences.

Donors were perhaps the first to show their hands. As Bob Woodward noted in *Bush at War*, the Coalition's decision to airdrop both bombs and humanitarian packages in the fall of 2001 was motivated, above all, by political aims.[2] There was almost no calculus, public or private, of how effectively those packages would relieve suffering compared to funding professional humanitarian agencies such as the UN's WFP.

Over the next twelve months it became increasingly obvious that donor governments considered humanitarian aid as just one more weapon in the war against terrorism. The global importance of what was going on in Afghanistan was hard to miss. The new rules for international engagement were being written here, and they posed interesting challenges for NGOs. In other post-conflict reconstruction contexts, NGOs had been strengthening governments for years. But this was different. An internationally orchestrated regime change had taken place, and state-building was clearly part of a larger plan to promote one type of regime over another. By accepting donor funds to strengthen the new government, NGOs would implicitly support this strategy and would jettison their pretensions at political independence from explicit donor agendas.

Perhaps NGOs should have been quicker to understand how the new government would view humanitarian space. In short, the new government found it arrogant that NGOs insisted on maintaining their autonomous decision-making capacity. As one Afghan minister said to me in late 2002, "What gave international NGOs the right or the capacity to determine what is best for Afghans? *We* are the elected representatives of the people." Anxious to prove their capacity to govern, they deemed humanitarian response a central part of the NDF and sought to control humanitarian resources as a result.

NGOs found themselves in a bind. If they stayed quiet, autonomous humanitarianism would be dealt yet another blow. If they spoke out, they risked being misinterpreted as anti-governmental rather than non-governmental. When they did attempt to clarify their concerns, in meetings or when asked to comment on the NDF, the arguments failed to convince. Officials willing to engage simply could not understand why NGOs did not want to support them. Faced with the abyss of Afghanistan's history, they felt that NGOs should have thrown their nagging doubts to the wind and their shoulders toward government efforts.

The government's concerns were not entirely unjustified. After all, humanitarian principles were designed for life-threatening emergency situations where the state was either unwilling or unable to function effectively. With Afghanistan trying to move from crisis to long-term reconstruction—the latter, an undeniably political challenge—the government had an understandable expectation that it would exert control over resources coming into the country.

Why didn't all NGOs sign up for this critical undertaking? Of course, some did. But others feared throwing their weight behind what was essentially a fragile political experiment. While most were comfortable participating in nation-building, they did not want to actively support the enfranchisement of one set of political actors over another. It was one thing to build the capacity of a state to function effectively—strengthening, for example, its ability to protect human rights, to monitor itself financially, or to hold free and fair elections—but it was another thing entirely to take on projects designed to popularize particular political actors while politically marginalized populations might be ignored. What if the situation reverted to crisis and the current political leadership was removed from power? NGOs were anxious to maintain their ability to work in Afghanistan regardless of who was in government.

Similarly, the international military Coalition did not understand NGO arguments for neutrality. Risking their lives to fight "bad guys," they had little time for NGO fence-sitting. "Aren't we all here trying to help the same people?" one US soldier asked me in early 2003. "We want to go out to places where you're not going, find out what people need, and get that information back to folks like you who can help them. What could be so bad with that?" he asked. When I tried to explain that our cherished relationships with communities depended on our perceived independence from military and political actors, he just wasn't buying. "Where do they think you get the money from?" he asked. "It all comes from donors. They know that." His perspective echoed a much wider sentiment among the military. From their standpoint, everything was, and always would be political. NGO infatuation with neutral humanitarianism, they felt, was a self-serving falsehood that undermined not just our effectiveness but the larger reconstruction effort in Afghanistan.

A notable irony of that time was the larger reaction of the media to NGO concerns. The days of "misery tours," where NGOs helped the media to tweak the compassion of the wider world, were long gone. The press in Afghanistan wanted more complexity for a readership that had had its fill of sob stories. NGOs knew that and tried to accommodate, but were surprised at how the media responded. On the politicization of aid question, few journalists had much interest in NGO concerns. NGO arguments couched in terms of long-term impact on communities were considered speculative and self-serving.

Perhaps most perplexing for NGOs was the perspective of our humanitarian siblings in the United Nations. The United Nations seemed caught between two mindsets in 2002. On the one hand, it wanted to be a major player in the reconstruction effort, to have a strong coordination role, and to help ensure its own legitimacy at a time when the UN's relevance was under serious political threat more globally. On the other hand, it had committed to a backroom role to ensure that the Afghan authorities took the reins. Often, this dilemma led to frustration for UN colleagues and sympathetic amusement from NGOs. But at other times it led to seriously negative consequences for NGOs.

NGOs were asked to contribute precious time and human resources to coordination initiatives that went nowhere. Internal wrangling over the heaviness of the UN footprint left huge holes in coordination that the military Coalition could legitimately use to show the need for its engagement in coordination. As an ally in the struggle for autonomous humanitarianism, the United Nations was compromised. Its dedicated staff voiced private frustration but could not speak out publicly to question the motives of donors or the government.

In 2002 Afghanistan was at a crossroads. One road to stable democracy demanded politics of principle that promoted transparent and accountable governance from the outset: protection of human rights, separation of powers, ethnically representative security forces, strengthening of the independent voice of civil society, respect for the will of the electorate, and so on. The other, the pragmatic path, recognized the nascent experiment that was taking place in Afghanistan and limited its expectations and its critique. Human rights took a back seat, glaring failures of representation in the Loya Jirga were ignored, "warlordism" and "spoils for the victors" were factored into decision-making as a given. The UN's commitment to coherence set it firmly on the latter road, an understandable decision perhaps, given the political constraints on the United Nations and the stakes for Afghanistan. But it clearly rankled many UN colleagues personally, and they turned some of their frustration on NGOs.

Aid politicization came at NGOs from all angles in 2002. We were threatened not just in terms of our principles but with respect to our two core concerns: the people we served were still getting the short end of the stick, and our own economic survival and relevance were now in question. How should NGOs respond? The next section argues that NGOs will have an important choice to make in Afghanistan over the next few years.

TWO ROADS DIVERGING

The Berlin Wall has been replaced by the World Wide Web as the metaphor for the modern era. So claimed Thomas Friedman in *Longitudes and Attitudes*.[3] He saw Cold War divisions replaced by the integrated reality of globalization, isolationism overcome by the reach of technology and terror. Interconnectivity had become the norm. In *Global Governance and the New Wars* Mark Duffield suggests a similar transformation and concludes that NGOs have yet to make the conceptual leap.[4] For too long, Duffield claims, NGOs have been driven by the simplistic cause-and-effect logic of Newtonian physics. We assumed that a given amount of inputs combined with a given amount of energy would produce given outcomes. Duffield argues that NGOs need to adopt the thinking of the new sciences, which describe the world organically rather than mechanistically. Whereas machines create predetermined outcomes, organic systems are concerned with self-renewal, and, as such, are more than the sum of their distinct parts.

Duffield concludes that NGOs are prone to see complex political emergencies as states of nature that can be understood and ameliorated through mechanistic problem-solving. Instead, NGOs needed to acknowledge the reality of "emerging political complexes" where fluid systems of actors and relationships play off each other politically, militarily, and economically, determining humanitarian well-being in ways beyond the conceptual capacity of humanitarian agencies.

Duffield's comments are part of a debate that is currently raging in the humanitarian world. The discussion grew out of the attacks against NGOs throughout the 1990s. People wanted to know why the grand development project was failing while endemic poverty survived. Northern governments were questioning the larger impact of development as corrupt regimes siphoned off aid dollars with entrepreneurial efficiency. Journalists, overwhelmed by compassion fatigue, wrote countless stories of NGO mismanagement. Jaded assistance workers reflected upon how it had all gone wrong.

Battered by those critiques, many international NGOs decided that a course change was necessary. They didn't want to be accused of naively applying band-aids to dying patients. They wanted to move from inadequately treating symptoms to getting at the underlying causes of poverty and suffering. If their programs were putting people in danger, they wanted to find out how and take steps to minimize unintended harms; if unending cycles of conflict were robbing generations of hope, then NGOs would promote peace through advocacy and "peace-building" programs; if corrupt regimes were impoverishing their peoples, NGOs would mobilize communities to protect their rights and pressure the outside world to act; if rich donor nations were not living up to their rhetoric or responsibilities to poorer countries, NGOs would use their moral authority and ground knowledge to educate donors and, if necessary, embarrass them into action.

In other words, these NGOs wanted to move toward "new humanitarianism." While preserving their right to serve communities apolitically, new humanitarians believed that NGOs had to become more politically astute and even take on the political causes of endemic poverty and suffering. Moving from a paradigm of charitable giving, those NGOs would aim to align themselves in solidarity with the human rights of the communities they served, holding themselves responsible to those communities and aiming to hold policymakers to their responsibilities as well.

Before new humanitarianism had truly found its feet, however, a backlash began. It started in British humanitarian policy think tanks like the ODI and the Institute for Politics and International Studies in Leeds. Its most influential recent advocate is David Rieff. In sum, thinkers like Rieff, Joanna Macrae, Mark Duffield, Fiona Fox, and co-author in this book Nicholas Leader are worried that humanitarianism has lost its footing.[5]

They argue that humanitarians need to get back to the basics of saving lives and relieving extreme suffering. Better to provide the suffering with "a bed for the night" than an empty promise that we could never fulfill. Our competency, our reason for being, was not to address the world's great problems. We would never bring peace to Afghanistan, end human rights abuses by warlords, or stamp out government corruption. In fact, as Duffield claims, faced with emerging political complexes, we didn't even have the capacity to understand the political impact of our work, and there was little point in our sitting around thinking about it. Nicholas Stockton said something similar in an informal presentation in late 2002 in Kabul. He had just come from the Eastern Congo, where he had watched humanitarians paralyzed by their "do no harm" analyses while millions suffered or died. He pleaded with us not to let the same thing happen in Afghanistan.

The choice for NGOs is this: Faced with the politicization of aid in Afghanistan, do we agree with this critique, get back to basics, and forget our pretensions to understand, let alone influence, the political environment around us? Or do we work harder to become more politically sophisticated and influential? In other words, should NGOs in Afghanistan dump or embrace new humanitarianism? This is not a choice between humility and arrogance, for there are people on both sides of the debate who overestimate the impact that NGOs will have on the new Afghanistan, either in terms of saving lives or in influencing policy. Doing advocacy, after all, implicitly recognizes that real power lies elsewhere with policymakers.

But it is a choice worth our serious consideration nonetheless. Afghanistan has become an "emerging political complex" par excellence. Gone is the ruthless simplicity of the Taliban. The new Afghan government is a multi-headed temptress with some players more progressive than many NGOs and others who would happily evict all international NGOs and divide Afghanistan into a feudal pie. Gone is donor indifference and media naiveté—every donor has an agenda, every story needs a twist. Gone too is the monopoly of compassion and humanitarian competence that not-for-profits once exercised in Afghanistan. On the heels of all the new money is an array of profit-oriented contractors, national and foreign, who threaten NGOs with their "doubtlessness" and "deliverables," not to mention the military, which has gone from engaging in the odd "hearts and minds" relief project to seeking a central coordination role in the overall assistance effort. The new Afghanistan is complex indeed.

All of these actors, in their own different ways, will make NGOs pay for making the wrong choice. NGOs are willing to adapt when their financial survival is at stake—some would say to a fault. But that does not mean we are prepared for this choice, or that we fully grasp what our role in the new Afghanistan is and ought to be. In 2002 there was enough funding going around that most NGOs were too busy even to think about making choices, even while they saw funding going to "competitors." But as the early signs of donor fatigue in Afghanistan emerge, the luxury of excess will soon disappear, and the choice will remain: new humanitarianism—love it or leave it?

A PLEA FOR TRADITIONAL HUMANITARIANISM: WHAT FOLLOWS THE ROAD WHERE IT BENDS IN THE UNDERGROWTH?

Not so long ago NGOs had lower ambitions in Afghanistan. They did not try to end the decades-long conflict with peace-building programs or seek to change the political direction of the Taliban. They did not think about the long-term political impact of their work or withhold their support for fear that it might actually hurt more than help. Far below the stratosphere of high politics, they aimed to relieve suffering and keep as many alive as possible through the dark years of Taliban rule.

There are some NGO staff who still believe that was not only our finest hour, but that it remains the path to our ongoing survival in Afghanistan. Those who have been here through many regime changes wonder how long this one will last and what will happen to the NGOs who get too close to the current regime. What if the world grows weary of its dramatic promises to ordinary Afghans? What if the peace dividend doesn't materialize soon enough for marginalized Pashtuns?

NGOs that maintain their political agnosticism, that refuse to work closely with the Afghan government or with the US military Coalition, are far more likely to remain trusted by communities and acceptable to any subsequent regime in the event of a violent overthrow.

Moreover, sticking with traditional humanitarianism does not necessarily make bad business sense. Finance Minister Ashraf Ghani, a former World Bank employee and leading strategist for the reformists, wants his government to be a lean machine. He aims to create a competitive environment for the provision of social services, and he doesn't see the Afghan government taking nationwide responsibility for education, health, food security, and shelter provision any time soon. If NGOs can mount competitive bids to provide these services, he is all in favor of them doing so, at least in the short to medium term. It may well be that NGOs who hear nothing, see nothing, say nothing, but do plenty will thrive in the new Afghanistan. To compete against for-profit contractors, they will need to be lean and results oriented. "Frills" such as policy advocacy, peace strengthening through projects, and benefits-harms analysis of new humanitarianism are a luxury.

While I would hope that not all NGOs would take this path, one cannot help but appreciate its force. There is a humility that rings true to acknowledging the minor role NGOs play in Afghanistan's grand drama. There is no proven case that new humanitarianism works. Nor can new humanitarians claim to be more politically sophisticated than their more traditional sister organizations. The ICRC, though not an NGO, can legitimately claim to be more politically informed *and* to relieve more suffering than any single NGO in Afghanistan. Yet it shuns the overt political agendas of new humanitarianism.

HAVING PERHAPS THE BETTER CLAIM:
NEW HUMANITARIANISM FOR A NEW AFGHANISTAN

NGOs that choose to embrace new humanitarianism may have the steeper climb, but their path is clear. They will have to start doing three things more effectively if they want to thrive in post-Taliban Afghanistan: First, they will have to strengthen their political acumen. The web of power relations in and affecting Afghanistan is incredibly complex and critical to fathom if they want to be an instigator rather than a victim of political change. Second, policy advocacy can no longer be the "spare time" activity of harried NGO senior management. Resources will have to be dedicated and the aim of influencing policy marketed as a central function of their activities and their mandate. Third, they will have to start taking real responsibility for the impact of their work. Workshops on "do no harm" and "peace-building" just won't do it. If new humanitarians are going to maintain the moral high ground in political debate, they will have to get their own houses in order. NGOs that have no women in senior management will never be effective voices for the marginalized in the villages where they work. NGOs that apply no objective standards to their programming will never be able to convince the military that it must submit its assistance interventions to the objective scrutiny of others. NGOs that claim every intervention as an unmitigated success will have little credibility in the world of pragmatic politics into which they are stepping.

What is the pot of gold at rainbow's end for new humanitarians in Afghanistan? Why invest in such a change? First, aid politicization in Afghanistan has left much of the field of political debate to NGOs. As so many other actors chose to align themselves "with" rather than "against" the political orthodoxy in Kabul, the potential stature and importance of *non*governmental organizations has grown. Those donors who believe Afghanistan needs civic debate, transparent governance, and public accountability are increasingly likely to look to NGOs that challenge the body politic to live up to its best aspirations.

A second reason for adopting new humanitarianism is that the nature of NGO work in Afghanistan is changing and demands political acumen. Emergency response is being replaced by peace strengthening as a donor priority. Donors need organizations with ground presence to mobilize war-weary communities to resist the short-term false promises of warlords. More than ever, NGOs need to understand local politics and the actors that would happily manipulate or threaten them to achieve economic or military gain.

With all parties looking to government to take the reins, the social safety net function of NGOs may become increasingly suspect—at least while this government remains in power and can garner donor support. Building government capacity is the urgent priority for most donors. What a paradigm shift! From not being able to give a free pencil to the Taliban, donors now want NGOs to strengthen government, seconding our staff to them, partnering with ministries, training them in our workshops. Every project should support the NDF, every NGO dollar should feed into the national budget.

For new humanitarians who not only acknowledge but embrace the political dimensions of aid, this presents a huge opportunity. Engaging with government allows NGOs to strengthen state mechanisms that address poverty and relieve suffering. Working alongside government, they can promote mechanisms to protect human rights, advocate for pro-poor public policies, strengthen public accountability to communities, and fight corruption through insisting on transparent dealings.

Once again, this may make economic sense as well. Our years as the social safety net has made NGOs indispensable, at least in the short term, as a capacity building partner for government. Perhaps donors would like to work solely through government, but they recognize that the human resources, technical expertise, and managerial experience are simply not there yet. Hence, the multitude of "arranged marriages" between larger NGOs and government ministries in 2002 and 2003.

Of course, this was and remains a delicate enterprise. There is a fine line between the politics of endorsing the particular political agenda of a government and the politics of helping the government to function as the legitimate representative of its people. Such an enterprise calls for considerable political discernment, and that is the challenge for new humanitarians.

The critics of humanitarianism think that NGOs are not up to the challenge. They urge NGOs to be more modest in their aspirations and humble about their capacity. Pretending that we understand the political motivations of other actors, or the humanitarian consequences of our own, is pure ideological vanity, they claim. If they are right, new humanitarians will soon sow the seeds of their own undoing in Afghanistan—and do untold damage in the process.

Some NGO staff believe that the critics are wrong. I am one of those staff. I believe that the frugality of their analysis of how organizations change sells new humanitarianism short. To use Mark Duffield's analogy, I think it makes more sense to understand NGOs as organisms rather than machines. We change iteratively over time, as different moral, economic, political, and emotional forces influence our thinking and practice. Without doubt, new humanitarians got it "wrong" in the early years, when they thought a "do no harm" workshop would yield massive organizational transformation or real change on the ground. But more and more often, we are getting it right. In Afghanistan since November 2001, NGOs have increasingly engaged in and influenced policy debate. By October 2002 several cabinet ministers, including Ashraf Ghani and co-author in this volume Haneef Atmar, were applauding the NGOs for their engagement in policy debates and recognizing the impact that it had had. My own organization, CARE, has advocated collaboratively with more than twenty different NGOs on different initiatives, both at the local level in Afghanistan and at headquarters in Europe and North America. Working together, NGOs can credibly claim to have raised the profile of human rights and gender equality in the NDF, stimulated political debate among donors on the need for more funding and better security in Afghanistan, and forced the military Coalition to curtail its plans to coordinate aid in Afghanistan to achieve military purposes.

Are NGOs sure they made a difference with these initiatives? No, they are not. Attribution of impact in policy matters is often a dubious endeavor. If, however, one recognizes that policy change occurs organically when a multitude of forces are brought to bear, then new humanitarians in Afghanistan can credibly claim to have influenced the development of policies in and on Afghanistan for the good of the Afghan people.

Some critics say the Achilles' heel of new humanitarianism will be peace-building. Whatever merit there may be to new humanitarianism, they argue, adherents really lost their footing when they thought NGOs could bring peace to conflict-prone contexts such as Afghanistan. But what if peace in Afghanistan is *not* a logical problem begging the "NGO solution," but rather (as co-author Norah Niland once said to me) "a hundred-year project" that will require the concerted efforts of a multitude of actors? What if peace in Afghanistan requires changing cultural attitudes, political practices, economic distribution patterns, global trends, the arms trade, the drugs trade, . . . and the list goes on. What if the world *is* as complicated as the critics suggest?

Perhaps NGOs who take on new humanitarianism have not *lost* their humility. Perhaps NGOs have realized their insignificance in the grand scheme, while also recognizing that it will take *all* of us, most of all Afghans, a very long time to inculcate the culture of peace in Afghanistan. Meanwhile, if there are two ways to do an intervention, and one exacerbates tensions in participating communities while the other helps to reconcile differences, why shouldn't NGOs choose the latter, *not* to bring peace to Afghanistan, but to be *part* of the larger solution, as we always should be.

MAKING THE CHOICE
WILL MAKE ALL THE DIFFERENCE

Why is this choice so urgent? Why must NGOs revert to the space of traditional humanitarianism or adopt the political agenda of new humanitarianism? Because of the two criteria that inform all our judgments: our utility to the people we serve, and our own business interests. Over the next few years neither the Afghan people nor donors will have use for fence-sitters. NGOs that try to do advocacy in their spare time will soon find themselves out of their league. There will no longer be funding or community support for NGOs who want to experiment with rights-based approaches or harms analysis without fundamentally changing how they do business as a result.

Which road should NGOs take? For my money, as long as Afghanistan continues to be a test case for international intervention and post-conflict reconstruction, where donors, the government, the military, and the United Nations experiment with new social change models, NGOs will make more difference as new humanitarians. It is critical, however, that we don't all abandon our roots. Our greatest strength has always been our diversity. Afghanistan needs NGOs both to engage *and* to disengage politically. It needs NGOs to address both underlying causes of poverty suffering *and* their symptoms. Only one thing is certain. The rules have changed utterly in Afghanistan, and NGOs must deal courageously with that fact, one way or the other.

NOTES

[1] David Rieff, *A Bed for the Night: Humanitarianism in Crisis* (New York: Simon & Schuster, 2002).

[2] Bob Woodward, *Bush at War* (New York: Simon & Schuster, 2002).

[3] Thomas Friedman, *Longitudes and Attitudes* (New York: Farrar, Straus & Giroux, 2002).

[4] Mark Duffield, *Global Governance and the New Wars: The Merging of Development and Security* (London: Zed Books, 2001).

[5] See, for example, Joanna Macrae and Nick Leader, "Apples, Pears, and Porridge: The Origins and Impact of the Search for 'Coherence' Between Humanitarian and Political Responses to Chronic Political Emergencies," *Disasters* 25 (2001), 290–307; Duffield, *Global Governance and the New Wars;* and Fiona Fox, "New Humanitarianism: Does It Provide a Moral Banner for the Twenty-first Century?" *Disasters* 25 (2001), 275–89.

CONCLUSION

11

Aid, Peace, and Justice in a Reordered World

BRUCE D. JONES

Throughout the modern era, the reconstruction of states and economies after war has been a tool used by intervening actors to shape international and regional order. This was so of the Allies' use of Marshall Plan aid to build liberal democratic regimes in Europe after World War II;[1] of the Soviet Union's aid to Vietnam after the fall of Saigon; and is true of the European Union's aid effort in Kosovo. International institutions such as the United Nations and the World Bank, shaped as they necessarily are by the politics of their member states, are agents of this effort, though they bring to it their own normative framework and distinct capacities and complexities. NGOs too play a role in what Alexander Costy calls the process of regime consolidation.[2]

Just so, relief and reconstruction efforts in Afghanistan must be conceived at least in part as an effort by key international actors—in particular the United States, but also Russia, Pakistan, Iran, and others—to shape the nature of the emergent Afghan state and economy within their own conception of regional order. Such efforts have bracketed the post–Cold War decade, exhibiting the flux and flow of international political change. Afghanistan has also been a test tube for experimentation by the United Nations and the humanitarian community, demonstrating all the vagaries and values of institutional politics and reform. In the most recent period Afghanistan has once again taken center stage, and once again the United Nations and the peace-building community have experimented in their efforts to provide relief, support to the state, and a measure of protection to Afghanistan's long-suffering population.

The chapters in this book have provided a series of perspectives on whether those experiments are working; on their benefits and possible unintended consequences, or the tradeoffs they require; and on their implications for different communities of actors in Afghanistan. The book as a whole reaches no overall conclusions, nor are any yet possible. Only several years hence will it be possible to measure the impact of recent aid and political decisions on Afghanistan and the surrounding region. As such, this chapter does not seek to draw conclusions for the book as a whole. Rather, it tries to locate Afghanistan and the early lessons of the current phase of peace-building within a wider analytical context. It places the account of the recent experience of regime consolidation in a broader comparative context; locates the questions about coordination arrangements within an ongoing institutional and policy debate; and asks what Afghanistan tells us about the place and role of humanitarian action and the United Nations in the post–September 11 system for multilateral conflict management and response.

REGIME CHANGE AND REGIME CONSOLIDATION

Though it is sometimes hard to recall, given the long litany of crises with which the world community was faced in the 1990s, during that decade more wars ended than started.[3] Thus, while the United Nations and the humanitarian community continued to be tasked with responding to humanitarian need and complex crises within war contexts, UN agencies and NGOs were also increasingly tasked with response in so-called post-conflict environments during the 1990s. These environments brought together a virtual alphabet soup of UN agencies, NGOs, bilateral agencies, and multilateral civil agencies. Together with major power actors and domestic state and civic actors, they formed the benignly named "peace-building community."

In the 1990s policy debates surrounding the peace-building community tended to derive from the nature of the community rather than from the challenge itself (that is, they were inductive, not deductive).[4] There were two major axes in this debate: one relating to overall coordination mechanisms; the other conducted under the rubric of "relief-development linkages" or, less optimistically, the "gap" between relief and development. These policy frameworks represented an institutional view of the issue and placed the institutions themselves at the center of the policy problem, especially in terms of the linkages between humanitarian relief agencies and their development counterparts.[5] The conversations reflected such concerns as the challenge of switching gears from operational to capacity building programming; the complexities for donors of funding two sets of activities within the same context; and the delay between pledges for development aid and its disbursement on the ground.[6]

In these conversations the recipient state has been largely absent, either as actor or as subject. State actors from recipient countries rarely participated in these policy debates, and the role of the state as both a responsible entity and a source of complexity was rarely the focus. There were some dissenting voices. But by and large the state remained largely on the periphery of post-conflict policy discussion. Increasingly, however, the state is being placed at the center of the transition debate, though not without associated challenges.

Such is the case in post-Bonn Afghanistan, where the state has been taking a lead role in planning and coordinating reconstruction aid. This has raised some tensions, particularly around the relationship between the state's responsibilities and the management of life-saving humanitarian aid (that is, humanitarian aid strictly defined). Agencies (most of the UN agencies and many international NGOs) that do both humanitarian (strictly defined) and broader reconstruction programming face dilemmas: how to maintain neutrality with your humanitarian left hand while helping a contested, if recognized, government with your reconstruction right hand? The dilemmas involved for humanitarian actors in the provision of emergency relief in contexts of weak state authority, or challenged state legitimacy, to the provision of capacity building assistance in the context of sovereign decision-making are central to the story of this book.[7]

These tensions reflect in part the normative and policy movement that occurred in the 1990s away from state sovereignty as the central organizing principle of international action. Doctrines such as humanitarian intervention, the right to protect, *le droit d'ingérence*, and more reflect the development of the concept of limitations on the role of the state and greater space for international actors to determine when and where state power should be limited.[8] Of course, even at their zenith (now surely passed) these concepts were applied unevenly at best; with few exceptions, humanitarian principles led rather than followed political action only where the offending state in question was both small and weak. That such concepts were developed at all is in part a function of the unusual nature of international politics in the 1990s—an issue explored in the last section of this chapter.

In Afghanistan the tensions between state capacity building and independent humanitarian action were clearly exacerbated by the fact that the policy driving the core political and military intervention—the forces that brought about regime change—was that of counter-terrorism, and the major actor was the US government. Although the United States was acting with UN authorization, it was also clearly acting in its own national security interest, while the policy framework around which the main aid institutions work are those of humanitarian relief and economic development. These objectives need not be in conflict, but they certainly generated both cultural and political tensions manifest in the humanitarian community's hesitancy about too-close association with the American-backed administrations in Kabul.

Afghanistan, of course, is not the first case where this kind of challenge has been faced. In several instances of post-conflict peace-building, the process of building state capacity to orchestrate, coordinate, and ultimately manage the flow of aid for reconstruction has been central to international efforts. It has also often been a contested process. In Rwanda, Ethiopia, East Timor, and elsewhere, new regimes or nascent states have at times asserted their role vis-à-vis NGOs and international organizations as the entity responsible for the welfare and rights of their citizens (as they are under international law). In all such cases nascent state entities have faced considerable challenges in imposing their own policy direction over the amorphous collection of donor agencies, UN agencies, and NGOs engaged in peace-building. Government ministers have often vented their frustration at the phenomenon of dozens of NGO workers with larger budgets than their ministries simultaneously talking about post-conflict reconstruction and resisting government "pressure" to design their operations around government policy. (A Rwandan minister once said, "Every time I turn around, there's another 'organization without borders.' Don't they realize we need borders?"[9]) At times, tension between governments and aid actors has resulted in the expulsion of NGOs and UN agencies and operations; more frequently, the major Western donors manage to pressure both governments and operational agencies to find common frameworks for coordination and management. But the tensions and dilemmas faced in some of these cases differ from those experienced in Afghanistan, in large part because of the differences (a) in the nature of the international intervention in the country, and (b) in the nature of the postwar regime.

This political context raises for aid organizations a series of questions about how to manage tradeoffs and dilemmas within a narrow choice set. The objective of strengthening the capacity and legitimacy of the central government is a valid and important one for humanitarian agencies—the only viable long-term strategy for protection of the Afghan population. Yet where vulnerable populations fall outside the writ of the government, those same agencies must negotiate with warlords and non-state military actors to gain access to populations. In so doing, their perceived close relationship with the Kabul government can be an impediment, throwing in doubt their neutrality. This tension is exacerbated for some humanitarian agencies by the UN's "integrated mission" structure for UNAMA, which brings together the

UN's humanitarian (as well as development) coordination arrangements and the UN's political mission under the mandate of supporting the central government. Closer integration with the political parts of the United Nations, and through it with the nascent Afghan administrations, raises uncomfortable questions with some humanitarians about their relationship to the principles stipulated by international humanitarian law.

Thus, the tensions and dilemmas faced in Afghanistan also reflect the nature of the Kabul government's capacity and its perceived legitimacy. One of the factors that shape the relationship between international aid actors and nascent state entities is the type of end-of-conflict process that brings the state into being, or back into a position of responsibility. Of the major post-conflict cases of the 1990s, some were characterized by comprehensive peace agreements, sometimes negotiated by the United Nations, that set out a political framework for power sharing among former combatants and the development of state and civil institutions.[10] Others were characterized by military victories by one party. And still others were characterized by more limited political agreements between a limited set of former combatants that collectively represented a majority of power or at least a political constellation that could (for shorter or longer periods) stave off organized competition. Afghanistan is clearly an example of the latter category.

The aid community would benefit from a comprehensive review of the comparative experience of building state capacity in various types of post-conflict situations. Such a study should start with a typology of cases, defined by three factors: the nature of the conflict (independence struggle, ethnic conflict, externally driven rebellion, and so forth); the nature of the intervening forces (none, peace-keeping, peace-enforcement, humanitarian intervention, invasion, and so on); and the nature of the postwar arrangements (comprehensive victory, partial victory, comprehensive political settlement, winners deal, ceasefire, and so forth). It should then identify both the commonalities and differences in the tradeoffs and challenges faced by aid actors in these contexts, as well as identifying good practice in building legitimate and effective state capacity.

BROADER ISSUES IN THE MANAGEMENT OF CONFLICT AND RECOVERY

Other issues raised in this volume touch on broader debates within academic and policy literatures on different aspects of conflict management. Among the issues raised are the role of NGOs in humanitarian and peace-building activity; tradeoffs between justice and stability in political contexts; the role of women and gender in conflict and recovery; the political economy of conflict and transition; and the question of winners and losers.

The increasing role of NGOs was a major aspect of the evolution of the humanitarian and peace-building communities during the 1990s. Yet many of the problems and challenges that attended the NGO sector in such watershed emergencies as the Great Lakes and Somalia remain with us today.[11] There are, first of all, continuing—perhaps deepening—fissures within the community as to what constitutes the proper role and basis for humanitarian assistance, what many have referred to as the Anglo-Gallic divide between US/UK NGOs, which tend to emphasize the practical, and French NGOs, which typically emphasize the political and the principled. Second, there is the continuing challenge of "herding cats"—the great difficulties involved in coordinating the activities of a diverse group of actors whose functions, funding bases, and philosophies differ widely, and whose organizational structures tend to emphasize and replicate an attitude of independence.[12]

A second question raised by the Afghanistan experience that has wider purchase is that of the place and role of human rights in transitional contexts.[13] Set in comparative context, Afghanistan is one of several cases in which both domestic and international actors have struggled to find the balance between efforts to (a) provide a measure of justice for past wrongs; (b) develop human rights protection for populations emerging from conflict, (c) stimulate or facilitate reconciliation among peoples that have been in conflict; and (d) solidify emergent, often fragile, state structures. In such cases as Sierra Leone, Guatemala, Rwanda, East Timor, Cambodia, Mozambique, and South Africa, different balancing points have been struck, some clearly emphasizing the important of stability, some emphasizing justice.

Here again, as in the question of state capacity building, much depends on the mechanism by which postwar governments are put in place, the nature of those governments, and the nature of the intervening forces. The kind of political pact among winning elites represented at the talks in Bonn and the early Sierra Leone agreements are unlikely to be conducive to heavy international models for human rights and justice. More robust human rights mechanisms are far more likely to emerge from comprehensive peace accords, while outright victory by one party brings risks that justice mechanisms will be more or less heavily tinged with retribution.

Part of the justice debate is about instruments. In cases such as Guatemala and Cambodia, international actors have emphasized investigation and accountability for past war crimes, with resistance from local governments.[14] In Rwanda, the government's own trials have themselves come under fire from human rights groups due to the paucity of the legal process and structure involved. In Sierra Leone, at an early stage, the United Nations accepted an amnesty for past war crimes as part of a peace agreement (though initialing its objection to the provision), while more recently it has backed the creation of an international criminal tribunal.[15] In contexts where peace was reached primarily through domestic, not international, action, South Africa's truth and reconciliation commission has created an influential model. However, there is no consensus among human rights actors on which instruments are more appropriate in a given context in spite of the lessons from these various cases. (It is worth noting that the first major comparative study of implementation of peace agreements in transitional contexts found no instance where a peace agreement had failed due to lack of implementation of human rights capacity building initiatives, but nevertheless saw long-term value in pursuing such strategies.[16])

In similar fashion, the peace-building community remains divided over what priority to give to questions of gender in managing conflict.[17] Institutionally, gender as a political concept has made substantial progress in the 1990s, reflected, for example, in a UN decision in 1999 to incorporate gender advisers into all UN peace-keeping operations, and to "mainstream" gender programming. In programming terms, if taken narrowly to refer to a greater emphasis on women's rights and roles, there is some evidence of limited progress in terms of hiring practices at the international level (for example, emphasis on hiring women within UN agencies, notably the WFP and UNICEF) but still a wide gender gap at the level of coordinators and special representatives (there is a list at the UN website) and at the level of consultative practices in local contexts (for example, the inclusion of women in traditional local councils in East Timor, but not in Somaliland). Conceptually, there is still a great deal of confusion and debate about what this really means, and what are the real political and programming implications of a gender focus.

One area where there has been a growing consensus both within the policy community and in academic research has been on the consequences for stability of large populations of urban, under-employed, young men. In broad comparative studies of conflict, this has been identified as a contributing or enabling factor in conflict. In policy terms there is increasing recognition of the importance of providing an alternative economy to a body of people who may otherwise find the practice of war more lucrative.

This leads to a broader question also raised by several chapters in the book, namely, the political economy of conflict.[18] Economic factors are important in shaping current political decision-making and security.[19] Here it is important to note that Afghanistan's political economy and security structure are intimately bound up with the subregion. Barnett Rubin and Andrea Armstrong have mapped important dimensions of what they term a regional conflict formation in south central Asia (among those countries bordering Afghanistan).[20] Similar to Mark Duffield's concept of network wars,[21] the idea of a regional conflict formation highlights trans-boundary economic, political, and security linkages that shape both the nature of conflict and the necessary features of post-conflict peace-building. Economic strategies for creating incentives to participate in the new governing arrangements outlined in Bonn must be framed within subregional terms, as must security arrangements. This is an important policy lesson as true of the Horn of Africa, West Africa, the Amazon Basin region in Latin America, and the Balkans as of south central Asia.

Most important, perhaps, is the question of winners and losers. Was the Bonn Agreement a winners' deal, forged between the strongest of the military factions and their international backers?[22] Comparative lessons can be drawn from other peace processes about the relationship between losers and peace deals. Comparative experience from Angola, Rwanda, Serbia, Kosovo, Guatemala, and other cases suggests that overcoming opposition from losers is a central challenge in regime consolidation and post-conflict peace-building.[23] Where spoilers are present—defined by Stephen J. Stedman as groups or individuals who will oppose any peace deal short of one that amounts to victory—the containment challenge will be particularly hard, often requiring the application of significant military capacity and force. Containing losers—groups who oppose a peace deal from which they are excluded but who can be induced to share power, if the terms are right—is also difficult, but there are important experiences of bringing losers into the fold, thereby broadening support for a given peace deal or new state arrangements. Through a deliberate strategy involving coordinated political, military, and aid initiatives, losers can be brought into the peace initiative. The challenge is to structure a political economy in which participation is more rewarding than opposition.[24] A combination of political cooptation, military containment, and economic innovation is usually needed to produce these circumstances. Large-scale external resource commitments will assist in the short term; but it is vitally important not to allow external aid flows to skew internal and regional markets in a way that leaves them fragile to collapse or contraction if and when aid flows are reduced. (The first British resident of Afghanistan, Alexander Burnes, learned this the hard way when he and his contingent were massacred by the Afghans in 1841, shortly after subsidies to various warlords were cut in half by London.[25]) Thus, though Bonn clearly had losers, it is not necessarily the case that the arrangements that resulted from negotiations in Bonn need predetermine the longer-term outcome of the political process.

It is primarily here that we find the clash of principle and effect between political and humanitarian actors. From a strict humanitarian perspective, the approach to political actors under whose control lie populations in need must of necessity be neutral. But from a political perspective, even neutral humanitarian assistance, if provided through the consent and facilitation of local challengers (as it must of necessity be), can strengthen the hand of those challengers vis-à-vis the central government, both in material terms and, more important, in terms of popular perception. This issue is at the heart of recurrent tension between humanitarian and political actors, including at the United Nations, and is central to a discussion of managing the tradeoffs among aid, peace, and justice. As Stedman and others have noted, managing such tradeoffs is an inherent challenge—perhaps *the* inherent challenge—in managing the implementation of peace agreements or managing regime consolidation in transition.

THE TECHNICAL ASPECTS OF COORDINATION

Within a UN context, and broadly within the peace-building and humanitarian community, the question of managing the potential tensions among peace strategies, justice strategies, and humanitarian strategies has often been tackled in fairly technical terms, as a question of structures for coordination.

The coordination debate at the United Nations (and among its supporting states and partner agencies) has a long provenance. In the contemporary period many relevant issues were raised by UN Secretary-General Boutros-Ghali's *Agenda for Peace* in 1992 and later in the revised *Agenda for Peace 1995*.[26] The challenge to enhance UN coordination, or "coherence," was given additional weight by the experience of Rwanda and the lessons learned (or mis-learned) therein.

At UN headquarters, enhancing coherence was cast primarily as a challenge of coordinating different elements of the United Nations— particularly the political, the humanitarian, the development, and the human rights elements of field operations—and it became one of the central policy discussions in the later part of the 1990s. It took shape in the form of institutional experimentation and policy discussion around two core concepts: strategic frameworks and integrated missions. These were linked by a common managerial perspective, namely, the role of SRSGs (essentially, political ambassadors of the United Nations) and their relationship to other coordinators, specifically the Humanitarian Coordinators that had been used in several emergencies in the 1990s and the Resident Coordinators that had been used by the UNDP in its field operations. A debate around the relationship between these alternative leaders/coordinators became surrogate for a larger set of discussions surrounding the appropriate roles and relationships for the various aspects of UN field operations.

Cutting a long and labor intensive story short,[27] through a long consultative process the political community around the United Nations, the humanitarian community, and the development community agreed to a memorandum of understanding on these relationships that was ultimately issued by the secretary-general as a standing note of guidance in 2000. It provided for overall mission leadership by SRSGs; for the integration of humanitarian and development coordination structures into broader political/peace-keeping mission structures *in post-conflict contexts*; and gave rough guidance as to the necessity for SRSGs to pay adequate attention to humanitarian principles and human rights concerns in executing their mandates.

Though this internal and uncharacteristically brief UN document (alongside literally dozens of others that tackled the same set of issues either through different lenses or in different UN forums) was fairly clear and received fairly widespread buy in, it did not address some of the more difficult potential challenges. Consider the following questions: Faced with a tradeoff between a key peace-building agenda and the necessity to provide relief to a particular population, where should priority be given? Faced with a tradeoff between lending UN support to measures that grant impunity to warring factions, and a collapse of talks, what choice should be made? Faced with funding constraints between short-term relief initiatives and long-term development activity, where should tradeoffs be made? Not only was no guidance given as to how to answer these questions, SRSGs were not in any serious sense given the tools to shape agencies' decisions in these regards. As a management tool the secretary-general's directives were more indicative and aspirational than they were operational.

In terms of the relevance and applicability of the note of guidance to the Afghan experience, the key phrase is the one highlighted above: that coordination structures are to be integrated in post-conflict contexts, and not in situations of conflict. This distinction was deliberately introduced in the note to create space for separate humanitarian operations in conditions where there were combatants, requiring agencies to approach the provision of relief assistance with neutrality, thereby ensuring their access to affected populations.

The challenge, of course, is that traditional distinctions between war and peace are often blurred in transitional contexts. Such is the case in Afghanistan, where the nature of the situation is especially contested. There, the question then becomes whether the "in conflict" or "in post-conflict" version of the SRSG directives should have applied. And the broader policy question becomes this: Are the policy coordination tools developed in the 1990s flexible and nuanced enough to provide credible options in the face of real-world variety in context? The answer to this latter question is clearly no.

Part of the reason relates to the existing tools for managing (and supporting) SRSGs. SRSGs as instruments of UN diplomacy are arguably increasingly important tools, and certainly growing ones; at the start of the 1990s there was a mere handful of UN SRSGs, but at the end of the decade there were more than thirty. Apart from being deployed to a growing number of conflicts, they are also responsible for a growing set of tasks within the United Nations, reflecting the spread of "multidimensional" missions, the "mainstreaming" of human rights, gender and children's perspectives into political and peacekeeping missions, and other outcomes of the increasingly labyrinthine interagency coordination mechanisms at UN headquarters.

Yet even in the performance of their core duties, SRSGs are subjected to extraordinary demands and work pressures stemming from the need simultaneously to manage a diplomatic process involving competing actors on the ground and a diplomatic process among (often) competing actors in the Security Council, key donor states, and key regional actors. The complexity of such negotiations is such that SRSGs can rarely be expected to engage adequately in the interagency negotiations that shape the broader facets of their mandates, though these facets affect their political roles. Moreover, SRSGs are often chosen from political and diplomatic backgrounds and tend to have little exposure to the (somewhat Kafkaesque) UN humanitarian and aid coordination bureaucracies.

In recent years there have been some efforts by UN headquarters to tackle these problems. Efforts include: the selection of SRSGs from a wider pool of persons, some with broader backgrounds, including experience in human rights and humanitarian affairs (for example, Jan Egeland, Sergio Vieira de Mello, Staffan de Mistura—each of whom had served either in NGO or UN positions dealing with human rights or humanitarian affairs prior to being appointed SRSG); the appointment of deputy SRSGs that come from aid coordination backgrounds and are thus able to assist the SRSGs in managing the aid community (for example, Nigel Fischer in Afghanistan, Alan Doss in Sierra Leone); periodic lessons-learning workshops for SRSGs, particularly the annual SRSGs forum managed by Connie Peck; and, most important, reporting lines through the under-secretaries-general (USGs) for peace-keeping or political affairs, or sometimes both (rather than directly to the secretary-general, the more common practice in past appointments—Lakhdar Brahimi in Afghanistan being one of the rare recent exceptions), which give SRSGs access to the secretariat support provided by the departments of peace-keeping or political affairs.

However, these recent managerial improvements are still limited. Put one way, it is clearly still the case that the majority of SRSGs are neither particularly knowledgeable about the UN humanitarian system nor held accountable for their performance on humanitarian issues (they do not, for example, report to the USG for humanitarian affairs, though some copy their reports to OCHA). Put differently, the headquarters systems for supporting SRSGs to fulfill the multiple functions assigned to them are still inadequate. There is no routine briefing process for SRSGs on their humanitarian or human rights responsibilities or available support mechanisms in these fields (though it is increasingly common for SRSGs to meet with the USG for humanitarian affairs upon being appointed, and to maintain a dialogue with the USG). And the process of appointing deputy SRSGs is far from reliable by the standard of providing officials with the requisite expertise to assist SRSGs adequately in the discharge of their many, sometimes conflicting duties. (Here, Brahimi arguably erred in rejecting an early offer from OCHA to appoint to his staff a senior humanitarian adviser.[28])

Moreover, although there are grounds to see as an important achievement the development of integrated mission structures under the management of SRSGs—of which UNAMA is the most advanced current example—there are grounds for criticism in two areas. First, the integrated mission structure is myopic, relating only to UN entities rather than to the broader universe of actors engaged in peace-building. This is true despite the fact that the United Nations has positive experience of broader coordination structures in a range of contexts (including, ironically, Afghanistan, but also in the Middle East and elsewhere). To take a basic fact: Except in Kosovo, integrated mission structures do not house the other key international organizations engaged in peace-building policy, such as the World Bank.[29] Second, the policy documents on which integrated mission structures are grounded are closer to a superficial interagency compromise than they are to a real mechanism for managing competing priorities. Thus, while the policy documents give some guidance as to how to handle the potential tradeoffs among political, humanitarian, and justice objectives, they do so only in extremis; they provide no real guidance for managing the constant and complex set of political and financial tradeoffs that are the bread and butter of real coordination.

The reasons for these shortcomings relate to organizational culture within the United Nations, which in turn relates to basic questions about the relationship among different UN bodies—particularly, about the relationship between the Security Council and the Economic and Social Council, and the question of to whom do various UN entities report. These issues are discussed further below.

THE ORGANIZATIONAL ASPECTS
OF COORDINATION AND COMPETITION

At UN headquarters in New York, the issues of integration and coherence, of coordination arrangements and management mechanisms for

SRSGs, are handled by three main departments: political affairs, peace-keeping operations, and OCHA. Additionally, through headquarters coordination mechanisms, UNDP and key UN humanitarian agencies (UNHCR, WFP, and UNICEF) have a voice on these issues. To whom do they report? To whom are they accountable? The answers vary between entities, both in de jure terms but, and more important, in de facto terms.

Of course, all of the above-mentioned entities are led by executive directors appointed by the UN secretary-general (though they have wider governing mechanisms). Under Secretary-General Kofi Annan this fact has become more salient than it has at times been, as he has used official inter-entity coordination bodies, such as the Administrative Committee on Coordination (now known as the Chief Executive Board) to try to bring greater coherence to the work of the specialized UN agencies. Moreover, within the UN secretariat, Annan and his deputy, Louise Fréchette, have placed a great deal of emphasis on enhanced collaboration between Secretariat departments, in part through the creation of executive committees that bring the department heads into regular contact and joint policymaking.

However, these efforts have not entirely erased two realities: one, that different departments and agencies report to different governing bodies (sometimes through the secretary-general, sometimes not); and two, partially as a result, the "cultural" experience of working in these different UN entities is very different. Working in the Department of Political Affairs, there can be no mistaking the weight of the Security Council in driving UN policy on peace operations. In the Department of Peacekeeping Operations, this is also the case, but the broader mechanisms of the Peacekeeping Committee (comprising 100 member states) and the involvement of a wide range of countries in peace-keeping missions as troop contributors create a slightly different political context. In the humanitarian department, by contrast, relations with the Security Council are slightly more arm's length, in part because OCHA's annual reporting function is to the Economic and Social Council (through the secretary-general) and because there is constant exposure to the UN humanitarian agencies and the broader humanitarian community, who create very different pressures and have different conceptions of OCHA's purpose and functions.

This differentiation plays out most particularly in terms of the authorization of missions. The process of authorizing a peace-keeping mission is, of course, largely in the hands of the Security Council. The UN Department of Political Affairs manages additional political missions and a range of political envoys, some of whom are authorized by the Security Council, but more of whom function under the secretary-general's good offices. Nevertheless, the Department of Political Affairs and the secretary-general's office are extremely careful to consult with the Security Council in the deployment of SRSGs or the creation of political missions. In the humanitarian sphere, however, there is no authorization process per se beyond that of the informal process for consulting agencies, within the Executive Committee for Humanitarian Affairs, the Inter-Agency Standing Committee, or, more often, through informal consultations with the key agencies and donors. Thus, member states' political control over the deployment of humanitarian coordination missions is far less direct than in the case of political missions—appropriately so.

All of this can cause a degree of tension among the core departments of the United Nations that at times can boil over into active disagreements about coordination arrangements on the ground—as have at times played out in Afghanistan. More broadly, they reflect the perennial debate around the question: For whom does the United Nations work? Or, to put the question differently: What is the relationship between power (represented by the permanent members of the Security Council) and principle (or the authorizing and regulating principles and laws of the United Nations, the Geneva Conventions, human rights treaties, and so on)? This question becomes central to understanding the nature of possible tradeoffs among aid, peace, and justice in future interventions (though we should explore it fully cognizant of the frequent and major lapses in principle that characterized UN and humanitarian action during the 1990s and before).

THE POLITICAL ASPECT OF "COORDINATION": POWER AND PRINCIPLE IN THE POST–SEPTEMBER 11 WORLD

All of these questions have become more acute in the post–September 11 world, the world in which the recent Afghanistan operations have occurred. The question of the relationship between power and principle has become more fraught because of the predominance of American power and its ability to use the veto in the Security Council, bilateral muscle with virtually every member state, and an expansive pocketbook to shape policy and practice at the United Nations, among some NGOs and some humanitarian agencies, and of many member states.

By contrast, it is worth looking back at the nature of world order in the 1990s, a world order primarily shaped by three distinct but interrelated phenomena: the collapse of the Soviet Union; the growing gap between US power and that of all other states; and the fairly passive role (relative to its disproportionate power) that the United States played in shaping the policies and institutions for multilateral conflict management.

The first two of these phenomena need no comment here; they are well documented in a large literature.[30] The third element is more relevant. The expansion of UN activities, roles, and capacities over the 1990s was importantly shaped by US attitudes. It is commonplace in the United Nations to refer to the collapse of the Cold War as having created an important new space for the United Nations. Less common is to reflect on the divergence between US and UN priorities during the 1990s.

From interviews with US officials, and a cursory review of US deployments, allocation of intelligence assets, and other sources, it appears that the strategic priorities of the United States during the 1990s were something like the following. Top of the list was clearly the business of attempting to shape the development of the post-Communist Russian regime (in the words of one former US cabinet official, "avoiding a neo-Weimar scenario") and to monitor the evolution of a potentially expansionist Chinese regime. Avoiding regime collapse in North Korea, with its potential for enormous destabilization and loss of thousands of American troops, was close behind. A great deal of energy was expended on the question of containing the proliferation of weapons of mass destruction, both in the form of containing the Iraqi regime (especially during the Gulf War) and more particularly in terms of controlling potential rogue access to nuclear material in the former Soviet Union. Tensions along the India-Pakistan border figured high. The Middle East was never off the agenda and consumed a substantial amount of presidential time and will. Toward the end of the decade there was a growing US concern about terrorism, as evidenced, among others, by the fact that President Clinton's 1998 speech to the United Nations was solely on that topic. The territorial unity and political stability of Indonesia was a priority, as was the relative stability of the Balkans—both arenas in which domestic conflict generated UN involvement as well as United States involvement (in one case, slowly but forcefully; in the other, swiftly but passively; in both of them, reluctantly). If there was space for other crises on the US policy agenda, they fell under a fairly general "contain crises in the rest of the world" category that occasionally bubbled up to the surface through a combination of the CNN factor, multilateral pressure, and sometimes domestic lobbies (as in the case of Somalia).[31]

By contrast, a review of the agenda of the UN Security Council reveals a majority of time spent on Africa; periodic intense focus on such crises as the DRC, Sierra Leone, Kosovo, and East Timor; and a great deal of concern with the protection of civilians and with humanitarian issues. A broader review of the United Nations reveals considerable energy going into such issues as the development of both bureaucratic and operational capacities to manage multidimensional peace-keeping operations; the expansion of the secretary-general's mediation activity, in large part through a proliferation of special representatives and special envoys; and a great deal of focus on the interagency management mechanisms for these operations. Some time was spent on counter-terrorism efforts, in the form of the passage of a series of ever more elaborate and sophisticated UN Security Council resolutions. Some time was spent on weapons of mass destruction, particularly within the Disarmament Committee, but far more was spent on controlling the spread of light arms; on the protection of civilians; and on the effort to ban land mines.

That the world's only superpower and a universal organization should have different priorities is hardly surprising. What *is* more surprising is that the organization was allowed to devote as much energy and resources as it did to those priorities without generating active hostility on the part of the United States. Of course, the 1990s were hardly a decade characterized by warm relations between Washington and New York. There was fairly constant carping between the two cities, and a US unhappiness that manifested itself through the suspension of its dues over more than half a decade. Nevertheless, the United States did not use either its political or its financial muscle to block or even sharply constrain the UN's increasingly important role in political spheres. Of course the United States did periodically block important peace-keeping deployments—with tragic consequences in such instances as Rwanda. But overall the US attitude to the United Nations—and perhaps even more so to the NGO community—was one that allowed a considerable expansion of their scope of activity. By the late 1990s the United Nations, its specialized agencies, its key donors, and the NGOs that also drew from those donor's budgets formed a kind of specialized conflict-management system that was the first line of defense for response to complex crises in lesser states— albeit one constantly marred by interagency turf battles, failure to learn key lessons, lack of real coordination, and lack of institutionalization of key financial mechanisms (such as funds for early recovery activities.)

The implication of this divide is that the 1990s was in effect a surprising and a unique decade, a decade in which the project of the United Nations and of the humanitarian community was allowed to grow and expand at an unsustainable rate. And among the strange characteristics of the 1990s is that questions of the relationship among political, aid, justice, and other interventions could be tackled as a technical question of coordination because, by and large, the principles that drove these interventions were, if not precisely the same, at least substantially overlapping. Thus, rather than having to fight out core strategic issues of (for example) whether or not to depose a given regime, or aid a given rebel group, by and large the challenges for intervenors were tactical ones of whether this or that strategy would work best to support a peace agreement negotiated between warring parties, or how to best function in the absence of a credible state or governing body. The disputes were tactical, not strategic or political, and thus amenable to technical rather than political solutions.

The implication is that as the world's superpower, or hyper-power, reawakens to its capacity to shape global order, the United Nations and the humanitarian community are facing a crisis, or perhaps a rolling crisis, over the clash between their priorities. The clash will take several forms (witness the debate over Iraq in 2002–2003), but among its forms is likely to be a deep challenge to existing coordination arrangements, de facto premised as they are on a convergence of political goals.

All of this means that Afghanistan is one part the first example of new relationship, and one part the last of a dying breed. The rapid convergence of US and UN priorities in Afghanistan after September 11 must be seen as a temporary aberration. Although the US national security strategy adopted in 2002 clearly highlights the important role played by peripheral states ("failed states," in the language of the document), their role is entirely derived from their potential to pose a threat to the United States—as distinct from a threat to their own citizens or to others in the region. This shift in policy was swiftly enacted in forceful military terms and remains the basis for the US military, political, and economic engagement in Afghanistan. Such is not the case for the UN humanitarian agencies and some of the NGOs, whose presence there in the 1990s was driven by humanitarian imperatives (as well as, arguably, institutional prerogatives). Thus, though there was a shared sense of the country being a priority, there were very different priorities in the country. Many of the tensions and concerns raised by this book are a reflection of this new phenomenon: divergent priorities within a context rather than between contexts.

CONCLUSION

Looking ahead, it is likely that the relationship between the United Nations and the humanitarian community, on the one hand, and the United States, on the other (and thus, very broadly speaking, between principle and power) will be characterized by two very different realities in two sets of conflicts. First, there will be those conflicts in which the case itself becomes a priority both for the United States and the multilateral community, but where their reasons for engagement are fundamentally different—such as Iraq, Palestine, and perhaps eventually North Korea. In these cases the divergent normative basis for engagement is bound to produce real tensions between the major powers and the humanitarian community writ large. Different segments of that community will respond differently. But there is little doubt that coordination challenges and similar managerial and political challenges will arise in these circumstances, as the peace-building "community" disaggregates into its component parts, each returning to preexisting mandates and conceptions to find grounding. Early reports of US plans for the rebuilding of Iraq call for a structure almost wholly directed by the US government and contracting parties—hardly an arrangement likely to foster good coordination around both politics and principles within the humanitarian and peace-building communities.

In other contexts the divergence among priorities will produce greater constraints on the multilateral community. Faced with the crisis in East Timor today, one can speculate that the US political effort to get Indonesia to consent to UN intervention—which was the basis on which the crisis was contained—would not be forthcoming, both due to other priorities elsewhere and to a shift in both policy and attitude that tends to reinforce the role of central state authorities over aspirant challengers. Would the United Nations and the humanitarian/peace-building community have been able to mount as effective an effort in East Timor today as it did in 1999?

There is certainly cause for doubt. We will doubtless watch these dynamics play out in whichever other peripheral states are unlucky enough to face crisis at a moment when the world's superpower is constrained and engaged in other priorities.

NOTES

[1] G. John Ikenberry, *After Victory: Institutions, Strategic Restraint and the Rebuilding of Order After Major Wars* (Princeton, N.J.: Princeton University Press, 2001).

[2] See Chapter 9 in this volume.

[3] *Annual Report of the Secretary-General* (United Nations, 1999).

[4] Necla Tschirgi, "Making the Approach for a Regional Approach to Peacebuilding," *Journal of Peacebuilding and Development* 1/1 (2002): 25–38; on the difference between inductive and deductive approaches to peacebuilding policy, see Elizabeth Cousens, "Introduction," in *Peacebuilding as Politics: Cultivating Peace in Fragile Societies*, ed. Elizabeth Cousens and Chetan Kumar with Karin Wermester (Boulder, Colo.: Lynne Rienner Publishers, 2001).

[5] This approach certainly characterized debates in the United Nations, and around such dialogues as the Brookings Initiative in 1999 (author's notes, UN headquarters, 1999–2000).

[6] Shepard Forman and Stewart Patrick, eds., *Good Intentions: Pledges of Aid for Post-conflict Recovery* (Boulder, Colo.: Lynne Rienner Publishers, 2000).

[7] These dilemmas and different perspectives on them are raised in particular in this volume by Alexander Costy and Nicholas Leader and Haneef Atmar (see Chapters 8 and 9).

[8] For an account of this evolution, see Jonathon Moore, ed., *Hard Choices: Moral Dilemmas in Humanitarian Intervention* (Lanham Md.: Rowman and Littlefield Publishers, 1998). For a critical perspective on this normative shift, see David Rieff, *A Bed for the Night: Humanitarianism in Crisis* (New York: Simon & Schuster, 2002).

⁹ Author's field notes, Rwanda, 1996.

¹⁰ Stephen John Stedman, Donald Rothchild, and Elizabeth Cousens, eds., *Ending Civil Wars: The Implementation of Peace Agreements* (Boulder, Colo.: Lynne Rienner Publishers, 2002).

¹¹ See Paul O'Brien, Chapter 10, in this volume.

¹² For perspectives on these issues see, for example, Michael Bryans, Bruce D. Jones, and Janice Gross Stein, "Mean Times: Humanitarian Action in Complex Political Emergencies—Stark Choices, Cruel Dilemmas," *Coming to Terms* 1/3 (Toronto: Program on Conflict Management and Negotiation, 1999), available online; Antonio Donini, "Surfing the Crest of the Wave Until It Crashes," *Journal of Humanitarian Affairs* (October 3, 1995); Larry Minear and Thomas Weiss, *Mercy Under Fire: War and the Global Humanitarian Community* (Boulder, Colo.: Westview Press, 1995).

¹³ See Norah Niland, Chapter 4, in this volume.

¹⁴ For an account of tensions in these two cases, see, for example, *Accord Issue 5: Safeguarding Peace: Cambodia's Constitutional Challenge* (London: Conciliation Resources, 1998) and *Accord Issue 2: Negotiating Rights: The Guatemalan Peace Process* (London: Conciliation Resources, 1997).

¹⁵ Author interview with former SRSG Francis Okelo (author notes, UN headquarters, 2000).

¹⁶ Stedman, Rothchild, and Cousens, *Ending Civil Wars*, 665.

¹⁷ See Sippi Azarbaijani-Moghaddam, Chapter 6, in this volume.

¹⁸ See Mats Berdal and David M. Malone, eds., *Greed and Grievance: Economic Agendas in Civil Wars* (Boulder, Colo.: Lynne Rienner Publishers, 2000); and Karen Ballentine and Jake Sherman, eds., *Beyond Greed and Grievance* (Boulder, Colo.: Lynne Rienner Publishers, 2003).

¹⁹ Nicholas Stockton in particular in this volume refers to the importance of the political economy in shaping the choices available to "warlords" and other actors that to date do not fall within the writ of the Kabul government (see Chapter 2).

²⁰ See Barnett Rubin and Andrea Armstrong, "Regional Issues in the Reconstruction of Afghanistan," *World Policy Journal* 20/1 (Spring 2003): 31–40.

²¹ Mark Duffield, *Global Governance and the New Wars: The Merging of Development and Security* (New York: Zed Books, 2001).

²² This question is argued by J. Alexander Their and Nicholas Stockton, and implied by several other authors in this volume.

²³ Bruce Jones, "The Challenges of Strategic Coordination," in Stedman, Rothchild, and Cousens, *Ending Civil Wars*, 89–116.

²⁴ See Nicholas Stockton, Chapter 2, in this volume.

²⁵ Karl E. Meyer and Shareen Blair Brysac, *Tournament of Shadows: The Great Game and the Race for Empire in Central Asia* (Washington, D.C.: Counterpoint Press, 1999) .

²⁶ Boutros Boutros-Ghali, *An Agenda for Peace 1995: With the New Supplement and Related UN Documents*, 2d ed. (New York: United Nations, 1995).

²⁷ For a fuller account, see Bruce Jones, "The UN and Post-Crisis Aid: Towards a More Political Economy," CMI Working Paper 2000:9 (Bergen, Norway: Chr. Michelsen Institute, 2000).

²⁸ Interview, senior official of OCHA, New York, February 2003.

[29] See Michèle Griffin and Bruce Jones, "Building Peace Through Transitional Authority: New Directions, Major Challenges," *International Peacekeeping* 7/4 (Winter 2000); also see Michael Doyle, "Strategy and Transitional Authority," in Stedman, Rothchild, and Cousens, *Ending Civil Wars*.

[30] For a collection of positions, see Andrew J. Bacevich, *American Empire: The Realities and Consequences of U.S. Diplomacy* (Cambridge, Mass.: Harvard University Press, 2002); Charles Kupchan et al., *Power in Transition: The Peaceful Change of International Order* (Tokyo: UNU Press, 2001); Stewart Patrick and Shepard Forman, *Multilateralism and U.S. Foreign Policy*, Center on International Cooperation (Boulder, Colo.: Lynne Rienner Publishers, 2002).

[31] Bruce D. Jones, *Interim Report, Project on Transitions in Multilateral Security Institutions*, Center on International Cooperation (forthcoming).

About the Contributors

Mohammed Haneef Atmar was appointed Minister of Rural Reconstruction and Development in the Afghan Transitional Administration following the emergency Loya Jirga in June 2002. Prior to joining the ATA, Mohammed Atmar was Programme Director, Afghanistan, for the International Rescue Committee, an NGO working for refugee relief, protection, and resettlement in conflict situations. He previously worked as Programme Director for Norwegian Church Aid, based in Peshawar, Pakistan, where he developed initiatives to strengthen the capacity of local NGOs. Mohammed Atmar has written on poverty, conflict, and development assistance issues. He was a member of the Overseas Development Institute team looking into aid, conflict, and peace in Afghanistan in 1991. Mohammed Atmar studied literature at the University of Kabul. He later obtained a master's degree in postwar reconstruction from the University of York, UK.

Sippi Azarbaijani-Moghaddam has been working as an independent consultant in the Afghan context since 1995. Her work focuses predominantly on issues of social difference, participation, and protection. She has authored a number of studies and reports for the United Nations, the European Union, and NGOs.

Kate Clark was the BBC Kabul correspondent from 1999 to 2002, the only foreign reporter to be based in Afghanistan under the Taliban. She was expelled in March 2001 and returned to Kabul in November of that year, walking into the city after the Taliban fled ahead of the victorious Northern Alliance forces. Kate Clark is now working as a London-based, foreign-affairs reporter for the BBC.

Alexander Costy served with the policy and planning unit of UNAMA during 2002–2003. Prior to this he worked in Iraq, Angola, and Mozambique, and has participated in several policy studies on conflict prevention and post-conflict reconstruction. He holds a Ph.D. in political science from the University of Toronto, Canada.

Antonio Donini is Visiting Senior Fellow at the Watson Institute for International Studies at Brown University, Providence, Rhode Island. From 1999 to the summer of 2002 he was Director of UNOCHA and Deputy UN Humanitarian Coordinator. Before going to Afghanistan, he was Chief of the Lessons Learned Unit of OCHA, where he managed a program of independent studies assessing the effectiveness of relief efforts in complex emergencies. In his twenty-seven-year UN career he served in a number of positions at headquarters and in the field, including the secretary-general's office, the Joint Inspection Unit, and an earlier tour of duty in Afghanistan (1989–91). In 1995 he was awarded a sabbatical at the Watson Institute for International Studies, where he prepared a monograph on UN coordination issues in complex emergencies. He has published a number of studies, evaluations, and articles on humanitarian and UN reform issues.

Bruce D. Jones is Deputy Director of the Center on International Cooperation, where he directs research on security issues. Previously, he was Chief of Staff to the UN Special Coordinator for the Middle East peace process; he was a member of the UN Advance Mission in Kosovo; and he worked on post-conflict policy issues at UN headquarters. Prior to joining the United Nations he was Hamburg Fellow on Conflict Prevention at the Center for International Security and Cooperation. Jones is the author of several articles and chapters on complex emergencies and UN responses, and of *Peacemaking in Rwanda: The Dynamics of Failure*.

Nicholas Leader worked for eighteen months for UNAMA in Afghanistan, where he worked as an adviser to the AACA and then to the Minister of Rural Reconstruction and Development. Before that he was a Research Fellow at the Oversees Development Institute in London, working on humanitarian principles and on the relationship between humanitarian and political action. He worked for Oxfam for five years as an emergencies manager in the UK and in Afghanistan, the Caucasus, East Africa, and the Balkans.

Norah Niland worked in Afghanistan as the Senior UN Human Rights Adviser from January 1999 to June 2002. She is currently a Visiting Fellow at the Institute of Human Security at the Fletcher School of Law and Diplomacy, Tufts University, Boston. She has spent much of her professional life with the United Nations, at headquarters and in the field, including assignments in Sri Lanka, Thailand, Cambodia, and Afghanistan, working on development, humanitarian, and human rights issues. She has a master's of philosophy (peace studies) from Trinity College, Dublin, Ireland. Niland has published several articles and study reports on land mines, Rwanda, and Afghanistan.

Paul O'Brien has been the Advocacy Coordinator for CARE International in Afghanistan since November 2001. Since graduating from Harvard Law School in 1993, he founded the Legal Resources Foundation in Kenya, practiced law with Cravath Swaine & Moore in New York, and worked as CARE International's Africa Policy Advisor. His publications include *The Benefits-Harms Package* (2001)—a handbook and facilitation tool designed to help humanitarian workers better understand and ameliorate the unintended impact of their work on people's human rights—and *A Training Manual on Human Rights and Rights Based Approaches* (2002).

Nicholas Stockton has worked in international development for over twenty-five years, of which seventeen were spent in Africa, first at Malawi University and subsequently as Oxfam's representative in South Sudan and Uganda. From 1994 to 1999 he was Oxfam's Emergencies Director, and then Deputy International Director until 2002, when he moved to Corsica with his family, taking up his current role as an independent consultant. In 1997 he was seconded to the Afghanistan Strategic Framework team, and in 2002 he undertook research into the strategic coordination of international assistance in Afghanistan for the Afghanistan Research and Evaluation Unit.

J. Alexander Thier is an Asia Foundation consultant to Afghanistan's constitutional and judicial commissions and has been a consultant to the International Crisis Group, the British Department for International Development, and the Governance in War-Torn Societies Project of the Watson Institute for International Studies, Brown University. He worked in Afghanistan from 1993 to 1996, was the Officer-in-Charge of UNOCHA in Kabul, and was Coordination Officer for the UN Iraq Program (Oil for Food) in New York. Thier holds a law degree from Stanford Law School, a MALD from the Fletcher School, and was a graduate fellow at the Stanford Center on Conflict and Negotiation. He is co-author of *Afghanistan's Political and Constitutional Development* (ODI, January 2003) and *Twenty-First Century Peace Operations* (US Institute of Peace, forthcoming).

Karin Wermester is currently working in the UN Resident and Humanitarian Coordinator's Office in the Sudan. Previously, she worked at the International Peace Academy on conflict prevention and peace-building. She is co-editor of *From Promise to Practice: Strengthening UN Capacities for the Prevention of Violent Conflict* and contributing editor of *Peacebuilding as Politics: Cultivating Peace in Fragile Societies*. During 2002 she conducted a study on the interaction of political and humanitarian action in Afghanistan for the Centre for Humanitarian Dialogue.

Index

# Also from Kumarian Press...

Humanitarianism

Famine, Conflict and Response: A Basic Guide
Frederick C. Cuny with Richard B. Hill

The Humanitarian Enterprise: Dilemmas and Discoveries
Larry Minear

Patronage or Partnership: Local Capacity Building in Humanitarian Crises
Edited by Ian Smillie for the Humanitarianism and War Project

Protecting the Future: HIV Prevention, Care and Support Among Displaced and War-Affected Populations
Wendy Holmes for the International Rescue Committee

War's Offensive on Women
The Humanitarian Challenge in Bosnia, Kosovo and Afghanistan
Julie A. Mertus for the Humanitarianism and War Project

War and Intervention: Issues for Contemporary Peace Operations
Michael V. Bhatia

International Development, Global Issues

Going Global: Transforming Relief and Development NGOs
Mark Lindenberg and Coralie Bryant

Governance, Administration and Development: Making the State Work
Mark Turner and David Hulme

Managing Policy Reform: Concepts and Tools for Decision-Makers in Developing and Transitioning Countries
Derick W. Brinkerhoff and Benjamin L. Crosby

New Roles and Relevance: Development NGOs and the Challenge of Change
Edited by David Lewis and Tina Wallace

Reinventing Government for the Twenty-First Century
State Capacity in a Globalizing Society
Edited by Dennis A. Rondinelli and G. Shabbir Cheema

Southern Exposure
International Development and the Global South in the Twenty-First Century
Barbara P. Thomas-Slayter

Visit Kumarian Press at **www.kpbooks.com** or
call **toll-free 800.289.2664** for a complete catalog.

Kumarian Press, located in Bloomfield, Connecticut, is a forward-looking, scholarly press that promotes active international engagement and an awareness of global connectedness.